POLICING PROSTITUTION, 1856–1886:
DEVIANCE, SURVEILLANCE AND MORALITY

Perspectives in Economic and Social History

Series Editors: *Andrew August*
                     Jari Eloranta

Titles in this Series

Residential Institutions in Britain, 1725–1950: Inmates and Environments
Jane Hamlett, Lesley Hoskins and Rebecca Preston (eds)

Conflict, Commerce and Franco-Scottish Relations, 1560–1713
Siobhan Talbott

Consuls and the Institutions of Global Capitalism, 1783–1914
Ferry de Goey

POLICING PROSTITUTION, 1856–1886:
DEVIANCE, SURVEILLANCE AND MORALITY

BY

Catherine Lee

Routledge
Taylor & Francis Group

LONDON AND NEW YORK

First published 2013 by Pickering & Chatto (Publishers) Limited

Published 2016 by Routledge
2 Park Square, Milton Park, Abingdon, Oxfordshire OX14 4RN
711 Third Avenue, New York, NY 10017, USA

First issued in paperback 2015

Routledge is an imprint of the Taylor & Francis Group, an informa business

BRITISH LIBRARY CATALOGUING IN PUBLICATION DATA

Lee, Catherine.
Policing prostitution, 1856–1886: deviance, surveillance and morality. –
(Perspectives in economic and social history)
1. Prostitution – England – Kent – History – 19th century. 2. Prostitution –
Government policy – England – Kent – History – 19th century. 3. Police –
England – Kent – History – 19th century.
I. Title II. Series
363.4'4'094223'09034-dc23

ISBN-13: 978-1-138-66184-4 (pbk)
ISBN-13: 978-1-8489-3274-6 (hbk)
Typeset by Pickering & Chatto (Publishers) Limited

CONTENTS

ACKNOWLEDGEMENTS

I have been living with Sarah Darge, Catherine Jackson and the other women who feature in this book for many years. This study was initially conceived as a postgraduate project, after I discovered that the corner of Kent where I then lived once enjoyed the notoriety of being at the centre of the controversies caused by the Contagious Diseases Acts in the 1860s. This discovery was all the more remarkable for being matched by near silence on the subject in local record repositories. The project has taken me in many different directions since then, but I have tried to keep Sarah, Catherine and the human dimensions of their experience in view throughout, and it is to them that the book is dedicated.

I owe a debt of gratitude to the Open University for the support I received whilst undertaking the original research on which this book is based, and to Debbie Brunton and Donna Loftus for encouraging me to believe that it justi-fied further development. Conversations with Suki Haider and with Julia Laite have stimulated and sustained me.

Most of all I would like to thank family, friends and colleagues, without whose forbearance and understanding the completion of this project would not have been possible. Finally, to Mick, for his tolerance, support and humour.

LIST OF FIGURES

INTRODUCTION

Soldiers and prostitutes assemble around the doors of two notorious beer houses, and their drunken laughter, uproarious conduct, and foul language, is perfectly disgraceful. On Thursday night I saw four of these shameless women near the passage leading to Mill Bay, and their conduct was most annoying to respectable persons.[1]

Perhaps no class of sufferers are more hapless than these poor women, everyone's hand being against them.[2]

These extracts, from the *Folkestone Chronicle* in 1870 and the *Chatham News* in 1873, encapsulate the conflicting discourses surrounding prostitution in the second half of the nineteenth century. The author of the letter to the *Chronicle*'s editor reflects one strand of this discussion in accentuating the alleged offence and nuisance caused by women, labelled as 'prostitutes' and described as 'shameless', to so-called respectable townspeople. The references to 'drunken laughter', non-specified 'uproarious' behaviour and 'foul language' suggest a rejection of conventional codes of acceptable female conduct on the part of the women themselves. They also reflect prevailing societal attitudes, intolerant of deviance yet at the same time prurient. In contrast, the speech given at the annual meeting of the Friends of the Chatham House of Refuge, as reported in the *News*, reflects a differentiated strand of discourse in highlighting misfortune, suffering and victimization, seemingly designed to elicit sympathy. The disparity between the two perspectives exemplifies the contradictions that permeated public discussion of prostitution at this time.

Prostitution was ubiquitous in the ports, dockyards and garrison towns of Kent in the second half of the nineteenth century, the consequence of a combination of supply and demand factors that took the form of poor employment opportunities for women and the presence of extensive naval and military installations. Under these conditions, complaints about soliciting and other behaviour deemed to be offensive, underpinned by fears of the breakdown of social order, filled the columns of the local press. In Sheerness on the Isle of Sheppey there were complaints of 'prostitutes walking the streets unbonnetted' and in Canterbury of 'flagrant toleration of immorality ... notoriously loose women promenade the principal walks and places of resort without apparently any surveillance'.[3] The

Vicar of St Mary's in Dover wrote of the 'open indecency and downright *assaulting* temptation ... nightly infesting our streets'.[4] Rescue and reform initiatives, such as those undertaken at the Chatham House of Refuge, introduced a more sympathetic tone into the discussion, as articulated in speeches made at the various institutions' annual meetings: 'To assist in rescuing any individual from such a life of horror as that of an "unfortunate" is a good deed'.[5] A variant of this theme was the motif of the betrayed, fallen woman, incorporated into the local debate by a Gravesend correspondent: 'those, who, having been once betrayed, sacrifice their once prized honour and a priceless soul for illicit gain or a nefarious livelihood'.[6]

The reflections of these commentators, articulated through the columns of the local press, indicate that community discourse surrounding the perceived problem of the 'social evil' encompassed the whole spectrum of contemporary attitudes, and the same tensions and inconsistencies that characterized the wider national and professional commentaries. The streetwalker was deemed to flout society's codes and conventions on female behaviour and dress; she 'swarmed' like an animal yet was at the same time a soiled dove; she was a victim of betrayal yet was at the same time predatory; dirty yet ostentatious, degraded yet assertive. She violated all notions of public respectability and impeded honest mercantile endeavour by obstructing the public thoroughfare, thus her offending behaviour ought to be restrained and her freedoms curtailed. The common theme was the call for surveillance, regulation and control. Local discourse therefore echoed wider debates in articulating the so-called 'social evil' in terms of a problem requiring action. Proposed remedies ranged from castigation and suppression, to rescue and reform.

The same themes permeated national and professional debates. Traditional, received accounts of the prostitute figure's inevitable descent into destitution, disease and early death had been challenged earlier in the century by French public hygienist A. J. B. Parent-Duchatelet, who suggested that, on the contrary, prostitution was a temporary and transitional phase through which some women of the labouring poor passed before being re-assimilated into the ranks of the respectable working classes.[7] His study of Parisian prostitution was the first scientific attempt to quantify and analyse the perceived social problem, and it concluded that prostitute women were not permanently excluded from the ranks of the respectable working poor, but possessed more self-determination than had previously been recognized.[8] This theme was taken up in Britain by William Acton, venereologist, member of the Royal College of Surgeons and prolific contributor to the *Lancet*, whose major 1857 work *Prostitution* was based on his own survey of the patterns of prostitution in London.[9] Acton challenged what he considered to be three 'vulgar errors' regarding the downward progress of the prostitute figure, namely that there was no escape from prostitution, that it led inevitably to moral and physical decline and that this decline was rapid. According to his twentieth-century editor, Acton challenged 'the conventional parable that prostitutes necessarily rotted in ditches, died miserable deaths in workhouses, or perished in hospitals'.[10] On the contrary, Acton argued that vast numbers of women who engaged in occasional and part-time prostitution merged inconspicuously into the mass of the working poor and were either re-assimilated back into this class after a few years on the streets or took advantage of the opportunity for upward social mobility. Acton concluded by arguing the case for state regulation as a means of containing sexually transmitted disease, thus focusing on a stratagem of legal containment rather than suppression.

The conventional parable refuted by Acton had associated prostitution with permanent social ostracism and an inevitable decline into disease, destitution and early death. It was endorsed by writers such as William Tait, William Logan and W. R. Greg, who each rejected Parent-Duchatelet's findings and reinforced the traditional, previously held 'downward spiral' stereotype. Tait was house surgeon to the Edinburgh Lock Hospital and secretary of the Edinburgh Society for the Protection of Young Girls. His 1840 survey of prostitution in Edinburgh had condemned male sexual license and identified poverty and unemployment as contributory factors. William Logan, a city missionary for over twenty years, wrote about his extensive first-hand experience in lock hospitals, Magdalen asylums and workhouses, most notably in Glasgow. Logan rejected Acton's thesis of prostitution as a transitory phase, considering it 'nonsense, absolute and unmitigated'.[11]

The 'downward spiral' model was further reinforced by W. R. Greg, contributor to the radical political *Westminster Review*, who made an emotive plea for a more compassionate attitude towards the prostitute, concluding, in agreement with Tait and Logan, that 'the career of these women is a brief one; their downward path a marked and inevitable one'.[12] Greg was amongst those commentators who identified the prostitute as a victim either of circumstances such as poverty or upbringing, of her own 'weakness', or of mistreatment by a male seducer. Urging a public attitude of 'grief and compassion rather than indignation and contempt' for the prostitute figure, Greg nevertheless concluded that prostitution was unavoidable and, like Acton, he proposed state regulation.[13]

The argument for regulation was strengthened by the association of prostitution with venereal disease and by the increasing authority of the medical profession. Thus, discussions of prostitution were additionally infused with themes of disease, contagion and contamination, which also informed wider sanitary reform debates. As prostitution became increasingly perceived as a significant social problem in need of a remedy, the image of the prostitute as a conduit of infection and agent of physical corruption was juxtaposed with that of the deserving recipient of compassionate charity. Whilst these stereotypes pre-dated the nineteenth century, they became more fully developed and more widely disseminated over time. The 'agent of decay and contagion' image combined concepts of both moral and physical contamination. Greg claimed that 'Prostitutes have been allowed to spread infection on all sides of them without control'.[14] Physical and moral decay were combined within the discourse by commentators who demanded a single standard of sexual conduct and a purity of sexual relations.

A contrasting stereotype, that of the prostitute as a deserving recipient of compassion and charity, was, it has been claimed, mobilized by reform workers to generate financial support for Magdalen homes, and in the words of one historian, 'to soften the hearts of potential benefactors'.[15] For example, William Dodd, preacher at the London Magdalen home, defined the prostitute figure as more sinned against than sinning, a victim of male exploitation and of the dual sexual standard. This approach to the public discussion of prostitution, as has been seen, was echoed in the debates conducted at a local level in Kent in the promotion of rescue and reform efforts. These initiatives, whilst couched in more sympathetic language, likewise represented regimes of surveillance and control over women involved in prostitution, albeit of a different character to state regulation.

A range of contradictory stereotypical images therefore emerged both to define the prostitute-figure and to account for her move into this way of life, reflecting the nineteenth-century predilection for classification and scientific analysis. These images were theorized in terms of sets of polarized opposites. One of the most enduring pair of images, that of 'prostitute as autonomous agent' in opposition to 'prostitute as helpless victim', was a recurring theme and one to which this discussion will return. It would be an over-simplification, however, to view the debate on prostitution in terms of the replacement of one paradigm by another. More accurately, a number of models co-existed in the professional and popular imaginations, which have been described as a 'loose and pluralistic collection of ideas and images'.[16] The degree to which the prostitute was the agent of her own destiny on the one hand, or a victim of circumstances on the other, was a persistent theme within nineteenth-century commentary and one that historians of nineteenth-century prostitution have revisited.[17] Remedial strategies, from repression and regulation to rescue and reform, took account of and corresponded to these pluralities within the dominant discourses.

These pluralities, as has been seen, were disseminated at a local level where the tensions and contradictions outlined above were rehearsed and reinforced. The Kentish press played a significant role in this process; reportage consisted of editorials, letters written to editors by members of the public, reports of speeches made at events such as the annual general meetings of rescue institutions, and of the transactions of Town Councils and their various sub-committees. Characterizations of prostitute women ranged across the spectrum from 'lost and fallen ones … whose youth, inexperience or misfortunes have laid them open to the seducer's artifices', to 'dirty groups of prostitutes parading the public streets', to self-directed offenders against standards of decency who 'congregated there for the purpose of luring victims of the opposite sex to some of the vile dens which are to be found at no great distance'.[18] This reportage also featured regular reports of magistrates' court petty sessions hearings, where wider societal attitudes were reflected both in the prosecution and sentencing decisions of agents of the criminal justice system, and in the discourse of the newspaper court reporters. The women's conduct in the public courtroom and the nonchalance with which they were frequently reported to have met the imposition of custodial sentence were accentuated, as if to emphasize the deviation from prescribed codes of acceptable female behaviour. The verbatim reproduction of Isabella Thompson's retort, as she was being led from the dock to begin a twenty-one-day custodial sentence for being drunk and using 'foul and disgusting language', that she could 'very easily do that' was typical.[19] Details of the circumstances of offences and arrests were also laid before the readership, where they provided entertainment and served a didactic purpose. The notorious Eliza O'Malley of Chatham, on the occasion of one of her numerous arrests during the 1860s, was described to the readership as having been 'running about the street, hollering like a mad woman, naked from the waist upwards'.[20]

This reportage continued largely unaffected at a local level by the passing of the Contagious Diseases Prevention Act ('An Act for the Prevention of Contagions Diseases at Certain Naval and Military Stations') in 1864. Introduced in response to the alarm generated by critically high levels of venereal disease amongst the armed forces, this piece of legislation reflected the dominance of medical and scientific authority in identifying prostitution as the cause of the problem. It provided for women's compulsory medical surveillance along similar lines to that long-practised abroad, most notably and enduringly in France, but also elsewhere in Europe and across the British Empire. That this measure was limited to districts surrounding military installations (and was not applied to major cities, nor, with one exception, to commercial ports) is a reflection of prostitution's association with the military, and thus by association with the imperialist project. Historians of regulationism point specifically to the military rationale for the CD Acts and to the centrality of regulated prostitution within the military apparatus of imperialist states.[21] In Britain, the 1864 Act was applied to eleven English and Irish districts, of which three were located in Kent and one in Kentish London. These consisted of key strategic military installations: Chatham, garrisoned naval dockyard town on the river Medway; Sheerness, garrison and naval dockyard on the Isle of Sheppey; Woolwich, site of the naval dockyard, garrison and Royal Arsenal on the River Thames; and Shorncliffe, a military camp on the south-east coast just outside Folkestone. The county of Kent thus felt the impact of the legislation particularly intensely, and the politics of prostitution in these districts reflects the association of regulation with the military. Members of the Parliamentary Select Committee appointed to investigate into the operations of the legislation, for example, heard evidence alleging that the provision of medically inspected women for the purposes of prostitution was understood by the ordinary soldier to be a routine part of barrack-room life.[22]

Under the provisions of the new legislation, a police officer was authorized to instruct any woman he knew, or suspected, to be involved in prostitution, and therefore likely to be infected with a sexually transmitted disease, to undertake to be medically examined. If she was found to be infected, she was to be detained for mandatory medical treatment for a period of up to three months. Women could choose sign a so-called 'Voluntary Submission Form' and submit to examination voluntarily, thus bypassing the requirement to appear before a Justice of the Peace in petty sessions. Those who did not comply were to be prosecuted through the magistrates' courts and sentenced to detention in prison. Additionally, brothel-keepers whom it was felt had reasonable grounds to believe that a woman was infected could be fined or imprisoned for allowing them to remain on the premises. An equivalent medical surveillance of the women's male sexual partners was not provided for under the law, though some regiments claimed to carry this out voluntarily.[23] The 1864 Act was limited to three years' duration and was replaced in 1866, following the investigations of a Parliamentary Select Committee that addressed itself largely to medical evidence. Invited witnesses comprised doctors, the military, police officers and civil servants. The amendment provided for the registration of women as prostitutes and introduced a regular medical examination, extended the geographical territories of some districts, and extended the provisions of the Act to Windsor.

Initially, the introduction of these measures into Kentish territories prompted minimal local public reaction, as measured by the paucity of comment in the local press. This deficiency may be a reflection of contemporary criticism that the legislation had been introduced surreptitiously to avoid publicity, with the result that it was little known outside of military and medical circles.[24] Over time, however, and with growing calls from the Association for Promoting the Extension of the Contagious Diseases Act to extend the legislation elsewhere in the country, press attention and wider awareness were generated. Public meetings in Chatham in early 1868, and in Gravesend a couple of months later, for example, attracted press comment. The *Chatham News* informed its readership that 'Chatham has taken a very prominent position in a question which is at this moment being discussed throughout the length and breadth of the land'. Amongst the 'influential gentlemen' of Chatham who accepted positions as vice-presidents of the association were the chaplains to the lock hospital and to the House of Refuge.[25]

Finally, in 1869, a third and final amendment lengthened the maximum medical detention period to nine months from three, introduced a clause enabling the temporary detention of women found unfit for examination (for example, menstruating or drunk), and authorized visiting surgeons to relieve women from examination in certain circumstances, after consultation with the police. Most significantly, for this study's focus on the impact of the legislation in Kent, the amendment extended operations to a further six districts, including the Kentish territories of Maidstone, Gravesend, Canterbury, Maidstone, Dover and Deal, whilst the Woolwich district was extended to include the parish of Greenwich.

The subjected districts of Kent have been described by Philip Howell as an 'archipelago', a series of island territories in which the CD legislation applied, surrounded by larger tracts in which it did not. When the 1869 amendment significantly extended this archipelago, the individual islands within it were made more differentiated. The newly subjected garrison towns were not dominated by the military to the same degree as the districts brought under the original 1964 legislation. The origins of Chatham, Sheerness and Woolwich lay with the development of their naval dockyards and associated military installations, and their civilian populations had grown to service them. The origins of the newly subjected areas, however, pre-dated their associations with the military. Gravesend was a river port and market town, Maidstone a market town and the county town, Dover and Deal were coastal resorts and sea ports, whilst Canterbury was a cathedral city. The economies of these locations were less dependent on government enterprise, and they were each incorporated boroughs with long-established rights of local governance. Thus one effect of the 1869 amendment Act was to introduce a much greater degree of heterogeneity into the territories in which the legislation now applied. These variations were related to factors such as economic structure, local governance, and arrangements for the administration of criminal justice and policing. The nature of the relationship between civic and military authorities provided a further level of variation. The politics of prostitution, therefore, operated differently from one location to the next, since the operational relationships between the military and civilian policing agencies, as will be further explored in Chapter 6, were characterized by variation rather than uniformity. Therefore, rather than constituting a single, standardized narrative, the impact of the CD Acts on the ground is more usefully conceptualized as a series of complex, diverse and interrelated ones. These differences necessitate a bottom-up approach to their study, to capture the disparities between one district and another, and to avoid the over-interpretation of singular circumstances.

The extension of the operations of the Acts beyond the naval dockyard towns by the 1869 amendment was also met with a corresponding increase in public and municipal awareness, as reflected in the columns of the local press. Here, the perceived merits and dangers of the legislation were rehearsed and debated, and its operations both at national and local levels noted. This commentary consisted of editorials, reports of local meetings, the routine reportage of local bureaucracy and the publication of letters written by the public to the editors. The impending inclusion of Gravesend under the law in February 1870 was met by a press editorial warning of a 'danger ... common to all women living in the districts to which the Act applies; and it applies to Gravesend'.[26] In contrast, the conservative *Kentish Gazette* printed a letter written to its editor declaring that: 'It is all rubbish about respectable women being interfered with'.[27] When the extension of operations to Dover prompted discussions at meetings of the General Purposes Committee on 17 May and of the Town Council on 16 June about whether or not the working of the Act had been 'productive of great benefit to the town of Dover', the debates were reported in detail in the pages of the local press.[28] Here, the civil and municipal authorities, as in other garrisoned towns, were protective of their independence from the military and from central government interference in local affairs. This mentality is reflected in the statement made in the pages of *Pike's Blue Book and Dover Directory* that 'We ordinary mortals are more concerned with the town as a place of business and a health resort, than as a military station'.[29] It is also evident in the observation of Wesleyan minister, Rev. Hughes, in relation to the CD Acts, that they 'set the military over the civil power, and the central over the municipal authority in matters of purely local government'.[30] This defence of local and municipal prerogative was to be a key factor in the development and organization of local opposition to the CD Acts.

A national campaign for the repeal of the legislation was mobilized following the 1869 Act. On New Year's Eve 1869, the *Daily News* published a protest drawn up by Harriet Martineau and signed by Florence Nightingale, Josephine Butler, penal reformer Mary Carpenter and the suffragist Lydia Becker. This led to the formation of the Ladies' National Association for the Repeal of the Contagious Diseases Acts (LNA), led by Josephine Butler. Thereafter protest against the Acts, based on a wide range of moral, libertarian and egalitarian objections, began to be articulated by a broad coalition of opponents. The propaganda war that ensued between supporters and opponents of the Acts, from the time that opposition to the legislation was mobilized in 1870 until their final removal from the statute book in 1886, generated a mass of documentary literature. Much of this was created by the campaign for repeal and notably by the LNA, consisting largely though not exclusively of its publication the *Shield* and of Butler's own voluminous writings. Other repeal publications included the Wesleyan Society for Repeal's *Methodist Protest* and the *National League Journal*, produced by the Working Men's National League, supplemented by an energetic publishing exercise that produced tracts, posters and leaflets as a means of influencing public opinion.[31]

Whilst opposition to the CD Acts was always fiercer outside of the subjected territories than within them, the growing momentum of the repeal movement, and its associated publicity campaign, was noted in the columns of the Kentish press. Here, public meetings were reported and commented upon, the views of interested parties were recorded, and editorials were used to set out the various publications' position in the ensuing debate. The *Gravesend and Dartford Reporter*, in reporting a public meeting in the town at which Josephine Butler had spoken, noted the 'startling' statements made about the operations of the Acts, whilst the *Kentish Gazette* observed in February 1870 that the legislation was 'exciting a good deal of highly virtuous indignation among certain estimable people'.[32] The *Dover Express* bluntly asserted that 'the opponents of the measures indulge in assumptions which are not warranted by facts'.[33] For the most part, then, the Kentish titles were reflective of the general tendency for opinion in the subjected districts to be in favour of the legislation, as will be more fully explored.

The subjected districts of Kent have received little attention in histories of the CD Acts, a field which has been dominated by Judith R. Walkowitz's celebrated work *Prostitution and Victorian Society: Women, Class, and the State*. Established as a core text on the Acts and also on the history of nineteenth-century prostitution more widely, its central narrative related the collaborative resistance to the 'technology of power' represented by the Acts on the part of middle-class women activists and women involved in prostitution. This reading was based on local studies of Southampton and Plymouth, districts selected on the basis that they experienced considerable levels of prostitution, vigorous repeal activism and significant levels of resistance. This combination of circumstances yielded voluminous documentary evidence that facilitated the examination of the workings of the CD Acts repeal movement, and thus the circumstances of Southampton and Devonport have come to represent the history of the legislation.

As a result, the CD Acts have come to dominate histories of the regimes of policing and sanction brought to bear upon women involved in prostitution. However, whilst this regulationist approach to the control of prostitution has attracted the majority of comment and attention, both from contemporary observers and from historians, the routine interventions of municipal and non-military authorities, which in some places had a more repressive impact on the day-to-day lives of the women directly affected, have attracted significantly less attention. The Kentish evidence, however, points to the control of prostitution being best understood within the wider contest for public space that took place following the reform of regional policing in the second quarter of the nineteenth century onwards. This development has been described as the 'extension into hitherto geographically peripheral areas of both the moral and political authority of the state'.[34] For historians of policing, prostitute women constitute less a unique category of targeted offenders as in specifically feminist interpretations, but are rather understood as part of a wider group of perceived transgressors against raised expectations of public order, respectable behaviour and decency.[35] According to this interpretation, a project addressed at the civilization of communal space was undertaken in the second half of the nineteenth century, which introduced the surveillance of the public arena and the regulation of behaviour on the street. Approached from this perspective, then, the CD legislation comes to be seen less as a uniquely punitive and repressive piece of legislation, but part of a much wider regulatory structure brought to bear upon the activities of those at the margins, whose conduct was construed as immoral and deviant.

The surviving records of Kentish petty sessions hearings of prosecutions brought against women publicly identified as prostitutes, together with newspaper reportage of those hearings, constitute a significant component of the source material on which this study is based. These reflect the lowering threshold of tolerance of public behaviour defined as 'immoral' and 'disorderly', in the wake of the introduction of the 'new' police from the second quarter of the nineteenth century onwards. Thus, for example, in 1856, the year in which the County and Borough Police Act established a framework for the mandatory extension of the 'new' police nationwide, the Head Constable in Gravesend supported the prosecution at petty sessions of a woman called Susan Claycroft, identified as a prostitute, on a charge of obstructing the footway. The precise nature of the offence was that Claycroft, together with several other girls, had allegedly been seen 'running the streets and courts and obstructing the paths'. The Superintendent's words in court, paraphrased by the *Gravesend and Dartford Reporter*, that 'they had been warned, he had had a great many complaints and intended to summon every one of this class found in future under similar circumstances', reflect the increasing levels of repression brought to bear on the public activities of women to whom the label 'prostitute' was applied, long before the introduction of the CD Acts.[36] In this instance, Claycroft was sentenced to seven days' imprisonment, in default of a fine of two shillings and sixpence.

Claycroft, together with the other women who are the focus of this study, went largely undocumented in the historical record except when they either came to the attention of the authorities, or into contact with the machinery of routine bureaucracy. The strategy adopted here, which takes these women's contact with the criminal justice system as a starting point, runs the risk, to an extent, of overlooking the everyday in favour of the extraordinary and of missing details about everyday life and social relationships. This approach is also biased in favour of those women who passed in front of the benches of the Kentish magistrates and towards the streetwalker who operated at the lower end of the prostitution market who was most visible and thus most vulnerable to the attentions of the police. However, when women were brought before the magistrates charged with a variety of street disorder offences including soliciting, a wealth of background information relating precisely to those areas of routine life and social relationships was often divulged, much of which was relayed in the local newspaper court columns. In the process of reporting a case of robbery, for example, court journalists frequently repeated the mass of additional detail that emerged during the court hearing and which was not routinely recorded by the court clerk. This often included, for example, the women's preferred haunts, which other women they kept company with, where and how they met clients, and sometimes details of the women's own backgrounds. Furthermore, both the newspaper reportage and the official records relating to the cases brought to petty sessions, which include the names of individual defendants and, frequently, an additional identifying feature such as an address, provide a foundation stone for a process of nominal record linkage. Using this methodology, women can be tracked between records and over time, thus allowing some life history reconstruction to be carried out.

This discussion opened with a consideration of the discourses surrounding prostitution in the nineteenth century, and of the processes of labelling and classification applied to those women whose public behaviour was perceived to flout agreed codes of respectability. Any exercise in writing about these women from a historical perspective, therefore, raises similar questions related to definitions and terminology. Previous historians in this field, faced with decisions about language, have responded in a variety of ways. Undoubtedly, as Linda Mahood has emphasized, the term 'prostitute' is not an objective, value-free category but a sociopolitical construct into which contemporary ideology is and was embedded.[37] Helen Self, whilst acknowledging the stigma attached to the word 'prostitute', has made the case for using both it and 'prostitution' in their historical context, since these are the terms used in legal documents and texts. Self has gone further in arguing for a differentiation between the terms 'prostitute' and 'common prostitute' (the latter first coined in the 1824 Vagrancy Act) to identify the group of women most vulnerable to arrest and prosecution for soliciting and loitering.[38]

Nineteenth-century commentators, as will be seen, used the term 'prostitute' in an empirical way, reflecting prevailing positivist modes of thought as well as the Victorian penchant for categorization. This, as has been noted, together with the term 'common prostitute', was the term recognized, although not defined, by law. In contrast, nineteenth-century sources employed a range of value-laden euphemisms when writing in a self-consciously more subjective mode, for example 'unfortunate', 'nymph du pave' and 'one of the frail sisterhood'. It is undoubtedly the case that this terminology was applied as part of a process of 'othering' a particular group of women who were deemed to defy social conventions and norms. The most significant difference between contemporary and modern usage is arguably the degree of permanence understood by the term 'prostitute' and, as will be further explored in this study, questions relating to the ease with which the lifestyle could be abandoned permeated much of the contemporary discourse of rescue and reform. Notably, many sources reflect a firm understanding of a subtle difference between the terms 'prostitute' and 'fallen woman'.[39]

Where possible, therefore, empirical use of the term 'prostitute' will be avoided here, except when used explicitly in the context of contemporary understandings of the term, whilst the term 'streetwalker' will be used in the literal sense of women who plied for custom on the street. The term 'prostitution' is used to describe the practice of exchanging sex for money, though it seems likely that alternative considerations, for example the purchase of alcoholic refreshment, may have been negotiated on occasion. Furthermore, the evidence relating to incidents of robbery of prostitutes' clients, which will be discussed in the following chapter, suggests that many women used the promise of sex as a means of luring clients into situations where they were more vulnerable to robbery without witness, and that the proceeds of such robbery constituted a significant portion of the woman's income. Thus, modern understandings of 'prostitution' are unlikely to equate precisely with nineteenth-century ones.

The focus of this study, therefore, is the web of surveillance and control measures brought to bear upon a group of women of the marginal poor whose way of life and public behaviour deviated from prescribed standards and norms. This web was an intricate one, and ranged from a process of 'othering' these women at one end of the spectrum, through to persistent arrest and custodial sentencing at the other. This wide variation dictates a range of perspectives and thus of methodological approaches. The first cross-section taken is a ground-level exploration of life lived at the margins. By definition, the search for the voice of those who have left so little record behind them risks misinterpretation and the taint of retrospection. It has also, in most cases, been filtered through the attitudes and language of those who created the evidence. Thus, one potential limitation of this empirical approach is that a socially constructed category, in this case 'prostitute', is evaluated, counted and discussed as if it were a tangible entity, thus validating the process of 'othering' that created the category in the first place. Whilst the problems associated with this methodology cannot be ignored, this strategy does allow, as far as is possible given the paucity and partiality of the source materials, for a closer approach to be taken to the lived experience. This bottom-up perspective is key to an understanding of the impact of the regimes of policing and control that are the focus here.

This study turns firstly to a search for the role of prostitution within individual women's survival strategies. Taking the conceptual framework of the makeshift economy as a starting point, Chapter 1 reconstructs the life histories of a number of women who came to the attention of the authorities as a result of their involvement in prostitution. This discussion uncovers patterns of life-cycle poverty, the workings of individual subsistence economies and the formulation of adaptable remedial strategies. Nineteenth-century street prostitution emerges as a more heterogeneous phenomenon than has usually been recognized, particularly by the Victorian state. Historians' debates about whether the step into prostitution represented the first on a slippery slope to disease and early death on the one hand, or was a transitory phase in the lives of women of the working poor on the other, have resulted in homogenous interpretations that tend to obscure the nuances and complexities of life at the margins of society. These complexities are interrogated further in Chapter 2, which examines prostitution in the ports and dockyards of Kent with regard to life cycle and ultimate outcomes. Taking as its unifying theme the questions of individual agency that lay at the heart of much feminist and social history, this discussion investigates the conditions in which women practised prostitution in the context of their immediate local communities, and the role of brothel-keepers and public house proprietors in what was, predominantly, a female subculture. With regard to age, degree of entrenchment into prostitution and ultimate outcomes, the women uncovered by this investigation represent a wider spectrum of experience than has usually been suggested by previous studies, a finding that has significant implications for the discussion of the impact of the CD legislation that follows in Chapter 6.

The discussion then turns in Chapter 3 to a consideration of the process of 'othering' brought to bear upon those at the margins, and of the role played by local newspaper reportage of magistrates' court hearings in this process. It explores the range of tropes and stereotypes, recognizable from wider professional and journalistic literature, used to label women whose behaviour was deemed to deviate from acceptable norms. These were disseminated at a local level and thus constituted a mechanism for surveillance of conduct deemed as deviant.

A contrasting perspective is adopted in Chapter 4, which employs street-level studies to explore the significance of locality and spatiality to an understanding of the operation of prostitution. With reference to scholarship in the field of historical geography, this discussion surveys the variable nature of towns' social and spatial boundaries. It maps prostitution geographically in the context of the contest for public space and the civic project to clean up the streets that took place in the second half of the nineteenth century. It takes as its main reference framework the questions of mistaken identity that were central to contemporary CD Acts repeal discourse. These stressed the possibility of so-called 'respectable' women and of 'virtuous women of the poor' being mistaken for streetwalkers and thus being brought under the jurisdiction of the Acts, and have been taken up uncritically in the modern commentary on the CD Acts. A national newspaper article claimed in 2006, for example, that 'any woman in designated military towns could be forcibly inspected for venereal disease'.[40] The spatial perspective adopted here allows such assertions to be challenged.

Policing strategies are more fully explored in Chapter 5, which frames its evaluation of the policing of prostitution within the narrative of the transformation of policing theory and practice that took place from the second quarter of the nineteenth century onwards. It is argued that in contrast to the received view, prostitution was not widely tolerated prior to the introduction of the CD Acts, and that in some locations the second half of the nineteenth century witnessed progressively more stringent regimes of control in line with the civic project to clean up the streets. In the districts made subject to the CD Acts, two parallel regimes of policing prostitution, carried out by different police forces, were in operation at the same time and on the same streets. Street prostitutes were exposed in many Kentish locations to repressive regimes of regulation and control at the hands of a local judiciary that was eager to keep the streets free and passable in line with raised expectations of public order and respectability. For women who lived by prostitution in many Kentish locations, routine polic- ing appears to have represented a consistently greater and more punitive hazard than the operation of the CD Acts, both before the latter were introduced and during the time they were on the statute book. Where this was not the case, it is argued that this had more to do with practical considerations such as polic- ing manpower and local judicial practice than with policies of tolerance. It is a central argument of this study that any consideration of the operation of the CD legislation must frame it within the wider narrative of the differing regimes of control brought to bear on women who practised prostitution at this time.

The notorious CD Acts and the long campaign to have them repealed have understandably earned an iconic place in the history of women's emancipation. The conventional narrative of the combined resistance of prostituted women and middle-class female repeal activists has highlighted opposition to, and non- compliance with, the provisions of the legislation as a demonstration of women's collaborative agency in protest against patriarchal and sexual oppression. The consensus view of the Acts, disseminated through the academic literature into popular history, is based largely on the findings of studies of the south coast ports of Portsmouth, Southampton and Plymouth. This reading asserts that the legislation was applied strictly and policed harshly, and that it met with the widespread opposition of working prostitutes who were encouraged and sup- ported in demonstrations of resistance and non-cooperation by middle-class female repeal activists. Chapter 6 demonstrates that the Kentish evidence sug- gests a more complex and nuanced pattern of response on the part of women who practised prostitution. In the light of the evidence related to heterogeneity revealed in Chapters 1 and 2, this discussion concludes that responses to the legislation were governed by the wide variety of individual experience of pros- titution. This reading is not, however, inconsistent with an interpretation that emphasizes agency, which was realized as much through practical calculations of best interest in the pursuance of individual survival strategies as through dra- matic and well-publicized demonstrations of non-cooperation. This chapter argues, in conclusion, that non-resistance should be viewed through a lens, not of victimization, but of marginalized practice.

This study's focus, therefore, is the broad complex of surveillance and polic- ing measures applied to women publicly identified as prostitutes, whose public behaviour was defined as immoral and deviant. The unifying perspective is the women themselves, and how these measures were experienced and resisted, rather than how they were understood and evaluated from above. Thus, this study adopts a bottom-up approach, turning firstly to an investigation of the day-to-day lives and working practices of the women who lived by prostitution in the naval ports, dockyards and army garrison towns of Kent in the third quarter of the nineteenth century.

1 PROSTITUTION, POVERTY AND THE MAKESHIFT ECONOMY

Emma Goodhall was brought before the Rochester bench of magistrates in June 1861, on a charge of drunkenness and using obscene language in a public place. Identified in court as a prostitute (though this had no bearing on the charges that had brought her to court that day), Goodhall publicly acknowledged that she earned a living in this way. She offered, by way of explanation, that 'she had no other means of obtaining a livelihood', before being convicted and imprisoned for fourteen days with hard labour.[1]

The supplementary details exposed by newspaper reports of courtroom hearings of cases like this one shed light on the difficulties negotiated by single or abandoned women living in the Kentish ports and dockyards to support themselves in the third quarter of the nineteenth century. Finding themselves in similar circumstances to Goodhall, other women pursued alternative courses of action. Thirty-six-year-old Mary Ann Jones, charged with breaking three panes of glass in Week Street, Maidstone, explained to the bench that she had committed the offence because she was 'hard up and had nowhere to go'. She was rewarded with fourteen days' accommodation at the county gaol.[2] When Georgina Cotsell, a twenty-nine-year-old single woman, found herself in a similarly destitute situation, she attempted to drown herself in the River Medway. Questioned afterwards as to her motive, Cotsell said that she had been 'thoroughly driven to it by want'; she owed three shillings and sixpence rent on her lodgings in Manor Street, Brompton, but had no means of paying it.[3] She volunteered that she 'had struggled on for two years and was determined not to struggle any longer'. Women with dependants were additionally vulnerable when they found themselves in similarly tightened financial circumstances. Gravesend widow Jane Collins, whose husband had died in the workhouse, was refused outdoor relief for herself and her two children in 1872 by Poor Law Guardians on the grounds that she was 'under the age'. Determined not to enter the workhouse where her husband had died because she believed the experience had contributed to his death, and unable to support her children, she abandoned them.[4]

It is clearly not possible, from the surviving evidence, to ascertain with any degree of certainty what might have prompted some women of the labouring poor, such as Emma Goodhall, to resort to prostitution when they found themselves in situations of exceptional hardship, whilst others, as demonstrated by these examples, pursued alternative strategies. Not all destitute women turned to prostitution, and yet, as this chapter will show, both the weight of evidence and the consensus of contemporary opinion suggest an associational link between material want and prostitution as practised at the margins. Commentators as profoundly divided on policy as Josephine Butler and Dr William Acton were united in the conviction that 'cruel, biting poverty ... the lowness of the wages paid to working women in various trades' was a significant causal factor in women's resort to prostitution in the second half of the nineteenth century.[5] Butler, with a characteristically rhetorical flourish, warned of women forced to 'embrace the career, the avenues to which stand ever wide open, yawning like the gates of hell, when all other doors are closed'.[6] Emma Goodhall was therefore not unusual in the course of action she adopted when faced with 'no other means of obtaining a livelihood'. Kentish philanthropist E. Buckhurst Taylor reflected the contemporary recognition of this causal link between prostitution and economic need in observing that: 'the once fair daughters of our poorer brethren resort to prostitution as a means to obtain their *daily bread*!'[7]

The Victorian state, in an expression of its faith in the power of statistics to reflect social reality, published yearly calculations of the number of women identified by the police as prostitutes, per head of population. The limitations of these statistics are numerous and have been rehearsed at length by historians of crime, yet they consistently show that the numbers of women who were believed to be earning a livelihood in this way were lowest in the manufacturing and textile districts (which offered alternative employment opportunities to women) and highest in the commercial ports and pleasure towns.[8] At the beginning of our period, for example, aggregates for the cotton, woollen and worsted manufacturing districts were one in 531, against one in 169 in the commercial ports.[9] The specific nature of the local economies of the Kentish districts under consideration here, as this discussion will show, was a key determining factor in limiting women's earning power. With no substantial textile production, little light manufacturing and numerous ports and pleasure towns, employment choices were restricted whereas opportunities to earn money from prostitution were plentiful.

Yet, whilst contemporary commentators evidently recognized this strong causal link between economics and prostitution, debates about the perceived problem and proposed remedies were dominated by moral rather than economic discourse. In the sixteenth Annual Report of the Dover Home for Young Women, for example, Honourable Secretary Caroline Hyde wrote of 'our present efforts to rescue the *lost and fallen ones* from a state of sin and misery' (original emphasis).[10] This emphasis served to create an overly simplistic dichotomy between the 'pure' and the 'fallen', and to obscure the complexities of the survival strategies pursued by women at the margins. In place of the dominant moralizing lens through which much Victorian commentary attempted to understand prostitution, the strategies adopted by many women in the Kentish dockyards suggest that an alternative interpretive framework might be more usefully applied. The concept of the economy of makeshifts has gained widening currency amongst historians since it was first coined in the 1970s, and is used to describe what have been called the 'patchy, desperate and sometimes failing strategies of the poor for material survival'.[11] Viewed in this way, prostitution becomes, in contrast to the conceptualization of contemporary moralizing discourse, less a necessarily discrete lifestyle or identity, than one resource amongst many within a flexible and mixed individual economy (alongside, for example, theft and applications for poor relief) by which women of the marginal poor sought to survive.

Previous studies have pointed to the ways in which underemployment, depressed living conditions and the large-scale displacement of populations from traditional communities into rapidly-expanding urban centres created material conditions in which many women turned to prostitution as part of mixed strategies of survival.[12] Under these circumstances, the prostitute figure became, as Judith Walkowitz has described, a 'highly visible symbol of the social dislocation attendant upon the new industrial era'.[13] More recently, the relationship between prostitution and other resources within makeshift economies have been explored in greater detail. Patterns of alternating applications for poor relief and charity with earning money from prostitution have been uncovered in Ireland and in eighteenth-century London, for example.[14]

Furthermore, as this and the following chapter will show, both contemporary and modern debates about the nature of nineteenth-century prostitution have questioned whether it represented a transitory phase in the lives of some women of the working or casual poor on the one hand, or the first step on the descent towards destitution, disease and early death on the other.[15] This dichotomy has taken on new meaning in the context of feminist readings of women's history that emphasize agency and eschew one-dimensional explanatory models of victimization. Each of these approaches, however, carries the risk of overlooking the heterogeneous character of prostitution. As practised in the port, garrison and dockyard towns of Kent, each of the models of prostitution offered by contemporaries and by historians can be shown to have been founded in some facet of the reality of the lived experience.

Reconstructions of the life histories of the casual poor are not without methodological difficulty since, by definition, this social group went largely undocumented except at moments of exceptional crisis. Survival rates of official records reflecting these crises, such as the minutes of petty court sessions, are variable, and local newspaper reportage of these proceedings, whilst contributing invaluable detail missing from the official record, involved a process of selection. These difficulties may explain why top-down approaches have been common in the field, since, as has been seen in the previous chapter, literary and documentary sources related to nineteenth-century prostitution were extensive. Nominal record linkage, based on a range of documentary sources generated as a result of routine, everyday administration and bureaucracy such as Poor Law Union records and census materials, goes some way to address these difficulties. Whereas single documents rarely provide more than a snapshot, a fuller picture can be constructed by tracing individuals between multiple sources. This methodology yields both quantitative and qualitative data, allowing statistical analyses to be illuminated by personal life-stories, and individuals to be tracked over time. The discussion that follows and the narratives throughout this study are partially based on this methodology. References to over 500 named women identified as having been involved in prostitution in the port and garrison towns of Kent between 1856 and 1886 have been uncovered in a range of records generated by the criminal justice and poor law systems, of whom some 200 can be linked between two or more sources. These women would otherwise have largely remained absent from the historical record. It is not possible to know with any degree of certainty how representative this 200 women were of all those who practised prostitution in Kent at this period. However, in the absence of alternative detailed documentary evidence, the methodology employed here allows the story to be told of a group of women who, by definition, had a vested interest in remaining as far as possible beyond the reach of officialdom and therefore might otherwise have remained largely unrecorded. These reconstructed life histories throw some light on the way of life and working practices of a number of women engaged in prostitution in the port and garrison towns of Kent in the second half of the nineteenth century, and on the regimes of surveillance and control brought to bear upon them. This chapter, then, turns firstly to the unravelling of the complexities of the economics of prostitution in the ports and garrison towns of Kent in the second half of the nineteenth century.

Life-Cycle Poverty

Women's recourse to prostitution within economies of makeshift was driven by a combination of circumstances, amongst which, as has already been seen, the difficulties they encountered in supporting themselves within particular local economic structures was a significant factor. As was suggested by the testimonies of Emma Goodhall and Georgina Cotsell with which this chapter opened, the earning capacity of single women in Kent in the second half of the nineteenth century was restricted on a number of counts. Long-term depression of wages, loss of economic status, occupational segregation under industrialism and the seasonal nature of agricultural employment were underlying factors.[16] Moreover, the development of the concept of the family wage, whereby women's and children's incomes were seen as supplementary to that of the main wage-earner, had a disadvantageous impact on women's earning power and particularly on the ability of single, widowed and abandoned women to support themselves and their children.

The material security of unsupported women of the labouring poor in Kent was put under additional stress by the structure of local economies. The cycle of the agricultural year, and particularly the growing of hops, continued to play an important part in local economies in Kent into the second half of the nineteenth century. In the 1870s, 11 per cent of the Kentish workforce was still employed in agriculture, compared with a national figure of 7.9 per cent.[17] Some 45,000 of the county's acreage was devoted to hops at the mid-century, and an estimated workforce of between 80,000 and 150,000 was required each year for the harvest. Women and juveniles were valued for their speed and dexterousness, and thousands of migrant workers were attracted into the county each year during the hopping season. However, the seasonal nature of the work drove the hoppers into the towns during the winter months, thus contributing considerably to the vagrancy problem.[18] Under these conditions, prostitution may have offered temporary relief from financial hardship, since, according to one contemporary observer, 'formidable and rampant was the vice commonly practised by the hop-pickers'.[19]

Occupational opportunities for women were little better in industry. Kent's wealth and population shifted over the second half of the nineteenth century from the rural southeast towards the industrial northwest of the county. Here the principal industrial activity was based around the Thames coastline and the Medway basin and consisted predominantly of heavy industry such as shipbuilding, armaments, munitions and building materials, sectors that offered employment opportunities predominantly to men. There was little light manufacturing industry. Where the county's small light industrial sector, such as Maidstone's well-established paper-making industry, did offer employment to women, this was restricted to poorly remunerated tasks. Maidstone's Turkey Paper Mill, for example, employed 263 women and twenty-six girls in 1865 (70 per cent and 7 per cent respectively of the total workforce). These statistics, however, mask the fact that processes such as sorting, cutting, macerating and boiling rags were defined as women's work, poorly paid and carried out in dangerous and unhealthy conditions. Those tasks demarcated as skilled work, on the other hand, were performed by a small number of well-paid adult males working fifteen-hour shifts.[20] Such was the paucity of women's earnings in the mills that Stephen Rimbault, who worked as a missionary in a Maidstone, maintained that 'many of those mill girls are clandestine prostitutes; they have very small wages and they increase their income by a common life'.[21] The case of twenty-two-year-old Harriet King, charged in 1860 with being drunk and disorderly, exemplifies Rimbault's contention. Described in the newspaper report of the court hearing as 'belonging to what is termed the unfortunate class', King was recorded in the following year's census as being employed at the paper factory. The fact that she was able to pay the ten shillings fine she incurred on conviction of the drunk and disorderly charge (see the following case for a discussion of monetary values) suggests that her wages at the factory were not her only means of income.[22]

Within this economic structure, adult female employment opportunities were restricted largely to domestic service, garment manufacture and laundry work. In the absence of a substantial industrial middle class, local domestic service was to be found predominantly in the numerous commercial premises rather than domestic settings. Employment in the clothing sectors, meanwhile, was irregular and intermittent, and dressmakers, milliners and makers of fancy items were employed casually as outworkers.[23] Wage rates in the needle trades were notoriously low, were based on piecework and subject to severe fluctuation in demand.[24] Some measure of the relative earning capacity of women from prostitution when compared with piecework in the needle trades can be gauged from the evidence thrown up by the press coverage of two events that took place in the early 1860s. Eleven of the fourteen seamstresses employed by Chatham machine clothing manufacturer Thomas Jackson refused to work in 1861 as a protest against insufficient rates of pay – one shilling for machining a dozen pairs of trousers. Whilst Jackson claimed that a good hand could sew twenty-four pairs of trousers in a day, equivalent to a weekly wage of ten to twelve shillings, other evidence suggests that the average weekly earnings of seamstresses in the Medway towns at this time was actually much lower than this optimistic figure, between six and eight shillings.[25] Indeed, so notoriously low were the wages paid to women in these sectors that Chatham philanthropist Frederick Wheeler claimed that 'in most cases, it is not that they are getting their living as much as supplementing ordinary wages by prostitution'.[26] As a point of comparison, sixteen-year-old Harriet Wood, who will feature in more detail in the following chapter, was paid half a crown for spending one night with a soldier. She was expected to give one shilling of this to her landlady as rent, and the remaining one shilling and sixpence was hers to keep. She was told that rent was due only if a man spent the night with her.[27]

Where individual Kentish women involved in prostitution are recorded in connection with other occupations, these activities reflect the scarcity of skilled and semi-skilled employment for women in the ports and dockyards of Kent at this period. This includes the occupations undertaken before, after or alongside making money from prostitution. Occupations are concentrated amongst the needle and laundry trades and in domestic service, as, for example, in the case of the Lucas sisters (mentioned below) who were recorded as dressmakers on census returns. Many others were connected with dressmaking and associated needle trades, some with domestic service and others with laundering or charring. The problems associated with using census data as reliable evidence of women's employment in the nineteenth century have been rehearsed at length and the data has to be approached with a measure of caution.[28] Furthermore, few women recorded their occupation as 'prostitute' for census purposes, though it was not unknown.[29] In the light of contemporary testimony that many women practised prostitution on a part-time basis to supplement income from other employment, however, these additional occupations may be assumed to have some measure of validity, and thus they shed some light on the makeshift economies practised by marginal women.

In addition to the paucity of employment opportunities offered by the local economy, what has been called the 'aggressive insistence' on workhouse relief pursued in the later part of the nineteenth century was especially punitive to women.[30] They bore the brunt of the shift in poor law policy and subsequent economy drive aimed at lowering the burden of parish poor rates in the 1870s because they had previously constituted the majority of recipients. The number of women supported by outdoor relief (that is, financial support to live outside of the workhouse) was reduced from 166,407 to 53,371 nationally between 1871 and 1891.[31] In Kent the number of people in receipt of poor relief was reduced from 4.53 per cent of the population in 1857, of which 81 per cent was outdoor relief, to 3.12 per cent of the population 1886, of which 66 per cent was outdoor relief.[32] Single, able-bodied women were denied this type of assistance except on a labour test. A twenty-nine-year-old Sheerness widow was refused outdoor relief in March 1870 on the basis that she was 'better off than the persons to whom relief was usually granted'. With three children aged four years and under, the woman earned nine shillings working in the dockyard, out of which she paid two shillings in rent and gave another one shilling to a girl to look after her children. She said that she had difficulty feeding four on what was left.[33] The same year, the Sheppey Guardians refused outdoor relief to a sixty-year-old widow whose husband had died only three weeks previously, demonstrating the broad interpretation of the categories 'single' and 'able-bodied'.[34] Historian David Englander, referring to cases such as this, observed that large numbers of widowed or abandoned women 'struggled to sustain themselves and their dependents on starvation wages'.[35] As part of this economy drive, the character and conduct of claimants were increasingly taken into consideration by Poor Law Guardians when making decisions about relief. The Medway Board, for example, 'readily granted' outdoor relief and a holiday to an old lady of seventy-six in 1859, but refused it to a girl 'of a certain character, aged sixteen, who began her frightful profession at fourteen'.[36] The search for the role of welfare in the makeshift economies of single able-bodied women must therefore be pursued within the workhouse, as the following discussion will show.

Life-cycle poverty was a common factor in the lives of women identified by this study as having been associated with prostitution in Kent. The paternal occupations of women for whom this information can be ascertained reflect the spectrum of urban, water-based and rural economies of these districts and their agricultural hinterlands. They include labourers, a shipwright, mariners, watermen, a pilot, a cordwainer (leather worker), a farmer, a pig-dealer and gardeners. Others were the daughters of skilled or semi-skilled workers and traditional tradesmen, including shoemakers, tailors, bakers and a bricklayer.[37] The father of the felicitously named Mary Ann Hooker, for example, was a biscuit maker who moved his family between Sheerness, Chatham and Sittingbourne before settling in Gravesend. The family was admitted to the workhouse in March 1858, where they stayed for seven weeks before applying to be discharged. During the following years James Hooker found employment as a journeyman baker, whilst Mary Ann, by the age of seventeen, was named in court as a prostitute and convicted of drunkenness and indecent behaviour.[38] She subsequently moved to Dover and took employment at a beer-shop. The background circumstances of Sarah Finnis, 'who said she was under sixteen years of age but who, it seemed, was leading a life of prostitution', were disclosed in court when she was brought before the bench charged with stealing a pair of boots.[39] Sarah was the eldest of six children whose labourer father was described as being 'in poor circumstances'. Sentenced to one month with hard labour, Sarah entered and left the dock in bare feet, having been arrested whilst wearing the boots in question. These women's backgrounds suggest that the temporary or permanent tightened financial circumstances of families of origin were a contributory factor in their own recourse to prostitution.

A critical event such as the death of a parent frequently triggered the precipitation of the daughters of many working families into the ranks of the destitute. Orphaned and broken family home status is a common theme running through the family backgrounds of prostitute women in Kent, indicating that the death of a parent was a significant cause of life-cycle poverty. Of the Kentish women for whom this information can be established, only half still had both parents living when they reached the age of twenty.[40] The individual life-histories of sisters Leonora and Clara Lucas, reconstructed by a process of nominal record linkage, help bring the relationship between widowed parent or orphaned status, prostitution and life-cycle poverty into sharper focus. The material circumstances of the family were very much reduced on the early death of Robert Lucas, who, according to census records, had farmed one hundred acres and employed four labourers in rural Boxley near Maidstone.[41] His eldest son William remained working in agriculture, whilst his widow Eleanor moved into Maidstone with two of her younger daughters and supported herself as a charwoman.[42] Leonora, aged in her early twenties, was already living independently of the family by this time, and whilst it is unclear at what age she became involved in prostitution, she was described in this way by police when she made an appearance at the Maidstone magistrates' court some five years later.[43] In 1871 she was captured by the census at the age of twenty-five, resident in the Chatham Lock Hospital, suggesting mandatory medical treatment under the CD Acts for suspected venereal disease.[44] Her younger sister Clara lodged in Camden Street, Maidstone, with Elizabeth Cripps, who is also recorded as having been involved in prostitution; the two women were captured by the 1871 census, Lucas's occupation described as 'dressmaker'.[45] Clara was convicted later that same year of being a 'disorderly prostitute' under the Vagrancy Act, for which she served a seven-day custodial sentence.[46] Clara died at the age of thirty-one, and the following year's census records Leonora living alone in Woollett Street in Maidstone, a neighbourhood that was home to several other women involved in prostitution, her occupation also officially recorded as 'dressmaker'.[47]

Whilst the death of a bread-winner precipitated many families into poverty, the early death of a mother was a causal factor in other cases. The mother of Selina Calver, for example, died in or shortly after childbirth. Since Calver's father was a fisherman, she was sent to live for some time with an aunt and uncle in Southwark, and subsequently at the home of neighbours in Gravesend, where she was employed as a nursemaid.[48] Selina's father married again some time prior to her fifteenth birthday, and shortly afterwards she ran away from home. She was discovered by police sleeping in a closet, an incident that resulted in an appearance at the magistrates' court, where it was disclosed that this was an established pattern. Calver's father blamed her behaviour on the 'bad habits and bad companions' she had acquired, but her uncle informed the court that it was the result of 'ill-usage' by her stepmother.[49] Nevertheless the authorities discharged Selina back to the care of her parents. In the following months Selina was admitted to the Gravesend Union Workhouse twice, once on the order of the magistrates and once as a consequence of 'distress'.[50] Over the course of the following three years, Selina was arrested on numerous occasions for soliciting and for being drunk and riotous. She was convicted and served two custodial sentences, being publicly identified in court as a 'common prostitute' on both occasions.[51] She subsequently went to live in Chatham, at the Admiral Rodney public house, which was notorious with the police for its association with prostitution.[52] This case therefore introduces a number of additional factors into the broad explanatory canvas against which prostitution in the second half of the nineteenth century must be examined.

Economies of Makeshift

Whilst the role of prostitution in some women's makeshift economies has long been recognized, their precise workings come into sharpest focus when scrutinized in relation to life cycle. Snapshot approaches tell only part of this complex story, but individual women's life histories demonstrate both the diversity and the precarious nature of personal economies over time. Many Kentish women appear to have practised personal survival strategies that combined streetwalking with applications to boards of poor law guardians for poor relief.[53] Twenty-year-old Elizabeth Spauls applied for admittance to the Gravesend Union Workhouse in July 1873, her occupation being recorded as 'field labourer'. The second child and eldest daughter of a tailor, Elizabeth and two younger siblings had been left motherless two years previously.[54] Elizabeth remained only a short time in the workhouse before being discharged at her own request after four days, which suggests that her application was a short-term stratagem formulated in response to acute want.[55] When her elderly father became indebted to the guardians for medical relief the following year, Elizabeth appeared in his place before the bench of magistrates because he was too sick to attend.[56] Soon after this, Elizabeth was charged and convicted as a 'common prostitute' for disorderly behaviour and the use of abusive and obscene language, and spent fourteen days in Maidstone Gaol.[57] Elizabeth subsequently disappears from the records, but reappears at the time of her marriage in 1892, at the age of thirty-nine.[58]

This pattern of alternating applications for relief with making money from prostitution appears not to have been an uncommon practice. Mary Putt, who was described by the local newspaper as a 'member of the frail sisterhood', was arrested on the streets of Dover at the end of March 1861 on a charge of disorderly behaviour.[59] Though the case was dismissed, Putt was able to pay the costs, but by the time that the census was taken just one week later, she had sought admittance to the Buckland Union Workhouse where her occupation is recorded as 'prostitute'. The occupations of three other women amongst the institution's female inmates aged between sixteen and forty-five were also described in this way. It is not clear on what basis the authorities made this classification, but the fact that Putt was similarly identified in the courtroom adds some validity to the suggestion that prostitution had some part to play within these women's makeshift economies.[60] Lydia Jarvis, described as an 'unfortunate' and arrested in Dover in 1863 for 'loitering and obstructing the footway', is recorded as having been resident at the Dover Union Workhouse for a period in 1861.[61]

For many women, an application for relief represented a response to a period of exceptional crisis such as sickness or pregnancy. Seven of the women who entered the Gravesend Union Workhouse during the month of September 1863, for example, were admitted on grounds related to venereal disease.[62]

Likewise, the Medway Guardians heard several such requests in the early 1860s from women described as 'unfortunates'. One, who had been living at a public house, requested admittance to the Medway workhouse for her lying-in but was refused. Another pregnant young woman, who had been living 'a life of sin' for two years, promised to 'forsake her evil courses after getting over this trouble' if she were to be admitted, suggesting a strategic approach to material survival.[63] In a similar case, Lydia Cripps of Gravesend, giving her occupation as 'servant', sought admittance for herself and her infant child Emily at the end of March 1873.[64] She discharged herself after staying only three weeks. Two months afterwards, and by now living at the White Hart Tap, Cripps was convicted by magistrates on a soliciting charge.[65] Another Medway applicant, described as being in a 'destitute state', had travelled from Haverfordwest in pursuit, according to the local newspaper report, of a detachment of soldiers.[66] On this occasion the Guardians decided to refuse relief and remove the girl from the town.

Begging was used by some women as an alternative resource within the makeshift economy. When twenty-four-year-old Annie Green was sentenced to fourteen days with hard labour for begging in 1873, it was her second appearance before the bench inside the month. On the previous occasion she was a witness in the prosecution of a publican for allowing his premises to be the resort of prostitutes, due to her having been discovered on the premises in a bedroom with a man. In giving evidence Green did not dispute that she lived by prostitution, and volunteered that she had spent some time in the lock hospital.[67]

The case of Sarah Darge further illustrates the relationship between life-cycle poverty, prostitution and the makeshift economy. Darge was fourth of the nine children of a Gravesend fish hawker who drowned himself due to financial insolvency when Sarah was eleven years old.[68] Her mother took over the family fish-dealing business, but found it difficult to support the family. One child was sent to a reformatory at the age of ten for two years, but on returning home he resumed stealing from his mother; the following year eleven-year-old twins were brought before the magistrates for stealing half a crown. In court, it was reported that: 'The poor woman wept bitterly when appearing in the witness box. She said she had five children to support, and she found it hard work to keep them'.[69] Sarah, meanwhile, had become, according to police, a well-known prostitute by the age of eighteen.[70] During the following few years she was arrested on a variety of charges, from loitering for the purposes of prostitution to drunkenness, to fighting on the streets with other women named as prostitutes. On one occasion, having been summoned for an assault, Sarah came to the police court drunk.[71] During this period she applied for admittance to the Gravesend Union Workhouse, where she was recorded as having no occupation. She discharged herself after two weeks. By the 1880s Sarah was still a regular visitor to the magistrates' court; during the hearing of one soliciting charge in September 1880, it was noted that that was her fourth that year.[72] At this time she was lodging with a childless couple called Edward and Hannah Cross, her occupation recorded as dressmaker.[73] Here, on one occasion, Sarah and her landlady were both threatened with having their throats cut by a drunken client whom Sarah had brought home, after he thought Sarah had stolen some money from him.[74] The money was subsequently found in his pocket. Nine years later, at the age of thirty-eight, Sarah's death is recorded in the registers of the Gravesend Union Workhouse.[75]

Each of these cases casts some light on the operation of the makeshift economy. For these women, prostitution appears to have constituted one means alongside others by which they made ends meet. The additional link between the administration of the poor law and the moral reform of prostituted women is brought into sharper focus by an 1866 Medway case involving two sixteen-year-olds who had attended midnight meetings. There they were informed that if they gained admittance to the union for a 'short while' they would be offered a home in London. 'Promising to amend their ways', the girls complied and were accommodated, but one left after three weeks, despite being pregnant and 'still suffering from the disease', again demonstrating that the recourse to relief frequently represented a short-term, crisis-management response to acute want.[76]

Clientele

Whilst prostitution may have offered these women a means of survival or temporary respite from material hardship, it did not represent an escape from poverty. Women identified as having been involved in prostitution and street-walking in the ports and dockyards of Kent at this time operated predominantly at the lower end of the scale, dealing with men from the same social class as themselves. For these women prostitution evidently represented a means of making ends meet rather than being a lucrative practice or providing upward social mobility, as had been seen was suggested at the time by Dr William Acton. The material conditions experienced by women who practised prostitution in the Kentish ports and dockyards were characterized by hardship and privation, which necessitated opportunistic approaches to survival. These women were, as local historian Brian Joyce has noted, 'neither elegant nor cheekily precocious, but women of the labouring poor attempting to earn a precarious living'.[77] One example is Mary O'Donald, who was prosecuted for sleeping in an outhouse and wandering about without any visible means of existence. Publicly identified during the court hearing as a prostitute, O'Donald was convicted and sentenced to twenty-one days with hard labour.[78]

The socio-economic status of these women's male clients is captured only when their liaisons came to the attention of the police. Whilst this methodological approach is necessarily biased towards those men who associated with street prostitutes and those who passed before the benches of the Kentish magistrates, such evidence as there is suggests that on the whole, the men were of the same status as the women themselves. The majority were soldiers and sailors, and men involved in commercial enterprise connected with the sea. The next biggest group were labourers and those with other unskilled or semi-skilled occupations. None of the men mentioned belonged to the professional classes.[79] It would therefore be overly simplistic to view prostitution in terms of class exploitation, which was a common theme in contemporary moralizing discourse.

Evidence relating to the amounts of money received by women for sexual services is scant. Clara Greenstreet of Dover was paid one shilling by fly driver James Etall for an open-air encounter in 1861, Ann Legge of Gravesend three shillings by groom Willoughby Johnson in 1856 for 'going home with her', and Mary Anne Burke five shillings by a man to 'go upstairs with her' at the Earl of Cardigan beer house in Chatham in 1867.[80] These sums take on additional meaning when contextualized by the sums of money mentioned in other cases discussed in this chapter, for example the three shillings and sixpence owed by Georgina Cotsell that prompted her to attempt to take her own life, and the six shillings on which the Sheerness widow had to feed herself and three children for a week.

Theft

Petty and opportunistic theft featured alongside making money from prostitution in many women's makeshift economies. Traditional associational links between prostitution and criminality had been substantiated by Parent-Duchatelet's detailed research undertaken in Paris in the early nineteenth century. Evidence relating to the Kentish ports and dockyards fifty years later corroborates the suggestion that theft constituted prostitutes' 'second profession.'[81] By definition, prostitution and theft operated as closely aligned practices within makeshift economies because the promise of sexual liaison lured many potential victims into situations where there was only circumstantial evidence and no impartial witness to the theft. Nevertheless, the Kentish magistracy frequently imposed substantial custodial sentences upon conviction and, in some situations where appropriate, referred such cases to quarter sessions to be tried by jury.

The theft perpetrated by Kentish prostitutes ranged from crimes of subsistence to those involving items of considerable value or sizeable amounts of cash. At the lower end of the value scale, petty theft as perpetrated by juveniles often appears to have been a transitional stage through which some teenage girls passed en route to prostitution. Elizabeth Coppin, for example, who will feature again in Chapter 6, first came to the attention of police for stealing scarves at the age of sixteen. She was discharged, but was arrested again within a short time for stealing a plum cake, and was sent to a reformatory for four years. Six years later, she was named among the inmates of the Chatham Lock Hospital undergoing treatment for venereal disease.[82] Over ten years later still, and having accrued twelve previous convictions, Coppin was once again admitted to Maidstone Gaol after being found guilty of being a 'riotous' prostitute. The gaol admission register notes that, by now aged twenty-nine, she could both read and write (possibly a consequence of the four years spent in a reformatory), and that on this occasion she was sentenced to fourteen days with hard labour.[83]

In a similar case, Martha Bright was brought before the magistrates at the age of fourteen for stealing a loaf and a currant cake. When she was subsequently charged with another offence three years later, she was named in court as a 'common prostitute'.[84] Likewise Mary Ann Ridley, who was born in 1856 and who first came to the attention of the police at the age of fifteen, when she stole ten shillings from a neighbour in Bath Street and was sentenced to one month's imprisonment.[85] The following year she was back before the bench, this time having stolen a pair of sheets from her parents, which incurred a three-month custodial sentence with hard labour.[86] Evidently at some point over the next two years Mary Ann became involved in prostitution, since in early 1874, aged eighteen, she served fourteen days imprisonment for failing to attend for a regular examination under the provisions of the CD Acts.[87] The following year she was once again convicted, this time on a soliciting charge.[88]

With the exception of cases involving juveniles, incidents of theft by women identified as prostitutes generally involved items of considerable value or substantial amounts of cash. Cases passing through the magistrates' courts in Kent involved sums of money upwards of ten shillings, many of which were of over three pounds and in one case of six pounds and ten shillings. Items of value include the gold watch and chain that Margaret Green attempted to steal from a Gravesend beer-shop keeper. Rose Richards of Maidstone allegedly bought herself a pair of white boots with the proceeds of a pick-pocketing spree in which William Saunders from Faversham had five pounds in gold stolen from him at the Castle Inn.[89] Other items include articles of property to the value of seven pounds, including his waistcoat that John Cairns awoke to find missing, having spent the night with Annie Ledger, a prostitute living in Eden Place, Gravesend.[90]

In many instances women operated with an accomplice. Mary Ann Martin was charged with theft from the premises of Edward Bryant, linen draper, jointly with Bryant's middle-aged male employee. The items missing from Bryant's shop were all discovered at Mary Ann's lodgings, but the case was dismissed when Bryant declined to press charges.[91] Rural labourers with money in their pockets who went into town for some entertainment appear to have been particularly vulnerable to theft. Thomas Botton, a waggoner's mate from Coxheath, had twenty-six shillings in silver when he met Charlotte Smith and her sister, both later identified in court as prostitutes, together with a male friend called George Wood in the Little Star beer-shop in Maidstone. The group invited Botton to join them and, having drunk some beer, they all moved on to the Eagle where he bought them all rum. Botton's recollection of what happened after this was apparently somewhat confused, since by the time the police arrived he was 'insensible', but witnesses attested to having seen him being physically beaten by Wood and to Smith having stolen his money.[92]

Thomas Phelps was similarly robbed when he went to Gravesend for a day's holiday. Phelps and his brother James, two working mechanics from London, went to 'a house of questionable character'. Thomas had three pounds and ten shillings in his tobacco box. According to his own version of events, he went to bed intoxicated and woke in the morning to find Joanna Smith, described as a 'girl of ill fame', in bed by his side. There were two other women sleeping in the room, and he found he had only half a sovereign left. The case, as frequently happened when there was no independent witness to the alleged crime, was dismissed by the magistrates for lack of evidence.[93] One can only speculate as to how seaman Thomas Row got home after his encounter with Ellen Marshman in Chatham. Having spent the night with her in a cottage in the yard at the back of the Lord Nelson Public House, Row woke the next morning to find Ellen, his trousers, and the one pound, eight shillings and sixpence that had been in his pocket all missing.[94] A comparison between these values and the amounts of money mentioned earlier as having been paid for sexual encounters underlines the significance of opportunistic theft within some women's makeshift economies.

Whilst the local magistracy usually dealt severely with the perpetrators of these offences, the press reportage of the incidents reflects the attitude that the victims had only themselves to blame. Sentencing Jane Ladd of Sheerness to six months with hard labour for stealing three pounds, seven shillings and six-pence from a sailor, the magistrate commented that 'the prisoner belongs to that class of persons who seemed to avail themselves of the opportunities offered by improvident seamen, to plunder them'.[95] The chairman of the Maidstone bench similarly admonished victim Henry Thornley when sentencing Elizabeth Parker to six weeks with hard labour for stealing his purse and its contents. He expressed the hope that the experience 'would be a caution to the prosecutor not to enter such company in future'.[96] As historian David Taylor has observed: 'Men buying sexual favours, or simply allowing themselves to be bought drinks by women, ran the risk of being robbed, and with no guarantee of a sympathetic hearing should they overcome their embarrassment and bring the case to court'.[97] James Brown, who said that a porte-monnaie had been stolen from him at a brothel in Three Tun Yard Gravesend, for example, was informed by the bench that 'if he kept such company he must expect to be robbed'.[98] A Maidstone man called Briggs was exposed to a more acute humiliation when he 'left the witness box amidst the laughter of the court', having prosecuted a case in which he discovered fourteen shillings missing when he woke up after spending the night with Kate Davis. There being no evidence to trace the money to Davis, the case was dismissed.[99] Gravesend Magistrate Robert Oakes took the opportunity to tell theft victim Patrick Goodfellow that the 'bench were disgusted at his behaviour' for falling into company with two prostitutes and agreeing to go to a room with them, before sentencing the women to three and four months with hard labour, respectively.[100] It is likely, for the reasons Taylor indicates, that these incidents were under-reported to the police. Nevertheless, given sufficient evidence and especially in the case of repeat offenders, prostituted women were punished severely for theft from customers. Mary Ann Golding of Chatham, for instance, was finally sentenced to ten years' penal servitude after twenty-two previous custodial sentences for the theft of money and a silver watch, chain, seal and key from a client.[101]

Residence

Makeshift economies are further reflected in the residential patterns and living conditions of women involved in prostitution in the Kentish ports and garrison towns. Those who rented their own lodgings lived predominantly in cheap housing in districts characterized by poverty and over-crowding. In Gravesend, for example, this was often amongst the common lodging houses in the crowded courts and alleys of tenement housing that led off of High Street on the south side of West Street, as will be more fully explored in Chapter 4. Evidence relating to precise addresses is scarce, but was often given during petty sessions hearings and has therefore been preserved where the court records survive, or on those occasions where it was reported by the press. Additionally, street addresses can sometimes be ascertained through census records where some other detail is already known. Where comparative sources also survive, they contribute towards some understanding of these localities. For example, four women reputed to be prostitutes made their homes in the neighbourhood of Back Garden Row in Gravesend during the 1870s. Mary Ann Loft, the fourth of ten children of a tailor, who was described as a 'common prostitute' during numerous prosecution cases brought against her, lived at number three in 1871 with fellow prostitute Sarah Curtis and with Antony Armstrong, a boiler-maker.[102] The census of that year records Mary Ann as head of the household, but it is unclear which, if either, of the women was cohabiting with Armstrong. Next door at number one, meanwhile, Louisa Collins, who was also associated with prostitution and with whom Mary Ann enjoyed less than cordial neighbourly relations, cohabited with Thomas Elford.[103] Elizabeth Surman, who was referred to by the police as 'a woman of loose character' and who likewise was prosecuted on charges related to prostitution on a number of occasions, was living at number four in 1877.[104] An impression of the neighbourhood at this period is revealed by an 1879 newspaper report of a local investigation into poverty, revealing the circumstances amidst which these women lived.[105] Resonating with imagery familiar from the better-known national social explorers, the report highlighted the living conditions experienced by residents, for whom one room per family was the average accommodation.[106] Investigators found a widow with five children, who all survived on parish relief and the six shillings per week earned by one of the children. Nearby in another room, they found a woman apparently very ill and lying on an old mattress, her unemployed husband and three children grouped round a small fire, and the only furniture in the room being one chair, one stool and a table.

In Maidstone, the description of the home of Elizabeth Jones (an account of whose death is given in the following chapter) provides another example of the material conditions in which many marginal Kentish women lived and practised prostitution. Jones lodged at what was described as 'a very destitute abode in Wharf Lane, tenanted by a vendor of water-cresses', where, according to the local press, she did not even have a bed to lie on.[107] In Dover, similarly, one brothel was situated in Hawkesbury Lane, a location described at a local Board of Health meeting as being in 'a filthy state', and having overflowing surface drainage making it 'almost impassable'.[108]

Occasionally, a rare glimpse is offered of a different class of prostitution taking place in the Kentish ports and garrisons; for example, a letter written to the *Gravesend and Dartford Reporter* referred to 'fine residences, with large knockers and brass-plates on their doors, with framed invitations suspended in their windows, where the girl of fifteen with hoary old sinners meet'.[109] Similarly, missionary Stephen Rimbault, who worked among the poor in Maidstone for twenty-eight years, spoke of women who, whilst not necessarily operating at a more lucrative end of the prostitution market, were discreet in their general demeanour and way of working. These, he claimed, dressed soberly, went to church regularly, conducted themselves quietly and demurely, yet did no work and were well known in the town as living by prostitution.[110] A further example is revealed by the evidence uncovered during the prosecution of Matilda McDonald, landlady of the New Inn in Gravesend. PC Cox told the court that at about a quarter past eleven he saw a cab stop at the New Inn, and the door was immediately thrown open and 'two gentlemen and two prostitutes alighted from the cab and entered'.[111]

However, the references to 'fine residences' and 'gentlemen' or 'cabs' in the Kentish evidence relating to prostitution are few. The majority of the women identified as having been associated with prostitution were women of the labouring poor who used this means of making ends meet within economies of makeshift. They were, in common with those women identified by Judith Walkowitz, 'members of the social "residuum", the casual labouring poor who inhabited "the nether regions" of society'.[112]

Outcomes of Prostitution

Whether prostitution was a transitional phase in a working woman's life or whether it inevitably led to further destitution is a question that lies at the heart of a long-standing and ongoing debate. As has been seen, physician Dr William Acton claimed that women who practised prostitution not only lived well when compared with their counterparts who worked long hours for little pay as dressmakers or laundresses, but often also made marriages that offered some measure of upward social mobility.[113] This reading was challenged by Acton's contemporary critics and more recently by historian Frances Finnegan, who argued that on the contrary, streetwalkers' irregular and dissipated lifestyles exposed them to general poor health, disease and unwanted pregnancies, which, in the absence of husband or friends to support them, often resulted in destitution, commitment to the workhouse and early death. Finnegan questioned 'why the popular image of the prostitute as demoralized creature treading the downward path ending in drunkenness, destitution and disease, was one which was so widely held if it was untrue?'[114]

Acton's thesis has been resurrected by Judith Walkowitz, who has argued that prostitution was a transitional stage through which many women passed before being re-assimilated into the ranks of the respectable poor and working classes. According to this reading, women turned to prostitution as a temporary 'refuge from uneasy circumstances', and the majority spent a limited time on the streets.[115] The implication is that women were able to opt in and out of prostitution as economic circumstances dictated. Contemporary commentators, therefore, constructed a somewhat over-simplistic dichotomy, in which prostitution was seen either as the inevitable precursor to dissipation, illness and early death on the one hand, or as a casual and temporary occupation that was followed by rehabilitation into the ranks of the respectable poor on the other. This debate has been revived and developed by historians who have been similarly divided. The situation in Kent, however, was more mixed than either of these theoretical models allows for. Makeshift economies were fluid and flexible, and over-generalization risks missing both their inherent complexities and the wide range of individual circumstances. Analysis of the intervals of time between the first and last documented mentions of ninety-seven women identified from court and other records as having been involved in prostitution suggests how long each might have spent on the streets. Of the total, 61 per cent appear in the documentary records within a timeframe of less than two years, supporting the hypothesis that for these women prostitution was a transitional phase. Clearly this methodology is not fool-proof, since if a woman ceased to be arrested it does not necessarily follow that she had ceased to practise prostitution. However, arrest records such as that of Emma Preston, who appeared in court on four occasions in the space of two years and is then mentioned no more, or of Emma Goldsmith, five times in fourteen months and then no more, or Emma Bennet, arrested for soliciting three times in seven months and then no more, do strongly suggest that significant changes may have taken place to these women's lives and individual economies.[116]

A substantial minority of the women did, however, remain engaged in prostitution over a longer period. Of the identified Kent group, 15 per cent were arrested periodically on prostitution-related charges over periods of longer than five years, suggesting that they were involved in prostitution for at least that long. In one case, that of Emma Smith, the length of time between the first and last documented arrest was eleven years and four months. Indeed, it was the opinion of several contemporary observers in Kent that the regime of medical care introduced under the CD Acts served to improve the health of women who practised prostitution and was therefore a contributory factor in extending their careers on the streets.[117] Rev. Hugh Baker, for example, whose missionary work brought him into contact with the Woolwich Rescue Home, observed that 'these women continue in this life for years; they keep coming back over and over again ... they are very old, many of them'.[118] Meanwhile James Baxendale, manager of the Greenwich Women's Refuge, believed that based on his experience, prostitutes spent an average of three years on the streets.[119]

The pattern of recidivism alluded to by Baxendale suggests that there was, however, some substance to the 'downward path to destitution' stereotype, and his testimony substantiates the evidence of individual examples. The reconstructed life histories of Catherine Jackson and Emily Huntley add qualitatively to our understanding of the way in which, in some cases, the move into prostitution does appear to have represented a significant step on a downward path. Jackson, of whose origins little is known, was born in 1851. By the age of sixteen, Poor Law Union records capture her on a rotational course between the Sheppey Union Workhouse, the Kent County Asylum at Barming and the county gaol.[120] At the age of seventeen, already having 'scarcely been out of the prison or the asylum', she was once again brought before the Sheerness magistrate for swearing at the Master of the Sheppey Union Workhouse.[121] A previous spell in the Barming Heath Asylum had resulted in Jackson's discharge after the surgeon had given his opinion that she was perfectly sane and just had an 'ungovernable' temper. Two years later and this time arrested as a prostitute, whilst in police custody she attempted to commit suicide by tying a piece of tape around her neck. She served a three-week sentence on this occasion and one of three months the following year, following which she disappears from the court records until the end of 1875.[122] After this, however, she was regularly summoned before magistrates on charges of being a riotous prostitute. Typically these charges alleged that 'being a common prostitute she did wander in a certain public street and did there and then behave in a riotous manner'.[123] Between 1875 and 1878 Catherine served seven sentences of three months and one of two months, each time with hard labour. Therefore during this period she spent twenty-six months out of thirty-six in Maidstone Gaol. Eventually Catherine was referred again to a doctor to be examined as to her state of mind, and was sent back to the County Lunatic Asylum, where she is captured by the 1881 and 1891 censuses.[124] She died in the asylum at the age of forty-nine.[125] The explanatory framework of the makeshift economy allows for an interpretation of these events that incorporates victimization as well as agency.

The similar case of Emily Huntley, who ended her days in the Sheppey Union Workhouse, likewise contributes to an understanding of nineteenth-century prostitution in which access to a variety of resources over the course of the life cycle reflects agency even on the part of women whose lives ended in apparent destitution. Born in Chepstow, Monmouthshire in 1845, by the age of seventeen Emily was living in Bristol with George Huntley, a cooper's labourer whom she subsequently married.[126] The couple lived next door to George's family, Emily earning a living as a hat-box maker, as did George's sister Mary. Evidently the couple separated some time after this, since by 1871 Emily had moved to Aldershot in Hampshire, a garrison town and a subjected district under the CD Acts, where she lodged next to the Army and Navy Hotel and her occupation was recorded as 'general servant'. The likelihood is that she was already living by prostitution at this time, since after arriving in Sheerness at some point in the following few years, she was arrested on a number of charges mentioning prostitution, riotous behaviour, drunkenness and assault, to which she pleaded guilty.[127] Between December 1875 and October 1877, Emily served four custodial sentences of three months each, and one of one month.[128] By the 1881 census, at the age of thirty-six, Emily was living in the Sheppey Union Workhouse, described as a prostitute and a pauper.[129] It is likely that she resorted to the workhouse as a result of sickness, since she died there a few months later.[130]

These examples suggest a more varied picture than some previous theoretical models have allowed for. Whilst for a substantial number of women in the Kentish ports, dockyards and garrisons prostitution did represent a step towards disease, further poverty and even admission to the workhouse or the asylum, for many more it did not. Statistics relating to the Greenwich Women's Refuge which was mentioned earlier, for example, show that of the 147 women from Greenwich, Woolwich and Deptford who passed through the institution's doors between 1872 and 1882, twenty-four (16 per cent) subsequently married, thirty-five (24 per cent) went into service, thirteen (9 per cent) went back to family or friends, whilst twenty-one (14 per cent) returned to a life of prostitution.[131]

The Greenwich statistics on subsequent marriage are supported by the evidence of recorded marriages of a number of other Kentish women who had previously practised prostitution. This group does not include a separate group of women who earned money by prostitution whilst already married or having separated. For reasons that have been explored by historians, it is likely that a substantial additional number of women contracted common-law marriages that were undocumented and therefore cannot be traced.[132]

The cases of Emma Partlett and Harriet Herrington are typical of women who married legally, in that they married within their own class and immediate community. Herrington came to the attention of Gravesend police on two occasions at the end of 1870 and beginning of 1871 on charges of drunkenness, and on both occasions was described in court as a prostitute.[133] At this time she was lodging in a house occupied by a labourer's family and describing her occupation as a nurse.[134] Two years later at the age of twenty-six, Harriet married Reuben Ransley, a fellow lodger at the Pattens', and they moved to rural Upchurch, where Reuben took work as a brickfield labourer.[135] Harriet died childless fifteen years later at the age of forty-one.[136]

Likewise Emma Partlett, who was the fourth of six children of a labourer and was brought up in Bull Yard in Gravesend, one of the crowded courts behind the High Street that was inhabited mainly by labourers and watermen.[137] Emma's father died whilst she was still in her teens, following which the family moved the short distance to Market Alley, where Emma's mother Elizabeth supported the family through dealing in rags and bones.[138] Two of her brothers found work, as a coal porter and an iron moulder. Around the age of seventeen, and by now described in the local paper as 'a young prostitute, living in Market Alley', Emma was charged with being drunk and disorderly, shortly after which she sought admission to the Gravesend Union Workhouse on account of 'sickness', where she stayed for two weeks.[139] Two years afterwards Emma married Isaac Ambrose, a pot man at the Waterman's Arms, a public house that had associations with prostitution.[140] Isaac took employment as a steam-boat stoker, and they had a family. Emma's mother Elizabeth continued to live with them, still dealing in rags and bones.[141] In the late 1870s Isaac spent some time in the county gaol, and was represented in his absence by Emma at a court case for not sending the children to school.[142] After Isaac's death, Emma took lodgings in Swan Yard with her youngest two children, the elder two being at industrial schools, and she earned a living dealing in marine stores.[143] The unions of these women did not, as William Acton claimed, represent improved social status, nor did they ensure a complete escape from poverty, but they did provide a measure of security against outright destitution.[144] Furthermore, marriage within their immediate communities suggests a high level of integration and absence of social ostracism.

The makeshift economy therefore provides an illuminating interpretive framework through which to examine street-level prostitution. It allows for a greater degree of variation and heterogeneity in women's circumstances than either of the long-established 'prostitution as transitory phase' or the 'prostitution as downward path' stereotypes have previously allowed for. It seems clear that Kentish women who engaged in prostitution did not conform to a single model; on the contrary they encompassed the full range of archetypes recognizable from the contemporary literature. In terms of total length of time spent on the street, degree of entrenchment into prostitution as a way of life, and ultimate personal outcomes, the women identified in this chapter represent the complete spectrum of circumstances. Furthermore, this reading poses a challenge to simplistic 'victimization' models of prostitution. Whilst these women were undoubtedly the victims of socio-economic circumstances and of official policy, many appear to have demonstrated a degree of agency, as demonstrated by the pursuit of individual survival strategies within makeshift economies, and by decisions made about their own life course, albeit that this was often from a limited set of alternatives. Questions of agency are pursued further in the following chapter, which turns to a ground-level exploration of the conditions of life amidst which women who made money from prostitution in the Kentish ports and dockyards lived in the third quarter of the nineteenth century.

2 PROSTITUTION, LIFESTYLE AND LIFE CYCLE

Emily Baseden, the twenty-one-year-old landlady of the Princess Royal public house in Chatham, was brought before the bench in March 1861 charged with 'knowingly allowing prostitutes to assemble' on the premises.[1] Notwithstanding her defence counsel's strong objection to the alleged 'crusade' waged against certain public houses by the authorities, the bench found Baseden guilty and imposed a fine of five pounds plus thirteen shillings costs, the maximum possible for the offence. The evidence uncovered during the petty sessions hearing was such that the Parish of Chatham was prompted to bring a further prosecution later that month, this time against Baseden together with William Payne, the landlord of the premises whom Baseden claimed was her uncle, on the more serious charge of 'keeping a house of ill-fame'.[2] This time the case was referred to Quarter Sessions.

The details thrown up during the various hearings related to this case, together with those of the numerous similar ones prosecuted through the courts, open a window onto the everyday workings of prostitution in the Kentish ports and dockyards in the third quarter of the nineteenth century. Frequently reported by the local press in some depth, the evidence laid before magistrates in the form of testimonies of defendants and witnesses (albeit that these were mediated through the language and attitudes of the court reporters) nevertheless affords a closer scrutiny of the workings of street-level prostitution than those offered by most alternative contemporary sources. It casts light on factors such as the ways in which women were recruited into prostitution, where they lived and how they met their clients, their sexual health and public behaviour. This chapter, then, explores the ways of living and modus operandi of the women identified through the surviving sources as having practised prostitution in the Kentish ports and dockyard towns. The discussion takes as its driving theme the question of individual agency, that is to say the degree of control exercised by these women over their own histories. This approach avoids viewing women who fell into prostitution through a one-dimensional lens of victimization, and thus replicating the simplistic dichotomies that permeated nineteenth-century discussions of the subject.

One expression of agency was through decisions made about living accommodation, and thus this discussion turns firstly to a consideration of the function of the brothel. This term was applied by the authorities to any premises where prostitution took place. It does not imply any particular relationship, financial or otherwise, between woman and proprietor, nor that the woman necessarily lived on the premises. Evidence related to what were also known as 'houses of ill-repute' in Kent, as uncovered by prosecution cases, paints a broad and varied picture. Kentish prostitute women predominantly lived either in public houses and common lodging houses, shared lodgings with other women who made their living in a similar way, or cohabited with men, but there is little evidence of pimping. Some premises were run much the same as other common lodging houses, and the named tenant knowingly sub-let rooms to women who used them for prostitution, presumably risking prosecution in exchange for a regular rental income, rather than being directly financially involved in the transactions that took place. Alternatively a woman rented her own lodging, which she may or may not have shared with one or more other women, and took clients there.

The evidence given by Harriett Wood, the sixteen-year-old chief prosecution witness in the Princess Royal case, casts some light on the role of licensed premises in the operation of prostitution and provides one example of the financial agreements entered into between women and their landlords. Wood had evidently left her position in service and had been introduced to the Princess Royal by another girl. Having applied to Baseden for a room, Wood was told that she might have one to herself together with a key, provided that she conducted herself 'as other girls in the house'. Whilst she would not be 'boarded' and no mention was made of there being rent to pay, she was told that one shilling would be due when a man slept with her. She reported that the two other girls who lived there both handed over money to the landlady after men had gone with them to their rooms. Wood's evidence was corroborated by Ann Connor, who had also spent some time at the Princess Royal. Connor had also been told that a shilling would be due when 'a chap stopped all night' with her.

A similar account was given to the Medway Board of Guardians by a twenty-three-year-old girl 'of a certain class' who was described as being 'in a dreadful state' and who applied for admission to the workhouse.[3] She told how she had slept at four named public houses with men, but stated that she had not had regular lodgings at any of them, thus reflecting a recognition of the legal distinction between this arrangement and being 'harboured' by the landlords. In a similar arrangement, Mary Ann Burke was charged no rent for her room at the Earl of Cardigan, also in Chatham, but clients paid three pence at the bar 'for going upstairs' and then paid Mary Ann directly for the sexual transaction, between two and five shillings.[4] These financial deals whereby landlords took a fee per transaction in lieu of rent were evidently devised as a means of circumventing the legal restrictions on publicans 'harbouring' prostitutes.

Other testimonies heard by the Kentish benches by way of evidence in pros-ecution cases related to prostitution paint similar pictures with regard to the role of public houses in prostitution. In another Chatham case, Jackson Fryer was convicted of 'harbouring' prostitutes on the evidence of Elizabeth Foster, Elizabeth Bowen and Annie Spicer. Giving evidence, all acknowledged living by prostitution and to having lived at the premises.[5] Newspaper reports of Annual Licensing Day hearings at petty sessions provide additional insight into the rela-tionship between public houses and prostitution. In Dover in 1870, for example, the license was withheld from the Crown after local residents had presented a petition and given evidence that 'common prostitutes' resided on the premises.[6] In other arrangements, publicans let rooms on a non-residential basis. Annie Hearnden, landlady of the Two Brewers in Week Street Maidstone, let rooms to women for the night, although the house was not licensed as a lodging house.[7] The Bee Hive Inn in Dover was brought to the attention of magistrates when publican George Eastman permitted a customer to 'retire' to a bedroom with a woman whom he took there.[8]

The varied picture painted by this evidence is substantiated by police statistics relating to the operations of the CD Acts. These classified the premises known to the police as 'brothels' into the categories 'public houses and beer houses', 'private houses in which women reside and practise prostitution', 'private houses in which accommodation is let indiscriminately to all comers for the purpose of pros-titution', or 'other locations such as coffee houses'. The proportions of the total accounted for by each class of premises varied markedly both from place to place and over time. Whilst 'licensed premises' and 'private houses where women live' were the two most common categories across locations and dates, public houses played a much larger role in Chatham than in any other town (60 per cent of the total in 1865), and none at all in Woolwich and Greenwich where private houses predominated (9 per cent and 61 per cent respectively in 1865). The most marked change over time was the overall decline in prominence of public houses and beer-shops, and the proportionate rise in 'others' such as coffee houses. The most likely explanation for this change is the Licensing Act of 1872, which gave magistrates increased powers over the way public houses were run.

Turning the spotlight onto the way in which private properties operated as brothels, the primary distinction made by the police was between those where women lived on the premises and those where rooms were let, according to the official description, 'indiscriminately to all comers for the purpose of prostitu-tion'. An example of the latter is North Cottage in North Street, Gravesend. Ann Elizabeth Court rented the house in early 1859, claiming that she intended to live by taking in washing and renting out beds, allegedly not knowing that the house had previously earned a reputation as a brothel. A man who 'engaged' a bed was subsequently visited in his room by a young woman known to the police as a prostitute. The fact that Court herself was involved in the attempt to sell an item stolen from the man at a pawnbroker throws some doubt on her assertion that she was unaware of the use to which the room was put.[9] The same house was named as a brothel during court hearings in 1862 and again in 1865, both of which incidents involved thefts from clients perpetrated by the same woman, Elizabeth Mitchell. The newspaper report of one of these incidents described the address as 'the notorious North Cottage'.[10] Several years later still, Sarah Jael and James Lane were separately convicted of running the house as a brothel in 1871 and 1873 respectively, the prosecution of Jael being supported by the evidence of neighbours.[11] That Lane was described in court as a 'labourer' contributes to our understanding of how a brothel was defined, since this would suggest that he was not directly involved in the transactions that took place there but collected rent as the landlord, and that this was not his sole income.

The majority of Kentish brothels identified during petty sessions hearings were run either by women on their own or as part of a couple, supporting the hypothesis of prostitution as female subculture. Catharine Gladwell, who frequently came to the attention of Gravesend police, was a married woman whose husband was in the lunatic asylum. Gladwell, who attempted to support her family of four teenage daughters by hawking, was herself described as a prostitute in court on one of the many occasions when she was arrested for drunkenness. Evidently she supplemented her income by sub-letting rooms to women who used them for prostitution. Elizabeth Burton and Ann Page, both identified in court as prostitutes, were said to have lived there, and the latter appeared to give evidence as a witness for the prosecution.[12]

Further examples include Thomas and Sarah Day, who will be discussed further in Chapter 5, and who ran their home in Three Tun Yard in Gravesend as a brothel for over five years in the early 1870s. Sarah Day herself had a conviction for soliciting and had served two months with hard labour.[13] Other examples include Ann Woodford, who ran a 'house of ill-fame' in Ifield Street in Gravesend, and who said that she was married but did not live with her husband, and Ann Gurney, who was convicted for running a disorderly brothel whilst cohabiting with a common-law husband, thus suggesting that the police recognized that she was the proprietor and responsible for the business.[14]

The picture painted by the evidence related to the premises used for prostitution, therefore, is a broad and diverse one, in which both public and private houses played a significant role. On the whole, women appear to have enjoyed some measure of autonomy and some element of choice with regard to their living arrangements, albeit from alternatives restricted by socio-economic circumstances. The occasional piece of evidence corroborates suggestions that some public house landlords exercised an abusive power over the women who lodged on their premises. William Payne of the Princess Royal, who has already been mentioned, was alleged by Police Superintendent Everist to have turned women onto the street in order to 'have a fresh lot'. Similarly in Dover, it was apparently the case that when a beer-house was sold, 'the wretched women living there were sold with the furniture to the next owner'.[15] However, it would be too simplistic to interpret these incidents in terms of sexual exploitation, since female licensees appear to have been equally unscrupulous. Sarah Stroud, who ran the Buffalo's Head in Rochester as a brothel, enticed young women to take up residence there on the promise of being able to make a good living. A young witness identified only as Elizabeth claimed to have been thrown out by Stroud because she did not make enough money. This allegation was corroborated by Anne Wanstall, who stated that when the man with whom she had cohabited there left to seek work, she had been told that she must 'do as the others did' in order to pay her rent.[16] These incidents help explain why some women appear to have preferred the independence of their own lodging.

In Sheerness, the suggestion that prostitution operated as a female subculture is even stronger. Norina White, who herself had convictions related to prostitution, let lodgings to other women, whilst Sarah Charlesworth and Elizabeth Tremain, both of whom were frequent visitors to the magistrates' court as defendants on charges that publicly identified them as prostitutes, lodged in the household of Marianne Hall, who described herself as a 'stationer'. Rachel Levy, a soldier's widow who herself had numerous convictions as a 'riotous prostitute', lived in Fountain Passage and let lodgings to other women who also passed before the magistrates' bench on charges related to prostitution. One of these, Mary Bennett, was a long-term tenant inherited from a previous landlady. The 1881 census captures several cases of Sheerness women with recorded associations to prostitution apparently cohabiting with sailors or marines; in these instances the woman is listed as the head of household and the man is the only lodger in the house on census night. Cecil Workman, for example, a seaman in the Royal Navy, was lodging with Hannah Clasper, who had been convicted on more than one occasion as a prostitute, and Edward Owens with Martha Stimpson, who also had convictions for prostitution.[17] Likewise, Royal Marine George Jennings spent census night 1881 lodging with Emma Williams, whose occupation is recorded as 'prostitute' and who is designated as head of household.[18] Williams lived in the same building as Marianne Hall, mentioned previously, who by this date lived with her two teenage sons and a 26-year-old sailor lodger. Thus the picture painted by this body of evidence is one of women who practised prostitution with some degree of autonomy and agency.

The inference that prostitution was largely a female subculture at this point in place and time is further reinforced by evidence relating to the collaborations in crime between prostitute women and their female landladies. Examples include Sarah Brown, described as a prostitute, and Sarah Goodyer, a brothel-keeper, who jointly robbed a client of six pounds and ten shillings, an occurrence that according to the police was not the first to have occurred at the house.[19] Similarly, as was seen previously, when prostitute Sarah Rouse stole a 'pin' from a client, it was her landlady Ann Elizabeth Court who offered the item for sale at Munn's pawnbroker. The women were described by the courtroom reporter as 'Mrs Court and her friend Sarah Rouse'.[20]

Prostitution and Life Cycle

The prosecution cases against Emily Baseden and William Payne for keeping a house 'of ill fame', as has been seen, threw up detailed evidence that sheds light on the way in which the Princess Royal public house operated in the procurement of prostitution. Amongst the details disclosed in the courtroom was the fact that Harriett Wood, the prosecution witness, was sixteen years old. The alleged extreme youth of girls recruited into prostitution was a central thread in the dominant discourse in the second half of the nineteenth century, and questions related to the ages of prostituted women preoccupied much of the contemporary commentary. The press campaign waged by the *Pall Mall Gazette*, which culminated in the notorious 'Maiden Tribute of Modern Babylon' scandal of 1885, did much to nurture the belief that large numbers of very young girls were being forced into prostitution. This notion has, however, been challenged by Judith Walkowitz, who concluded that 'the throngs of child prostitutes so highly advertised during the white-slavery campaign of 1885 must be dismissed as imaginary products of sensational journalism intended to capture the attention of a prurient Victorian public'.[21]

The light cast onto this question by the Kentish evidence is somewhat opaque, since reliable data relating to the ages of Kentish women involved in prostitution is both scant and contradictory and has to be approached with a measure of caution. The forty-one patients at the Chatham Lock Hospital on census night in 1871, for example, had an average age of twenty years and eleven months, the oldest being thirty-two and the youngest sixteen.[22] Of the 590 women admitted during the six months to March 1871, furthermore, only thirty-five (6 per cent) were under twenty years old.[23] However, the length of time taken from first risk of infection to diagnosable symptoms means that the average age of this group of hospitalized women would be expected to be higher than the average. This group was therefore not wholly representative of the population of women who lived either fully or partially by prostitution.

However, turning to the admission records of Maidstone Gaol, the absence of very young offenders is again apparent. The average age of the seventy-six women admitted during the twelve months ending 31 December 1883 and whose occupation was recorded by prison authorities as 'prostitute' was twenty-five years and five months. The oldest was forty-two-year-old Sarah Nash of Rochester, and the youngest were two seventeen-year-olds, Ellen Freeman and Catherine Howard, both of Chatham, convicted for drunkenness and vagrancy respectively. Once again, this picture is likely to have been distorted by policing and magisterial policy and practice with regard to juvenile offenders on the one hand, and the incremental custodial sentences imposed on recidivists on the other. Nevertheless, this average is higher than might be expected, and challenges contemporary narratives of the prevalence of juvenile prostitution.[24]

Statistics compiled by the Metropolitan Police in relation to the workings of the CD Acts suggest that the majority of women registered as prostitutes under this legislation were aged between twenty-one and twenty-six. Of the 844 women registered in the Kentish subjected districts as at 31 December 1871, 41 per cent were aged between twenty-one and under twenty-six, and 23 per cent were twenty-six and under thirty-one, but only 16 per cent were aged under twenty. Once again, however, these statistics have to be approached with caution, since considerable doubt was cast on their accuracy by many contemporaries. William Krause, a missionary with eighteen years' experience working in the subjected district of Woolwich, for example, claimed that a considerable number of young prostitutes there were aged under eighteen, some as young as thirteen and fourteen.[25] Similarly, in Chatham, fifty-six residents presented a petition to Parliament to the effect that the Metropolitan Police statistics in respect of juvenile prostitutes underestimated the problem.[26]

The accuracy of the police statistics in respect of the ages of women identified as prostitutes is likely to have been affected by the operation of the register. Officers responsible for overseeing the operation of the Acts in the subjected districts were, according to the Metropolitan Police's own account, charged with making efforts towards reclamation and rescue where possible, before registering a woman as a prostitute. Clearly this was more likely to happen with younger women who were less well entrenched in prostitution and were therefore believed to stand more chance of rehabilitation. Seventeen Kentish girls under the age of eighteen were apparently 'returned to friends' in this way in 1874, and a further seven cautioned by the police and not registered. One example, as reported in the Assistant Commissioner's report for 1874, concerned a fourteen-year-old called Harriett, from Gravesend. Harriett was apparently 'found in the company of prostitutes' by police, 'her mother was seen and made re-acquainted the following day, and she has not been seen in bad company since'.[27]

Whether or not these reclamation and welfare efforts of the police were exaggerated for the purpose of cultivating positive public relations, the number of young teenagers engaging in prostitution is likely to have been under-recorded when other evidence is taken into consideration. Yet the Metropolitan Police statistics relating to teenagers do conform remarkably closely to national judicial statistics that purported to quantify the women known to local police forces as prostitutes in the period before the commencement of the CD Acts. These also suggest that the numbers of very young girls who practised prostitution were small, the percentage of the total represented by under sixteen-year-olds across Kent for the year 1862, for example, being fourteen. This aggregate masks a wide variation from place to place, however, for example only five out of 206 women in Dover were noted to be under the age of sixteen.[28]

Newspaper reportage of petty sessions hearings of prosecution cases related to prostitution helps to flesh out the picture drawn by statistical evidence. Sarah Cunningham of Folkestone, for instance, was fifteen when she got into the company of 'bad characters' and went to live at a house 'of bad repute'.[29] During the trial of Fanny Blunt, described as an 'unfortunate', for stealing a porte-monnaie containing nine shillings, it emerged that she had been 'on the streets' since the age of twelve.[30] Often, it was the point at which landlords were prosecuted for running premises as brothels that the involvement of very young girls in prostitution was uncovered. At the hearing of the case against Jesse and Sarah Dunster for keeping a house 'of ill fame' at the Earl of Cardigan public house, one of the key witnesses was Mary Anne Burke, mentioned earlier, who was thirteen years old at the time.[31] In another case, ten girls were found by Dover police in the upstairs room of the Marine Arms in the company of thirty soldiers. One of the girls was fourteen years old, and the rest aged between fifteen and eighteen, according to the police officers' testimony.[32]

Thus the anecdotal evidence suggests that a number of young girls did become involved in prostitution at some level, though it does not help towards an understanding of how deeply entrenched they became nor how long they remained involved in that way of life. References to thirteen- and fourteen-year-olds in the records are remarkable not for their frequency but for the fact that their ages are mentioned at all, suggesting that local newspaper reportage both reflected and contributed towards the dominant discourse.

Some young women were still living in the family home at the same time as practising prostitution, suggesting that this way of life did not necessarily involve estrangement from their families. Mary Jane Brown, Eliza Belcher, Lavinia Pearce and Emma Partlett are examples to be found in Gravesend; the former was still living with her parents some six years after her first conviction as a prostitute.[33] Other women practised prostitution whilst married or cohabiting with common-law husbands. Magistrates in Dover, for example, expressed themselves of the opinion that 'The state of morals revealed by this case was most revolting', after hearing the case against Jane Williams for stealing from a client. Having had sex with mariner Thomas Davis, Williams stole money from his trouser pocket and returned home to go to bed with the man 'who lived with her as her husband'.[34] The members of the Parliamentary Select Committee heard, in 1882, from Stephen Rimbault, town missionary at Maidstone, that from his knowledge married women practised prostitution, often with their husbands' knowledge, 'for the sake of obtaining dress', and that prostitutes who married soldiers or 'common men' did not leave what Rimbault referred to as 'the profession'.[35]

Other women who earned money by prostitution were single mothers, once again underscoring the link with poverty. Jane Boorman and Jane Waters, both of Maidstone for example, alternated their appearances at the magistrates' court for prostitution-related offences with summonses for not sending their children to school, whilst Mary Ann Brown, alleged to be a prostitute by a neighbour, lived with her thirteen- and eleven-year-old daughters in Woollett Street in Maidstone, and described her occupation as dressmaker.[36] Amelia Hearn was distinguished by being mentioned twice in the local press in the space of five months in 1879; the first was to report the death of her two-year-old child from convulsions in the workhouse, and the second to report her conviction as a prostitute for disorderly behaviour.[37]

Numerous instances of what might be considered 'professional' prostitution, that is, women of the same family working in prostitution, are thrown up by the Kentish records, thus providing a corrective to the thesis of prostitution as a transitory phase of life cycle. Examples include Fanny Blunt of Dover, mentioned previously, whose sister had 'led the same life', and Dover brothel-keeper Susannah Tolney, whose own twenty-year-old daughter was herself prostituted, according to the press. The mothers of Harriett Crossthwaite and Sarah Martin, young Gravesend girls who practised prostitution, both kept brothels. Sister groups include Priscilla and Patience Roland of Gravesend, the Lucas sisters Leonora and Clara of Maidstone who were discussed previously, and Elizabeth and Margaret Jones, also of Maidstone, who are discussed in more detail later in this chapter. The role of family relationship is reflected in the careers of sisters Mary Ann and Hannah Simpson of Gravesend, who were the second and third of six children of an Essex shoemaker. The family relocated to Kent when Mary Ann and Hannah, just one year apart in age, were young children, and set up homes in Brewhouse Yard and subsequently in Clarence Street, Gravesend. In 1856 the girls, described erroneously as twins, had appeared at the magistrates' court as witnesses in the prosecution of sixteen-year-old William Clements for what is described as a 'criminal assault' on them. In October 1866, at the ages of sixteen and seventeen respectively, the girls were arrested in High Street. Hannah, described as a prostitute, was arrested for using obscene language and Mary Ann for being drunk and disorderly. They were both sent to Maidstone Gaol for fourteen days with hard labour. One week after their release, having made their way back to Gravesend, the girls were again found together, drunk and creating a disturbance in West Street, between one and two in the morning. Described as prostitutes at the subsequent court hearing, they were returned to Maidstone for one month. Over the following years both girls were involved in a number of court cases, both as defendants and complainants. Mary Ann served two sentences of one month each in 1870, each time for obstructing the footpath, admitting in court on one occasion that she did not know how many times she had been to Maidstone Gaol. The level of recidivism reflected in the records of both sisters, both separately and together, suggests a degree of entrenchment into prostitution at this stage, although each disappears from the records shortly afterwards.

Agency

These cases, together with the others in this chapter, raise the question of individual agency. In the case of the Princess Royal public house with which the chapter opened, it was seen that sixteen-year-old Harriett Wood had left a position in service to take up what we must assume represented a preferable alternative. Thus Wood's move to the Princess Royal can be interpreted as self-determination. In the previous chapter it was seen that whilst it would be over-simplistic to view the relationship between poverty and prostitution as a matter of cause and effect, the latter nevertheless constituted a prominent resource within the mixed makeshift economies of many women of the casual poor. Whilst both the weight of evidence and the consensus of contemporary opinion therefore link prostitution overwhelmingly with poverty, the connection is associational and begs the question as to why some women took this route and others did not. It is far from clear, from the surviving evidence, what distinguished the women who chose this option from others in similar circumstances who did not. The same interpretive difficulty, as has been seen, initiated extensive contemporary speculation. The conclusions that were offered were frequently based on explanatory frameworks that highlighted personal morals, victimization and seduction.

Eschewing modes of interpretation popular in the nineteenth century, modern approaches to this question are able to draw on theoretical debates in the fields of sociology and women's studies to arrive at a reading that identifies human agency as the determining feature. That is to say, despite the link with poverty, the move into prostitution was rarely made at the point of absolute destitution or starvation, and an element of self-determination or choice was what distinguished those women who included prostitution within their own personal makeshift economies and those who did not. Once again, individual case histories serve to illustrate this point. Kate True, for instance, was born in Devon and was brought to live in Gravesend at the age of four. She had evidently held down several situations in service, before leaving her employer 'to follow her present dissipated course of life'.[38] It is clearly impossible to determine Kate's motivation for leaving service for a life on the streets, or indeed whether this move was one of her choice at all, since the interpretation we are offered is mediated through the discourse of the courtroom. However, since she had seemingly previously held down more than one position in the past, her move into prostitution could be argued to reflect some element of agency. Likewise Jane Brown, who was admitted to the Dover Home for Young Women following a court appearance, who had subsequently 'quitted and gone back to her old course of life', suggesting that she preferred life on the streets to that in an institution.[39] Mary Ann Burke of New Brompton, who was mentioned earlier, worked at a school before reportedly leaving home to live at the Earl of Cardigan beer-house, having got into conversation with a girl who took her there.[40] The case of Harriet Wood, with whom this chapter opened, is even more persuasive. Harriet had previously been in service at rural Wouldham, but left and had taken to frequenting 'low public houses' and robbing her mother of money and clothes. Despite her mother having gone to look for her and having taken her home twice, Harriet, it would appear, preferred the apparent bright lights of the public houses in Chatham to living with her parents, since she left home once again to live at the Princess Royal.[41]

A comparison with the lives of siblings from the same background, where such evidence is available, helps throw additional light on the question of self-determination. The difference in personal outcomes suggests a degree of individual agency and deliberate choice, albeit from a restricted set of alternatives. Jane Garlinge of Canterbury, for example, was the youngest of the five children of a market gardener. Jane's parents Richard and Mary both survived into old age, and Richard worked as a gardener into his seventies, indicating that whilst the family may have been poor, they were not destitute. Jane left home to live in Canterbury, where she came to the notice of the police on at least two occasions for offences relating to prostitution. She is captured on the 1871 census resident at the police station, described as a prostitute and awaiting the hearing of a charge of being at the barracks for immoral purposes. Her sister Charlotte, meanwhile, pursued a different course, marrying a labourer and giving birth to seven children. She lived with her family in the same rural village for thirty years.[42]

The parallel stories of Sarah Darge, who was mentioned in the previous chapter, and her sister Clara provide a further example. It will be remembered that Sarah gained the reputation as a prostitute after numerous arrests on the streets of Gravesend. Her younger sister Clara, meanwhile, went into service, firstly in Lee and subsequently with the family of a German merchant in Brixton.[43] She married a railway clerk called William Jackson, and at the 1901 census was to be found living with Jackson and their child in Bermondsey, south London, in a working-class neighbourhood where fellow residents included a sorter at the post office, two police constables, a teacher and a commercial traveller.[44] As was seen previously, the girls' family of origin suffered a reduction in financial circumstances on the death of the main breadwinner. Arguably the children were victims of an economic system that was structured in such a way that their widowed mother was unable to maintain the family adequately on her own, and of a social system that failed to provide alternative support. However, one sister took the route into service, the route often advocated as a pathway into the ranks of the 'respectable' working classes, whilst Sarah took to life on the streets, a course that does not appear to have led to improved prospects, but rather to a death in the workhouse.

A further example is that of Mary Jane Harriet Brown, who was born in Lewes, Sussex in 1846, the eldest child of a labourer. The family moved frequently during Mary Jane's childhood, possibly in pursuit of work, between locations across Sussex and Kent before settling in Gravesend, where Thomas Brown found work as a coal labourer and took accommodation in St John's Place, one of the crowded courts of poor-quality housing behind West Street.[45] Mary Jane became known to the police before the age of fourteen after a series of petty thefts, on one occasion of a pound of cheese, and on another a length of lead pipe, the latter of which earned her a custodial sentence of two months.[46] By the age of eighteen Mary Jane was being arrested for drunkenness and prostitution-related offences on a regular basis, and her twelfth appearance before the bench, for being drunk and acting indecently with a man, resulted in a custodial sentence of three months.[47] The following year, having been caught pilfering from a fellow customer at the Brunswick Arms, it became apparent that her mother Harriet had also been involved in the incident, and they were both imprisoned.[48] Mary Jane complained to the police that her father had 'knocked her about', expressed a wish to enter a reformatory or penitentiary because she could not remain living at home, and threatened to take her own life.[49] Evidently this did not happen, since shortly afterwards, now being described in court as a 'disorderly prostitute', Mary Jane was found drunk and insensible lying in a pool of water and mud and had to be carried to the police station.[50] Three months after this, a case of theft of a loin of lamb involving both mother and daughter was referred to quarter sessions, where Mary Jane pleaded guilty and her mother not guilty. In sentencing Mary Jane to twelve months imprisonment, the magistrate said that at twenty-one years of age she had lived the life of a profligate, but conceded that 'the evil example set to her by her mother might have influenced her to become a bad woman'.[51] Evidently on her release Mary Jane returned to the family home, resumed her old lifestyle and was back before the bench on a drunk and disorderly offence within a few months.[52] The family relocated to Canterbury at some point over the next few years, Mary Jane accompanying them, after which she disappears from the records.[53] Albeit made from a limited set of alternatives, Mary Jane's decision to re-join her family rather than to seek admittance to one of the numerous rescue institutions might be seen as indicative of some level of independent action and, as with the other examples, it would be an oversimplification to view her purely through a lens of powerless victimization.

Public Demeanour

The public behaviour of women who earned local reputations as prostitutes often contributed to this process of labelling, since, as Judith Walkowitz noted, they often displayed a degree of independence and assertiveness rarely found among women of their own social class, and which was certainly unknown amongst middle-class women.[54] The press reportage of petty sessions cases often contains vivid narratives of prostitutes' conduct within the courtroom, frequently combined with a description of events surrounding the case. Whilst these narratives should be read with caution, for reasons that will be outlined in the following chapter, they nevertheless enable some impression to be formed of the women's general public demeanour. It is certainly the case that the majority of streetwalkers do not appear to have conformed to prescriptive mid-Victorian notions of respectable feminine public behaviour, and that on the whole they displayed a marked lack of intimidation by authority figures. Sarah Valentine of Dover, for instance, having been convicted on a charge of assaulting a police officer and given the option of a fine, retorted to the bench that she would instead 'go to gaol and lay it out'.[55] However, it is evident that such female independence and assertiveness was not exclusive to women identified as prostitutes. Drinking in public houses, public brawling and drunkenness, swearing and a lack of intimidation by authority appear to have been characteristic of a wider group of women of the casual poor who were mentioned in the local press, both those who earned money by prostitution and those who did not. Physical assertiveness is illustrated by the case of Mary Ann Hicks of Chatham, who bodily intervened when a man abused her husband in the Cricketers beer-house, as a result of which she suffered a severe beating.[56] Verbal defiance in the courtroom reflects an anti-establishment subculture; Catherine Smith, a Maidstone woman who was arrested for drunkenness over twenty-five times but was never alleged to be a prostitute, on being sentenced to one month's hard labour informed the bench that she could 'do it on her head'.[57] In a similar vein, after prostitute Emma Smith had been charged with an assault, she was informed that there was another case to answer and was asked if she would consent to its being heard then and there; Emma's reply to the bench was: 'Yes, if you like, I might as well be hung for a sheep as a lamb; go on, mate!'[58] The impression created by this evidence contrasts with the representations disseminated through the CD Acts repeal campaign literature, which mobilized a discourse of powerlessness and victimization in its description of prostitute women. The stereotypes suggested by descriptions such as 'poor wretched creatures', 'the enslaved', 'defenceless women' or 'unhappy victims' are not, on the whole, endorsed by the Kentish evidence.[59]

Venereal Disease

Poor health contributed to the decline of many prostitute women from poverty to outright destitution. The Kentish evidence relating to venereal disease, whilst scant, does not support the claims of contemporary CD Acts repeal activists that medical help was sought voluntarily prior to the introduction of the Acts.[60] Edward Swales, visiting surgeon to the Lock Hospital for Sheerness, for example, testified to the Parliamentary Select Committee in 1869 that in his experience prostitutes had been reluctant to seek medical attention when infected.[61] Hugh Baker, Vicar of Woolwich, likewise reflected with hindsight that 'it was impossible in those days to get a poor girl in that condition in a hospital'.[62] These impressions are supported by the statistics of the lock ward at St Bartholemew's Hospital in Chatham. During 1866 the hospital was treating fifty patients from Chatham and twenty from Sheerness, districts where the CD Acts applied and for whom hospitalization was therefore mandatory.[63] At the same time there was only one patient from Gravesend and two from Maidstone, towns not yet subject to the Acts, which means that these women's hospitalizations were not mandatory. Even accounting for differences in the population of women who were most vulnerable to infection, this notable difference in numbers of voluntary and mandatory patients suggests that relatively few women sought medical help voluntarily, since the medical treatment provided under the Acts was free of charge, whereas voluntary treatment, other than that provided under the Poor Law, was not. The admissions registers of Poor Law Union workhouses, together with statistical data generated by central government, both suggest that many women sought admittance to those institutions in order to seek treatment for venereal diseases. Annual Returns relating to indoor medical relief recorded cases of gonorrhoea under the category of 'Diseases of the generative system'.[64] These statistics are supported by anecdotal evidence. The Medway Board of Guardians received numerous applications for welfare help from sick women, identified as prostitutes, prior to the enactment of the CD legislation. One such, a twenty-three-year-old, was described as being 'in a dreadful state, and had been for several months'.[65] Another was apparently 'almost dying from disease and starvation', and the Board had been obliged to send a 'conveyance' to bring her to the Union, suggesting that she was too unwell to walk there.[66] The young woman in this case had previously been 'frequently in the house', supporting the hypothesis that women who lived by prostitution used Poor Law Union workhouses as a resource of last resort in times of exceptional hardship. In another Chatham case, two young women reported to be 'afflicted with a frightful disease' had been admitted to the workhouse.[67] They told magistrates that they had been living at public houses, but had not been allowed to remain once the state of their health was known. Their landlord had apparently told them that he could not find doctors for them. In the light of this experience, the Chairman of the Chatham Board of Health Adam Stigant gave evidence in 1881 to the Select Committee on the Administration and Operation of the Contagious Diseases Acts to the effect that in his opinion, the majority of women would not avail themselves of voluntary medical care, and thus the mandatory treatment provided under the legislation was advantageous.[68] Prior to the Acts, according to Reverend Tuffield of Woolwich, infected women had to 'submit to a cross-examination by a number of maiden ladies and others', which was not conducive to their willingness to volunteer for hospital treatment or examination.[69] In Greenwich and Woolwich, according to James Baxendale of the Greenwich Women's Refuge, it was common practice for diseased women to go into Shooters Hill Woods to live once their health had deteriorated so badly that they were no longer able to earn money by prostitution.[70] Here, echoing the account of the 'wrens of the Curragh' given by Maria Luddy, they were supported by food donations brought to them by women who remained working on the streets.[71] These women's resort to this extreme measure calls into question the premise that a voluntary system of medical surveillance would have been more effective than the CD legislation.

Alcohol

Drunkenness and the excessive consumption of alcohol are striking features in the lives of numerous women who lived by prostitution, as reflected in levels of prosecution for drunkenness, and in the narratives surrounding them. The associations between prostitution and alcohol were remarked upon by a number of contemporaries, including William Logan, who in 1871 claimed that 'the evil is all but universal among prostitutes'.[72] Excessive alcohol consumption had been perceived as a considerable social problem since the early part of the century, when a rise in real wages had coincided with a reduction in spirit duties. This situation was exacerbated by the shift in population from the countryside to urban environments, where large masses of people were crowded into inhospitable and unsanitary housing. In contrast, pubs provided a warm and convivial meeting-place. In these circumstances, it has been argued, 'public drunkenness was an everyday fact of life'.[73] The per capita consumption of both beer and spirits rose to all-time highs in the mid-1870s, as did the figure for expenditure on drink per head of the population.[74] *The Times* believed that 'It is drunkenness which fills the poor houses and lunatic asylums, the hulks and the gaols', an opinion clearly shared in Kent, where the Recorder at the Gravesend Quarter Sessions deplored the large increase in arrests of habitual drunkards in 1872, stating that 'There was no doubt that the greater part of the crime of the country originated in drunkenness'.[75]

It is difficult, from the evidence available, to ascertain with certainty the direction of the cause and effect relationship between alcohol and prostitution.

Logan was certainly of the opinion that in many cases women turned to prostitution to fund their addiction to alcohol. Whichever the case, evidence from Kent
clearly supports historians' observations that taverns and public houses played a
key role in women's procurement of clientele for prostitution.[76] Local authorities in many of the Kentish subjected districts, as will be seen in the following
chapter, controlled street solicitation firmly, and thus public houses provided
an alternative opportunity to ply for trade. One third of prosecutions brought
against prostitutes in Gravesend, for example, between 1864 and 1875 were for
offences related to drunkenness.

Whilst a 'scientific appreciation of alcoholism' was only beginning to become
general during the second half of the nineteenth century, it is clear from contemporary police data, which differentiated between 'drunk and disorderly' convictions
and those of 'habitual drunkards', that the severe, persistent inebriation of apparently alcohol-dependent individuals was beginning to be perceived as a unique
category and as posing a greater problem.[77] Of the named women identified as
prostitutes who were charged with drunkenness-related offences in Kent during the period under study, one-third were arrested twice or more for the same
offence. Eliza Bennett of Gravesend was charged with drunkenness at least seven
times within three years, whilst Elizabeth Ann O' Mally of Chatham appeared in
court so many times on drunkenness charges (forty-nine or fifty as at June 1861)
that the press reporter indulged his talent for word-play in describing her as 'a
regular customer at the bar of justice'.[78] The courtroom narratives surrounding
prosecutions for drunkenness suggest that many women drank to the point of
helplessness. Elizabeth Laws, named in court as a 'common prostitute' on being
charged with drunkenness and causing a disturbance in Rochester High Street,
on being asked for her plea, replied that she 'supposed she must be guilty, but that
she couldn't remember anything about the incident'.[79] When Clara Greenstreet
of Dover was found drunk and disorderly, she was apparently 'extended across the
pavement' and was conveyed to the station by two constables 'in a paroxysm of
rage'.[80] Margaret Cowl of Sheerness was so drunk the arresting officer had to take
her to the lock-up on a truck.[81] Evidently there was no truck to hand when PC
John Jayne arrested Mary McGarth for drunken and noisy conduct in Peppercroft
Street Gravesend, since he had to carry her, whilst in Greenwich Ellen Walter,
who had previously been a nurse but was now leading 'a dissolute life', was found
lying drunk across the footway in the Greenwich Road. These women clearly
jeopardized their own safety; Mary Ann Chiton of Sheerness and Rosella Groves
of Gravesend both tried to take their own lives by drowning whilst intoxicated.

As was seen previously, alcohol played an additional contributory role in the
modus operandi of women who lived on a combination of prostitution and theft
because it provided a means of befuddling the wits of intended victims such that
their testimony could not be later relied upon in court. Sarah Brown of Graves-

end, for example, met a young labourer called George Beaumont who was a stranger to the town, and they went to a public house together where they stayed drinking for two or three hours. Beaumont went home with Sarah, and on entering her bedroom he paid her. Shortly afterwards, Sarah took his watch and chain and disappeared from the house. She had therefore not only stolen his property but also taken money under false pretences for services not rendered. The three-month sentence imposed on Sarah for this offence appears not to have deterred her from repeating this lucrative practice. Within weeks of her release she worked the same routine on soldier Patrick Connellan, who became so drunk that the Police Superintendent had to send for the picket to get him back to the barracks. Once there and presumably sobered up, he missed seven pounds from his purse. However, his recollection of what had happened was so dim that there was insufficient evidence on which to convict Brown, and she was discharged.[82] Notably, as demonstrated in these and other theft cases, magistrates appear to have required the same weight of evidence as for other defendants, and thus prosecutions were frequently dismissed when such evidence was insufficient for conviction.

Violence

Physical violence constituted an occupational hazard for the street prostitute, and women who earned money in this way faced the constant risk of physical assault both at the hands of men (who might reasonably be presumed to be clients and would-be clients), and also from one another. Many of these women's apparently opportunistic custom of theft from, and deception of, clients or would-be clients created additional risk. Local press reportage of petty sessions in the subjected districts of Kent, which is filled with cases of assault inflicted on women named as prostitutes, strongly suggests that violence was a routine feature of life for those at the margins of society. Press reporters' descriptions of the injuries sustained during these assaults and fights are graphic and sensationalist, but can be presumed to provide a reasonably accurate account of the severity of the attacks. Chatham prostitute Maria Gates, for example, was assaulted by William Maine, a marine who 'was in the habit of visiting her'. He struck her in the eye, which remained blackened for some time afterwards, and she said he used other threats against her.[83] Gravesend prostitute Isabella Stewart appeared before magistrates twice within eight months, first as the victim and then as the perpetrator of violent attacks. On the first occasion she had been assaulted by a man called Edward Brown in the Privateer public house, though we are given no further detail. Isabella was described as having 'a most desperate black eye besides scratches on her face, her lips cut, and various other marks'. The following year Isabella, 'a strong looking woman', returned to court accused of an assault on a neighbour, Caroline Morris. The assault happened after Morris had 'remonstrated' with Isabella for 'laughing and drinking' with the man she lived with, whom she described as her 'keeper'. The victim on this occasion was described as having 'both eyes black, evidently from heavy blows, a bite mark on her cheek and lips black'. This episode earned Isabella a fine of twenty shillings plus nine shillings and sixpence costs, which it might reasonably be supposed she could not pay, as the three weeks' custodial sentence was served instead.[84]

When Dover Police Constables Clark and Terry went to investigate the report of a street disturbance, they discovered two soldiers with belts in their hands 'greatly ill-using an unfortunate woman who was in their company'.[85] A particularly violent attack on Chatham prostitute Ann Kelly was considered sufficiently serious to be referred by the magistrates to the assizes. Kelly, who was thirty-nine, had been 'getting a living on the streets' for twelve or thirteen years before the attack. She and her child lived in one room at the rear of the Bell public house. On the night in question, while her child was being looked after by a neighbour, she returned to her room to find two soldiers already there. She told the court that when she asked them what they wanted, they said that she would soon see and threatened to kill her, putting a hand over her mouth to prevent her from screaming. The *Chatham News* deemed the details of the attack as described in court unfit for publication, and described the incident in its report as a rape rather than an assault, though it was prosecuted as the latter.[86]

When news of the 1857 murder of Elizabeth Jones was made public, Maidstone was, according to the press, 'thrown into a state of agitation'. Jones, who lived by prostitution, died as the result of an assault by a bargeman named Charles Chumley, who had beaten her on the back of the head with a broom handle. Jones and her sister Margaret had accompanied Chumley and another man on to a barge, but a quarrel had developed at the end of the evening, as a result of which both women were badly beaten. Margaret was found wandering by police in the early hours of the morning with her face covered with blood, and took them to the barge where Elizabeth was found partially conscious. She died four days later.[87]

Women who lived by prostitution were as much at risk from assault from one another as they were from men, and numerous cases were brought before the magistrates of violence perpetrated by one prostitute on another. Fights over territory or supposed 'slights' appear to have been common. Mary Taylor and Maria Mallowby of Gravesend, for example, were arrested having been found fighting in the street outside the King's Head public house. Mallowby told the bench that Taylor had started the fight because 'she was offended that some man had treated her' (Mallowby).[88] Quarrels often started with name-calling and bad language and escalated into physical fights, such as that between Mary Ann Simpson and Alice Linton, in which Mary Ann's silk jacket got torn, and that between Matilda Goodhew and Emma Goldsmith near the Black Horse in Prince's Street,

Gravesend, in which Matilda's bonnet was torn and her face scratched.[89] Elizabeth Brown, Ann Horgan and Ann Hickey of Chatham were all arrested having been found drunk and riotous in the Military Road. Brown and Horgan were 'stripped for fighting', whilst Hickey was holding their clothes, and urging them on. They were sentenced to twenty-one days, fourteen days and seven days with hard labour, respectively.[90]

Women named as prostitutes appear to have been conspicuously willing to prosecute both material and moral infractions through the magistrates' courts in pursuit of restitution, in line with previous historians' findings with regard to the strategies used by the poor to access the policing and criminal justice systems for their own ends.[91] This suggests that an appearance at a public court hearing in front of the local press, during which their occupation was invariably mentioned, was less daunting to these women as might be assumed, and challenges the thesis that the CD Acts condemned prostituted women to a status of permanent exclusion from their immediate community by disrupting their anonymous assimilation into working-class neighbourhoods.[92] Hetty Nash of Sheerness, for example, prosecuted Patrick Devlin, a seaman with the Royal Navy, for stealing five pawn tickets and a locket from her, in a case that was dismissed on grounds of insufficient evidence. Charles Currigan, a soldier in the RA, was likewise charged by Mary Ann O'Bryan with stealing four shillings and a penny ha'penny, a knife and a handkerchief from her and was convicted. In both cases, the women were named in court as prostitutes.[93] It is possible, of course, that in these cases where property was at stake the women had little option but to press charges and risk public identification, since they could ill afford to do otherwise. There are numerous cases, however, where no property was involved and quarrels between prostitutes broke out as a result of name-calling and the exchange of insults, developing into physical assault. Examples include the altercation between Louisa Collins and Mary Ann Loft at the India Arms, which resulted in Louisa being summoned for an assault. The case, we are told, 'introduced to the court several members of the frail sisterhood who variously stated the facts of the quarrel'.[94] In a similar case, Sarah Nightingale was summoned for assaulting Mary Ann Hoffner in the White Hart. Mary Ann told the court that the defendant and some other prostitutes abused her and assaulted her by spitting in her face.[95] Sarah Nightingale, in her turn, summoned Sarah Darge for an assault some months later.[96] When a fight broke out between Elizabeth Court and Jane Beeston at the Russell Arms after Jane and a friend, Harriet Crossthwaite, went there for a glass of brandy and water, the outcome was torn clothes.[97] Ann Inkpen charged Mary Ann Penman with using abusive language to her, the 'principal epithet being that she and her companion were "soldiers' trolls"'. The complainant's evidence in this case was supported by two other girls of 'similar character'.[98] The witnesses and prosecutors in these cases went through with a public appearance in the courtroom during which they were named and their way of life noted. The argument that the Contagious Diseases legislation was punitive because it publicly identified working prostitutes appears less persuasive in the light of this evidence.

Conclusion

The women identified by this study as having lived by prostitution operated at the lower end of the market, plying for trade in the street and in public houses. Cramped and squalid living conditions, drunkenness, poverty, disease and violence all appear to have been everyday facts of life. Unquestionably, not all women who practised prostitution in Kent conformed to a single model; instead they reflected the full range of archetypes recognizable from the contemporary moralizing literature. In terms of age, total length of time spent on the street and ultimate personal outcomes, the women whose lives have been uncovered here represent the complete spectrum of circumstances, thus contesting the over-simplistic explanatory frameworks advanced by contemporary commentators.

Furthermore, these findings pose a challenge to simplistic 'victimization' models of prostitution. Whilst these women were undoubtedly made victims by socio-economic circumstances and of official policy, many appear to have demonstrated a relative degree of independence and autonomy in response. They were agents in their own histories, as demonstrated by the pursuit of individual survival strategies, and by decisions made about their own life course, albeit that this was from a limited set of alternatives.

Themes of heterogeneity, agency and individual outcomes have significant implications for the discussion of women's experience of, and responses to the CD Acts, to which this study will turn in Chapter 6. Additionally, the findings relating to the backgrounds, personal circumstances and working practices of the women of Kent who lived by prostitution provide a framework against which the themes of regulation and control, which form the primary focus of this study, can be developed. In considering these regimes, this discussion turns firstly to explore a practice that may be interpreted as a first level of such policing and control, that is, the shaping of attitudes and process of 'othering' carried out in the columns of the local press.

3 REPRESENTATIONS OF PROSTITUTION

On Wednesday, 18 July 1860, Eliza Richardson was brought before the Gravesend bench of magistrates on charges of drunkenness and of physical assault. The *Gravesend Reporter*'s coverage of the case at that day's petty sessions, published under the subtitle 'A Virago', noted the police's terse description of Richardson in court as a prostitute and as 'the terror of the neighbourhood', before laying before its readership a dramatic narrative of the details of the alleged offence.[1] The defendant, it was observed, had made several previous appearances before the bench, usually for some alleged 'outrage'. The complainant, apparently obliged to give evidence from a chair due to her injuries, recounted how Richardson had knocked her down in the street and 'jumped up and down on her with great violence'. The narrative was rounded off with a physical description of the defendant. Richardson was, readers were told,

> a strong looking middle-aged woman, she as usual wore no bonnet but her hair was worn in a velvet not [*sic*] in the prevailing fashion, and her cotton dress of dubious cleanliness was also properly distended by the hoop so very important to female attire.

In the space of less than half a column, the writer had simultaneously alluded to multiple strands of the contemporary discourse surrounding the prostitute figure, which, as has already been seen, were propagated through a wide range of professional, journalistic and literary publications. From the mid-century onwards a proliferation of texts of all types, described by one historian as a 'sudden burst of books', had addressed itself to the subject of prostitution.[2] This literature set about the quantification and definition of the perceived problem, and the attempt to uncover and illuminate its causes and consequences. Prostitution was redefined both as a significant social problem in need of social action, and as a pathologically deviant pattern of behaviour. These debates crossed over multiple currents of contemporary social concern, engaging with medical discourses of disease control, moral discourses regarding the containment of dangerous sexualities, and legal discourses of crime, punishment and disorderly behaviour. Whilst much of this writing has been described as intellectually impoverished, and of comprising 'the impressions, opinions or bawdy anecdotes of middle-class gentlemen', the complex and contradictory myths it created nevertheless had a significant and lasting influence on wider popular representations.[3] A range of tropes and stereotypes emerged from these myths, reflecting the tensions and contradictions that permeated the wider professional debates. These were widely disseminated through popular media and would thus be recognizable to the readers of the *Gravesend Reporter*'s coverage of the hearing of the case against Eliza Richardson.

The newspaper's pen portrait of Richardson and its narrative of her case reflect a number of these themes. She is characterized as being physically strong and violent, in contrast both to respectable femininity, which was understood in terms of fragility, and also to 'the frail sisterhood', which stood as a widely recognized euphemism for prostituted women. She is described as being bare-headed in contravention of prevailing notions of respectable women's public dress, whilst a further tension is set up between her apparent observance of the dictates of fashion and the aspersions cast on her standards of personal cleanliness. The writer additionally alludes to questions of recidivism through reference to Richardson's record of previous appearances at the magistrates' court. Each of these themes, to which this discussion will turn in greater detail, was recurrent in the descriptions of women identified as prostitutes in Kentish newspaper court reports. Thus the sketch of Richardson, in common with those of numerous other defendants who passed before magistrates' benches at this time, contributed to a cultural process of 'othering' of the accused, through classification into crude but easily recognizable social categories. These groups were characterized and identified as outsiders because of their perceived deviance, whether or not they were subsequently convicted of a criminal offence.

Whilst historians have examined the role played by the nineteenth-century newspaper and periodical press in shaping and disseminating attitudes through political and social reportage, the routine reporting of local magistrates' court hearings has yet to be fully explored as a journalistic genre in its own right. In analysing the representations of women labelled as prostitutes in these columns, this chapter considers the little-explored contribution of the nineteenth-century local press in shaping and reflecting attitudes towards the social groups represented by defendants in local court cases. In addition, it interrogates the way in which these reports functioned to perpetuate the myths and caricatures constructed in the wider, multifaceted nineteenth-century discourse related to prostitution. These caricatures contributed to what has been described as the 'gallery of types that society erects to show its members which roles should be avoided and which should be emulated'.[4] That is to say, the written caricatures of defendants in the press coverage of magistrates' court hearings played a didactic role in the reinforcement of notions of respectability and codes of morality.

They identified and labelled transgressors, and held their behaviour up for public censure, ridicule and amusement.

Newspapers have always played an important role in the formulation as well as the reflection of social realities. At a time of restricted access to other types of media, the nineteenth-century press was a significant vehicle for the communication of ideas, and newspapers in this period played a vital role in the propagation of what has been called 'moral politeness'.[5] This was based on the standards and values of the 'middling sort', such as decent behaviour and moral improvement, and involved a process of what has been described as the 'striking of resonances to elicit a process of identification'. The press played an important role in the propagation of class ideologies in Victorian England, as earlier forms of local politics slowly gave way to ones based on broad bands of class stratification.[6] Between the 1860s and 1880s, what has been described as a 'crisis of representation' took place as respectable public appearance became increasingly problematic for those who assumed middle-class status.[7] As a result, as historian Simon Gunn argues, the periodical press engaged in a 'systematic process of categorizing and classifying "social types", providing a sociological guide to the streets and restoring order to the confusion of sense impressions'.[8]

Representations of offenders and prosecutors in Kentish petty sessions and police court reportage demonstrate these processes of classification. Appearance and behaviour was measured against standards of public respectability and morality, and resonances were struck to invite either identification or condemnation. In the absence of photographic images to facilitate this process, pen portraits were provided by many magistrates' court reporters. Thus George Hampson, appearing before the bench to prosecute Charlotte Oliver for stealing his silver watch, was described as 'a respectable looking mechanic', whereas Mary Jane Harriet Brown, convicted of stealing a florin, was 'a bold looking girl'. Stephen Wilson, charged with assault, was described as 'a man dressed like a navvy', Ann Williams, on a charge of being drunk and disorderly, 'a woman clad very indifferently', and Susan Pike, of being drunk and causing an obstruction, 'a woman of very miserable looking appearance'.[9] The categorization of these individuals into social types, recognizable to the papers' middle-class and respectable working-class audiences, served both to reinforce and reflect notions of public respectability. In some cases, however, the images presented in the press were characterized by ambiguity, as in the cases of Elizabeth Finlayson, described as 'a girl of interesting appearance and rather superior deportment' who was identified in court as an 'unfortunate', and Amy Austin, 'a respectable looking young woman' who was summoned for not reporting herself under the CD Acts.[10]

The extent of the influence exerted by the provincial press over the wider attitudes and mentalities of the past is, of course, difficult to quantify from the sources available. The ability of the press to reach beyond a purely middle-class

readership was clearly dependent upon such factors as literacy, cost and avail-
ability. Literacy rates in the nineteenth century have been shown by historians to
have been higher than were suggested by early research findings that were based
purely on individuals' ability to sign their name in marriage registers. Thus, the
myth created in the aftermath of the 1870 Education Act that literacy levels
prior to this date had been universally low has now largely been overturned.[11]
The 'final drive' to full literacy was, according to David Vincent, under way by
the 1830s, and the education provided by elementary schools had created a
demand for reading material.[12] Thus by the 1850s and 60s it was not unusual for
working people to buy a weekly newspaper costing one or two pence, and newspapers were regarded as a common and necessary feature of working-class life
well before the end of the century.[13] Furthermore, bare circulation figures are an
imprecise measure of the full reach of the newspapers' influence, since up until
the mid-century titles were recirculated and each copy of a newspaper might be
seen by half a dozen readers as well as being read aloud in public spaces such as
pubs and coffee houses.[14] The weekly reading club in Maidstone, for example,
met during the 1850s in the coffee room of the Roebuck Inn in Week Street.
Here, the news of the week was read aloud by George Nye, a local furniture
dealer whose commercial premises were located nearby.[15] As the century pro-
gressed, reduced production costs eventually led to disposable newspapers, but
the practice of recirculation continued until well into the 1870s.[16] The sphere of
influence of local Kentish weekly titles therefore extended beyond the provincial
middle classes, and the project of imposing standards of morality by means of
stereotypical representations of transgressors can be assumed to have reached, if
not to have been primarily targeted at, the respectable working classes.[17]

Newspapers were brought within closer reach of this group when prices were
dramatically reduced in the third quarter of the nineteenth century, following
the abolition of newspaper taxes. The period witnessed a proliferation of new
newspaper titles in direct response to this measure, one of the greatest areas of
growth being that of provincial weeklies. The birth of several new weekly titles
in Kent at this period reflects this general trend: the *Gravesend Reporter* was
founded in 1856, the *Dover Express* and the *Sheerness Guardian* in 1858, and
both the *Chatham News* and the *Maidstone Telegraph* in 1859. The *Kentish
Gazette* had an older pedigree, having been established in 1717 as the *Kentish
Post or the Canterbury Newsletter* after Canterbury was granted a licence to
operate its own printing press. Likewise, the *Kentish Mercury* had started life
in Kentish London as the *Greenwich, Woolwich and Deptford Gazette* in 1834.

The proprietors of these titles originated from a mix of backgrounds and
often incorporated the newspaper into family printing or bookselling businesses.
The proprietor-editor model was an established and enduring one in provincial
publishing.[18] Joseph Friend, publisher of the *Dover Express*, had undergone a

printer's apprenticeship and had previously trained on the *Dover Chronicle* before establishing the *Express* in 1858 at the age of twenty-seven.[19] Thomas Morell Blackie, founder of the *Gravesend Reporter*, originated from Ipswich and had previously completed a bookseller's apprenticeship.[20] His mission statement, as outlined in his first editorial, was to 'furnish a correct report of the Police and County Courts ... [from] ... an unprejudiced and independent standpoint', indicating that reportage of court hearings was, from the outset, one of his purposes.[21] The title changed hands in quick succession before being acquired in 1861 by William Stallworthy, a printer, stationer and bookseller who operated it until his death in 1866. Blackie's original stated intention of remaining politically neutral was not sustained after the title changed hands, however, and the result of the 1865 general election, in which the West Kent seat was taken by the Conservatives, was met with an editorial proclaiming that 'for a time we must be content to be *mis*represented in Parliament'.[22] The *Maidstone Telegraph*, according to its centenary celebration publication, was founded by the proprietor of the local library who, having concluded that there was a market for a local newspaper after hearing the news being read aloud in the Roebuck Inn, incorporated newspaper publishing into his existing business.[23] Like the *Gravesend Reporter*, the *Telegraph* developed strong liberal leanings. Reportage of magistrates' court hearings was, therefore, identified from the outset as central to the business of local newspapers, as demonstrated by Thomas Blackie's published mission statement regarding his intentions for his title. This objective echoed the assertion of political activist Richard Cobden, who in campaigning for the repeal of newspaper duties in 1854 had argued that it would be desirable if the ordinary man 'could read about a neighbour being taken to petty sessions for poaching'.[24] Cobden had thus recognized the potential influence, both in terms of deterrence and of informal social control, of publicizing the transgressions of individuals from within the community and in so doing, perhaps, fulfilling the aspiration of James Grant, former editor of the *Morning Advertiser*, who believed that the mission of the press should be 'to enlighten, to civilize, and to morally transform the world'.[25] At a local level, this civilizing process was often implemented by holding law-breakers together with offenders against codes of public decency up for disapproval, and by representing them in terms of recognizable social categories, or excluded groups, often along class or ethnic lines. Physical characteristics such as dress and accent were brought into play to facilitate this process of classification. Thus William Clifford, charged with throwing an egg at the hustings at the 1865 general election, was described as 'a youth, shabbily dressed', whilst Charles Rigby, described as a 'stalwart beggar', and William Lindsay, 'a wretched looking type of the vagrant class', were both convicted of begging.[26] Jane Stiff, who was convicted of drunkenness and using obscene language, apparently appeared before magistrates 'in a very untidy condition'.[27] The reportage of the cases involving Jeremiah Connell, 'a blackguard Irishman', for drunkenness and fighting, and Mary Ann Marlow, 'an unmistakable inhabitant of Erin', for drunkenness and using obscene language at the police station, demonstrate that as Jeremy Black has observed, press comment about excluded groups, such as the Irish in England, could be malevolent.[28]

Many of the pen portraits extended beyond descriptions of defendants' dress and general appearance in the construction of excluded groups, however. Graphic negative descriptions of individuals' countenances reflected the widespread popularity and scientific authority of physiognomy at this period. Revived by Swiss practitioner Johann Lavater at the end of the eighteenth century, this ancient art claimed a connection between an individual's facial features and character, instincts and behaviour. Professing to be both a science of the mind, and a source of moral authority, it has been argued that its emergence as a popular phenomenon in the nineteenth century, just at the time when fundamental questions were being asked about man's place in the world of nature, was largely due to the moral framework that it provided for everyday conduct.[29] Thus it was believed that character could be determined through expression, by means of classification into human types and social classes.[30] Kentish newspaper reportage of petty sessions reflects this interest, as seen in the coverage of the prosecutions of Ann Legge, described as a 'notorious prostitute of the town of most repulsive countenance', Margaret Harrison, 'a dissipated looking woman', Ann Chatfield, 'a prostitute of the lowest class and most forbidding appearance', and Mary Weldon, 'a woman with a peculiarly distressed-looking countenance'.[31] Mary Ann White, also identified in court as a prostitute, had, readers were informed, 'every appearance of dissipation in her countenance, her language and conduct was of the most violent description'.[32] The inference was that the 'repulsive', 'forbidding' and 'distressed-looking' faces and expressions of these women were the outward manifestation of their sinful and degenerate moral characters. The body of theory reflected by this association would be developed further at a later period by criminal anthropologist Cesare Lombroso.

Of all the excluded groups mentioned in the Kentish police court reports, women identified during magistrates' court hearings as prostitutes, like Eliza Richardson with whom this chapter opened, were represented in terms of their perceived transgression against codes of acceptable behaviour on numerous levels, whether or not the offences with which they were charged related to prostitution. Female offenders in the nineteenth century, as Lucia Zedner has argued convincingly, were held to have been doubly deviant since they had not only broken the law but had also offended against prevailing codes of socially acceptable feminine conduct.[33] Prostituted women, by extension, were multiply deviant as defined by prevailing ideologies of purity and morality. As has been seen, the reportage of the Richardson case made reference to multiple strands of conduct deemed deviant in women, including immorality, drunkenness, recidivism and physical aggression. The item opened by reporting that the police had tersely described Richardson in court a prostitute, thus labelling her and classifying her as a member of an excluded group and as a social type before the case had even been heard.

The term 'prostitute' was, as Linda Mahood has argued, a socio-political construct and a label or censure applied to those women whose 'dress, behaviour, physical appearance or vocation' marked them out as departing from the norms dictated by middle-class observers.[34] Clearly Richardson attracted comment in each of these categories. With regard to vocation, the term 'prostitute' was employed in Kentish newspaper court reports interchangeably with 'common prostitute' and a wide range of euphemistic terms. These included 'unfortunate', 'woman of the town', 'lady of easy virtue', 'woman of ill repute' and 'nymph du pave', all of which reflect the wide spectrum of ambivalent and contradictory attitudes towards the prostitute figure that characterized the wider discourse. As will be seen, the term 'common prostitute' was recognized, though not defined, by law, whilst 'prostitute' was one of the categories into which the 'criminal classes' were sorted by the government's Annual Returns of Judicial Statistics.[35] Reflecting what has been called the 'Victorian mania for classification', these statistics attempted to organize and codify offenders by type, other categories being 'Known thieves and depredators' and 'Habitual drunkards'.[36]

In the Kentish press, 'prostitute' and 'common prostitute' were used most often in reports of cases where the charge was related to soliciting on the street, thus 'Caroline Parker, a common prostitute', was 'charged with practising her calling', and Emma Evans, 'prostitute', was charged with obstructing the public streets.[37] In other instances, a range of euphemisms was brought into play by the Kentish court reporters, and these were often even more heavily value-laden. Ann Swift, for example, was described as 'a woman of bad character', Matilda Goodyer and Rosina Brown as 'girls of bad character' and Joanna Smith 'a girl of ill-fame'.[38] Louisa Gardener, charged with 'abusing' a woman named Smith and using abusive language, was described in her absence in court as 'unfortunately associated with the "Social Evil"', thus firmly identifying her with a value-laden label of censure.[39]

The theme of deviancy was further developed in the Richardson case with narratives of drunkenness and of physical violence, both types of behaviour that were judged unacceptable by prevailing codes of respectability, particularly when perpetrated by women. Our understanding of attitudes towards deviancy in the past and of the role played by the media in the creation and propagation of recognizable social types can be enhanced by considering what scholars have to say about these issues in the modern context. Howard Becker and others have defined deviance as behaviour that breaks the rules of the dominant group, to which a particular meaning is attributed by the reactions and interpretation of others.[40] Deviance is therefore created, according to this theory, by the for-

mulation of rules by certain social groups and the labelling of rule-breakers as
outsiders. Women such as Eliza Richardson, brought before the Kentish benches
in the third quarter of the nineteenth century charged with offences related to
prostitution, were identified and labelled in this way as a reflection of the meaning attached to their behaviour, which failed to adhere to codes of middle-class
morality and public respectability. In many cases a crime had been perpetrated,
but in many others it had not, and deviance proceeded from the responses of
others to that behaviour. Identification was carried out by agents of the criminal
justice system such as magistrates and members of police forces, but the rules
they imposed were regulated by wider codes of respectability. These codes were
imposed informally by what Becker has described as 'moral entrepreneurs' as well
as being policed formally. An example of moral entrepreneurship is the association founded in Maidstone in 1863, which took as its aim the abatement of 'that
class of public offences which consist in acts of indecency, prostitution, cruelty
to animals, drunkenness, profanity and open Sabbath breaking'.[41] Less formalized examples include the letters written to, and published in, the local press.
'The time is surely come', wrote one correspondent to the *Sheerness Guardian* in
1865, 'for the respectable inhabitants to stir in this matter ... surely the habit of
prostitutes walking the streets unbonnetted might easily be stopped'.[42] Thus the
writer called on the moral entrepreneurs of Sheerness to make a stand against a
particular type of behaviour that was held to be unacceptable, and which was
perpetrated by a social group identified as outsiders.

The reference to the unbonnetted status of the Sheerness women by this
letter writer echoes the same observation made in the description of Eliza
Richardson. The close correlation of bare-headedness with immorality can be
measured through an examination of the reaction to the increasing popularity of
the hat, in place of the bonnet, amongst fashion-conscious women at this time.
The hat was viewed by some as indicative of 'a loosening of morals', according
to one fashion historian, and only a bonnet, which covered more of the head
and face, was considered respectable enough to wear to church.[43] By extension,
going bare-headed was therefore interpreted as utter wantonness, and Judith
Walkowitz has argued that being bonnetless in public was part of prostitutes'
'dress code'.[44] When Sgt Broadbridge of the Kent County Constabulary was
called as a witness in the prosecution of Chatham publican William Clark for
'harbouring prostitutes', the fact that two women named in court as Riley and
Carr 'had no hats or bonnets on' constituted part of his evidence.[45] Ann Jones,
therefore, appears to have caused some confusion when she appeared before the
Gravesend bench charged with creating an obstruction on the footpath. She was
described as 'a young woman without a bonnet, but well dressed in a good morning attire, said by the police to be a prostitute'.[46] Jones' combination of 'good

morning attire' with a lack of appropriate head covering clearly challenged the bare-headed stereotype and sent mixed messages.

The representation of Eliza Richardson, together with those of women like her, was constructed in terms of the threat that she was believed to pose to the social order, based on her dress, demeanour and way of life. The role played by the popular media in reaffirming dominant conceptions of morality and in shaping attitudes towards deviant groups has been much explored in the contemporary context in the wake of Stanley Cohen's classic study *Folk Devils and Moral Panics*. This concept related to the way in which, at certain moments in time, incidents, individuals or groups of people (the folk devils) come to be viewed as threatening to societies' values and interests. According to Cohen, the mass media present stylized and stereotypical representations of them, as a result of which 'moral barricades are manned by editors, bishops, politicians and other right-thinking people', and diagnoses and solutions are offered by experts.[47]

This definition is helpful in contributing towards an understanding of the mid-nineteenth-century outpouring of concern over prostitution, to the extent that it became known as the 'great social evil'. The prostitute figure was deemed to represent both a physical (in the form of venereal disease) and a moral threat to society. Applying Cohen's conceptualization, therefore, the figure of the prostitute, in one of many incarnations, was cast as a folk devil, on to whom the perceived ills of society could be projected.

The folk devil concept has been further developed in a way that has particular resonance for any discussion of nineteenth-century prostitution. A specific group of deviants, David Garland has elaborated, 'is singled out for "folk devil" status, in large part, because it possesses characteristics that make it a suitable screen upon which society can project sentiments of guilt and ambivalence'.[48] Themes of guilt and ambivalence, of course, together with moral condemnation, have particular resonance in discussions of nineteenth-century women labelled as prostitutes. They are most easily demonstrated in the use of 'unfortunate', the euphemism most commonly used in the Kentish press for prostitute women. This term echoed one of the themes that ran through professional discourse, which was that these women were more sinned against than sinning.

The pen portrait of Richardson was even more ambivalent, however. The first image or stereotype to which the reporter makes reference is that of the virago, thus alluding to notions of physical strength and deviant agency. This was a common theme in reports of magistrates' court cases in the Kentish press, in contrast to respectable nineteenth-century femininity which was constructed in terms of physical weakness. Isabella Stewart, prosecuting an assault charge against a man called Edward Brown, was described as 'a strong looking woman with a northern accent', before the reporter graphically noted the extent of her injuries, including 'a most desperate black eye besides scratches to her face, her lips cut, and various other marks visible and invisible', and quoted her assertion that she was one mass of bruises from the waist to the top of her boot.[49] In sharp contrast, however, other women, such as Catherine Martin convicted of soliciting in 1870, were described as 'one of the frail sisterhood', thus constructing prostitution in terms of an opposing trope that was characterized by moral frailty.[50]

Victorian discourse surrounding prostitution featured a central dichotomy in which the prostitute figure was represented either in terms of agency on the one hand, or powerlessness and victimization on the other. The origins of this dichotomy can be traced to the ongoing debate conducted in the professional and journalistic literature regarding the outcome of prostitution. It would be an over-simplification, however, to view the debate on prostitution in terms of the replacement of one paradigm by another. More accurately, a number of models co-existed in the professional and popular discourses, and the degree to which the prostitute was viewed as the agent of her own destiny on the one hand, or a victim of circumstances on the other, was a persistent theme within the commentary. This ambivalence is reflected in the range of tropes to be found in the Kentish press. Mary Putt and Susannah Fagg were described as 'two fashionably dressed members of the frail sisterhood', thus creating conflicting images of the women.[51] The descriptions and narratives surrounding the cases concerning Lucy Witnall, 'a powerfully dressed young lady', Rachel Goatley, who had left home and 'turned prostitute', and Emily Harris, 'a lady of the same profession, lately returned from Maidstone', all contain suggestions of agency.[52]

By contrast, the description of Selina Boswell as 'a sister in misfortune' reinforces the victimization trope.[53] This stereotypical image of the prostitute as a deserving recipient of compassion and charity was constructed to elicit sympathy. Nevertheless, once having fallen, the Magdalen was unable to be rehabilitated into respectable society, and thus the most appropriate ending for the 'prostitute as victim' was an early, repentant death, a symbolic event that was repeated in numerous fictional accounts.[54] As has been seen, at a popular level, the victimization trope can be most easily seen in the widespread adoption of the euphemisms 'unfortunate' and 'one of the unfortunate class'. These were widely used in the Kentish press, as in the description of Rose Eliza Saunter, prosecuted for causing a disturbance at the Duke of York public house in Dover, as an 'unfortunate of tender years', and of the public disturbance caused by Eliza Bromley and Kate Horton as 'a street quarrel between two unfortunates'.[55]

A further strand of rhetoric, to do with contagion and disease, was mobilized in much of the contemporary discourse, influenced by the growing authority of the medical profession. The image of the prostitute as an agent of destruction and conduit of contagion was juxtaposed with that of the deserving recipient of compassionate charity. Whilst these stereotypes pre-date the nineteenth century, they became more fully developed and more widely disseminated over this time as prostitution was increasingly perceived as a significant social problem in need of a remedy. The 'agent of decay and contagion' image combined concepts both of moral and physical pollution and contamination. The physical dimension originated in the medical discourse on venereal disease, the spread of which was attributed largely to prostitutes, and contributed to wider themes of contamination that informed sanitary reform debates: 'Prostitutes have been allowed to spread infection on all sides of them without control', Greg argued.[56] At the level of popular stereotypes, this theme of contagion was most often associated with dirty clothing and poor personal hygiene, as was seen in the case of Eliza Richardson. As fashion historian Aileen Ribeiro has observed, morality was equated with cleanliness of attire, whilst soiled clothing was the sign of a depraved woman.[57] On a closely associated theme, decay was hinted at by the description of Ann Carter, appearing before magistrates on a charge of being drunk and disorderly, as 'a nymph of the pave, approaching the sear and yellow foliage'.[58]

The influence on readers of representations of women identified as prostitutes in the Kentish press is further illuminated by recent studies in the field of linguistics. These have pointed to the role of language in the creation of 'socially constructed' news.[59] Roger Fowler has argued that in determining the significance of news events, newspapers and their readers make reference to pre-existing mental categories, paradigms or stereotypes according to which events or individuals can be sorted. This reading takes into account the ideology embodied in the language used by the writer, and the reciprocal part played by the reader in recognizing and identifying with the values and beliefs conveyed in the language. This ideology is one of consensus, to the extent that it is assumed that the values and interests of the readership are unified. In the reportage of the Richardson case, 'terror', 'outrage' and, of course, 'virago' can all be assumed to have had a particular resonance amongst, and to elicit a particular response from, the newspaper's middle-class and respectable working-class readership. According to this analysis, therefore, the very modes of discourse adopted by newspapers encode the attitudes of the elite.

The selection process brought into play by modern newspapers in deciding what stories to print helps shine some light on the same processes in the past. Decisions about what is given prominence and what is omitted have been shown by Fowler to play an important part in constructing the news and thus influencing the views and attitudes of the audience. The newspaper reports of police court and petty sessions hearings on which this study is based represent a portion of the total number of cases heard in the twice-weekly sittings. In the absence of any evidence about the criteria on which selection was made, the personalization factor described by Fowler, in which individuals are used by the media as symbols with which readers are invited either to empathize, disapprove or identify, is persuasive. It can be seen to be particularly pertinent in the case of reportage of prosecutions of women named as prostitutes, as the following discussion will show.[60]

Earlier, it was seen that the pen portrait of Eliza Richardson emphasized her dress and physical appearance, which was a common tendency amongst the Kentish petty sessions reporters. Most notably, the women's style of fashionable and ostentatious dress attracted comment, as it was implied to be lacking in taste and inappropriate for women of their status, yet at the same time indicative of their occupation. Emma Ransley, for example, was described as a 'dashingly dressed' young lady, Clara Lucas as 'a fashionably dressed prostitute', Elizabeth Mitchell as 'a most showily attired unfortunate', and Mary Anne Martin, a prostitute, 'dressed in showy style'.[61] Other examples include Susan Pole, a 'showily attired unfortunate', and Rose Richards, 'nymph of the pave, attired in blue with hat and feathers'.[62] In addition to being targeted specifically at the women in the dock, the censure implied in these descriptions reflects wider contemporary criticism of fashion and consumer culture. The mid-1900s have been identified by historians of fashion as a period characterized by the creation and over-consumption of vast quantities of finery, and the 1860s more specifically as the moment when a more 'strident note (was introduced) into the fashionable wardrobe'.[63] Finery was associated both with vulgarity and with dissolute habits, and indulgence in personal luxury viewed as demonstrative of a 'relaxation in virtue'.[64] Yet, as Judith Walkowitz has perceptively observed, prostitutes eschewed the demure respectability of the middle classes and aspired instead to imitate the 'conspicuous display' of Victorian ladies, a nuance apparently lost on moralizing observers.[65] The tropes carried in the Kentish press focused on inappropriate displays of finery, and reflected the wider criticisms of this trend by juxtaposing descriptions of fashionable or showy dress with narratives of non-respectable behaviour. Thus Elizabeth Chapman, a 'stylishly dressed young woman', was convicted of creating a disturbance at two o'clock in the morning, and Mary Skinning, summoned for assault, was described as 'a young lady in hat and feathers, and a cloud'.[66] Georgiana Campbell, a 'nymph du pave', earned a particularly detailed and closely observed description when she was summoned in front of the bench on a soliciting charge. She was apparently 'dashingly dressed after the style of her class, in turban hat, mask veil, spangled hair net and silk dress'.[67] That this apparent finery was merely superficial is borne out by the fact that Campbell could not afford the 5s fine imposed on her on conviction, in lieu of which she served a seven-day prison term.

The reference to Campbell's turban hat was one of many similar observations of modish detail that demonstrate a consciousness of fashion, both on the part of the wearers and the Kentish court reporters. The appearance of Ann Hopper, 'unfortunate', brought before the Dover bench in 1862, was marked by the observation that she 'wore a pork-pie hat and feather and carried a small bunch of violets in her hand', revealing that Ms Hopper was extremely au courant, since the 'pork-pie' or turned-up hat was one of that year's fashionable developments.[68] The violet, meanwhile, according to contemporary dictionaries of floriography such as Thomas Miller's (published in its second edition in 1855), symbolized modesty. Whether the ironic touch can be attributed to Ms Hopper, or the court reporter, or both, is not possible to determine. Other references to fashionable hats include the description of Rose Brown, 'a dashingly dressed Cyprian', summoned for being drunk and using bad language, who appeared in court wearing a 'floperty hat and lace fall'.[69] The pen portrait of Emma Jones, described as being 'rather showily attired in a black hat and magenta feather', pinpoints her outfit to a particular historical moment.[70] The first aniline dyes (produced synthetically from coal products) were created in 1856, and brought into general use in the fashion industry around 1860.[71] Magenta was one of the first two available colours, re-named to commemorate the 1859 Battle of Magenta in Italy.[72]

In an even more striking reference to fashionable trends in clothing, Jane Boorman, a 'nymph of the pave' who was brought up in custody before the Maidstone bench in July 1872 on a charge of 'wandering, being a common prostitute and indecent behaviour', was described as being 'well known as "Grecian Bend"'.[73] This reference is to a trend in ladies' fashion of the late 1860s which marked a rejection of the crinoline-shaped skirt. A higher waistline and the revival of tight lacing, bustle at the back, high heels and hair piled on top of the head all combined to give the wearer a stooping, S-bend posture, a look that critics nicknamed the 'Grecian Bend', and which was satirized in an 1870 *Punch* cartoon.[74] Like these women, it was earlier seen that Eliza Richardson was represented as paying heed to the dictates of fashion, such that her dress was described as being 'properly distended by the hoop so very important to female attire', a reference to the development of the crinoline. Whilst the 1850s had witnessed a progressive increase in the volume of women's skirts, it was the introduction of the steel-framed crinoline by 1860 that was deemed by reactionaries and moralists to be demonstrative of the immorality of modern dress.[75]

That streetwalkers in the Kentish ports and dockyard towns such as Eliza Richardson, Georgiana Campbell and Jane Boorman should have been able to observe the dictates of fashion so faithfully is a reflection of the brisk secondhand clothes trade of the period. This was maintained by advances in technology, which enabled wealthy women to possess large wardrobes and to discard clothes frequently.[76] Wearing second-hand clothes was a common custom amongst the poor, and the fact that even crinolines were taken up by the second-hand market is borne out by social commentator Henry Mayhew's reference to 'huge, awkward, unwieldy hen coops which are hung out at the doors of cheap selling off shops'.[77] Thus, as is evidenced by the *Gravesend Reporter*'s comment that Richardson's dress was of 'dubious cleanliness', the apparent finery worn by some prostituted women was illusory and superficial, and not necessarily indicative of prosperity or upward social mobility. As was seen in Chapter 1, prostitution in these localities represented for many women a means of survival at the margins rather than an escape from poverty. Thus, the references to fine dress do not undermine interpretations of prostitution that emphasize poverty, but reflect the range of resources incorporated into individual makeshift economies.

Eliza Richardson's appearance before magistrates in July 1860, with which this chapter opened, was not her last. Her twelfth appearance, in January 1861, resulted in a ten-day custodial sentence, and she subsequently served increasingly long terms over the following years. On one occasion she was reported to have proclaimed in court that 'if it was not for the drink she would not have so mis-conducted herself', and on another she was found collapsed in the street by a policeman, apparently 'helplessly drunk, crying for her child'.[78] Thus Richardson had, through the columns of the local press and over the course of a number of years, been represented in terms of the full range of stereotypes through which nineteenth-century prostitution was comprehended. From 'virago' to 'helpless' and from 'terror' to contrite, it is impossible to know which of these, if any, came close to a realistic portrayal. Yet each corresponds closely to the wider discourse surrounding prostitution that was conducted through literary, artistic and journalistic media, and which would have been familiar to the newspaper's readership. Each also served a didactic, moralizing role in holding these women up for public inspection, whether for censure or for pity.

This chapter has considered the ways in which cultural representations of the prostitute figure were circulated at local level, and the way in which these contributed to a process of 'othering' those women perceived as deviant. This process was located at one end of the spectrum of surveillance and policing to which these women were made subject. This discussion turns now to consider questions of identity in relation to geographies of prostitution and the spatial dimensions of prostituted women's integration into their own communities.

4 GEOGRAPHIES OF PROSTITUTION

When Mary Patrick was brought before the Gravesend bench of magistrates in December 1857 charged with theft, the evidence thrown up by the resulting prosecution case, as detailed in the local press, charted the route of her encounter with her victim, labourer William King, through the town. According to King's testimony, Patrick firstly 'accosted' him in the High Street, where she asked him to buy her a drink (see Map 1). They then went together, firstly to the King's Head public house on King Street, and afterwards to her lodgings in Clarence Street, where she relieved him of his money, watch and chain.[1] In a similar incident brought before Dover magistrates, the route taken by 'unfortunate' Elizabeth Reeve, during the series of events culminating in the alleged theft of a purse of money from Private William Smith, can be plotted from the evidence outlined to the bench (see Map 2). From the White Hart public house in Dolphin Lane where the two met, they proceeded to the Bee Hive public house in Snargate Street, and then to what was later described in court as a 'house of ill fame' in Hawkesbury Lane, where Reeve lived.[2] The geographical references cited in the reportage of these incidents allow individual women's movements through the urban landscape to be plotted and individual cartographies of prostitution to be constructed for the localities under examination. These illustrate the ways in which urban environments were negotiated and differentiated by users, and highlight the spatial and temporal boundaries of contested sites.

Geographical approaches to the study of nineteenth-century prostitution been adopted more frequently over recent years, as the additional insights that they can offer have begun to be better appreciated.[3] These insights shed light on the ways in which urban space was used and negotiated, and on the boundaries erected between these spaces, by different groups of users and by the authorities. In the context of this study's focus on the control of street prostitution, this approach also highlights questions of policing knowledge and practice, and also of identity. Cartographies of prostitution varied between one location and the next, and were determined by a wide range of factors, including the size, historical development, economic structure and regulatory complexion of individual locations. As illustrated by the examples of Mary Patrick and Elizabeth Reeve, it is clear that women differentiated between geographical zones, between those where they initially met and socialized with men and those used for sexual transactions and/or robbery. The boundaries between these zones, whether physical and spatial, or conceptual and temporal, were essential to each location's individual cartography of prostitution. Thus, geographical perspectives add qualitatively to an understanding of the ways in which space was understood, used and negotiated in the pursuit of prostitution.

The surveillance of public behaviour and the suppression of street disorder, as was seen in the previous chapter, were carried out progressively rigorously as communal space became increasingly disputed from the mid-century onwards. These initiatives became central to what historian Andy Croll has described as the 'civic project', that is, the collection of strategies developed in order to 'order, civilize and rationalize the urban experience' in the second half of the nineteenth century.[4] The conflicting interests of different social groups were contested at sites of communal space, and this is where new standards of public behaviour were both imposed and resisted. This imposition and resistance is illustrated by the events surrounding the arrest of Mary Ann Hayes of Dover on a charge of drunkenness and standing on a corner. When asked to 'move on' by a police officer, Hayes responded that she had as much right on the pavement as anyone else.[5]

Central to this civic project were the strategies developed both by and on behalf of women to preserve a public display of respectable feminine conduct. One such strategy was the provision of communal space and places of amusement for women that served both to regulate and protect them in public. Those who flouted these conventions, most notably the streetwalker, were heavily penalized. Middle-class women, who took increasingly to the streets for recreation and shopping over the course of the later nineteenth century, were faced with the challenge of distinguishing themselves from other classes of woman commonly found there, in particular the street prostitute, whose very identity, as Simon Gunn reminds us, was derived from social space.[6] This need to distinguish between the respectable and non-respectable woman on the street, combined with the spatial and temporal restrictions put on middle-class women's freedom of movement through public space, led to its categorization into respectable or non-respectable, and the formulation of corresponding assumptions about the type of women to be found in each. These assumptions were also coloured by class, such that the lady of the middle and upper classes was deemed to be in need of protection, whilst the dangerous woman, in need of regulation and containment, came from the ranks of the poor and labouring classes. Thus the public environment and the urban streets in particular became sites of contest, not only between classes but between classes of women in particular. Gendered mind-maps of the urban landscape were therefore devised, which involved a dichotomous classification of womanhood into stereotypes. This dual classification, as will be seen in Chapter 6, has a particular significance in the context of the policing of the CD Acts, given the prolific and influential repeal campaign discourse on the question of mistaken identity.

This chapter, therefore, explores the urban landscape of prostitution at ground level in three Kentish locations during the 1860s and 1870s, thus contributing to an understanding of the ways in which the contest for public space was played out in individual locations. It touches on questions of identity and mistaken identity, and on the likelihood of women in public being mistaken by the police for prostitute women. This discussion once again takes surviving petty sessions records and the newspaper reportage of petty sessions hearings as its starting point. These, contextualized and supplemented with contemporary published sources such as local almanacs, together with census materials, allow details related to residential and recreational patterns, together with the itineraries pursued in the pursuit of prostitution through the urban environment, to be illuminated.

Prostitution and Urban Development

Street prostitution is by definition a feature of the urban environment. It was articulated by nineteenth-century commentators specifically as a symptom of urbanization, and by local officialdom specifically as a *local* urban problem in need of a solution. Whilst eighteenth-century debates about prostitution had focused on its moral and social hygiene aspects, the question of contested public space was specifically a feature of nineteenth-century discourse.[7] The articulation of a growing fear of the threat of street nuisance, of which street prostitution constituted a significant element, coincided with the period of major population growth in the first half of the nineteenth century. Contemporary commentators such as Greg and Acton emphasized the link between prostitution and the crowded urban landscape.

The very visibility and public nature of nineteenth-century streetwalking made it the focus of official and public concern, an effect described by Gunn as 'the perception of immorality on show'.[8] In Kent, prostitution appears largely to have been tolerated as a regrettable inevitability, but its visibility, alleged threat to public decency and the impediment that it represented to the swift navigation through the streets were deemed to be acute nuisances to be tightly controlled at best, and preferably banished beyond the civic boundaries. Individual geographies of prostitution were specific to place and were influenced by patterns of urban development. The case studies explored in this chapter help illuminate the influence of these patterns on the use of the urban landscape for the pursuit and practice of street prostitution. The cartographies of prostitution for nineteenth-century Gravesend, a garrisoned river port, Dover, a garrisoned sea port and resort, and Sheerness, a garrisoned Royal dockyard, highlight the significance and particularity of place.

Gravesend's origins as a river port were derived from its strategic location twenty-four miles to the east of London; its economy was therefore largely dependent on water-related trades and activities. In the second half of the nineteenth century, vessels departing from the capital took on their final stores here, and pilots and customs officials were taken on and set down, as evidenced by the 852 passengers and crew recorded by the 1871 census on board moored vessels awaiting a tide and full cargos. Thus the town developed outward from the area close to the river frontage, landing places and town stairs in response to the need for ships to be provisioned and supplied, and to cater for the accommodation and refreshment of travellers. Inns and public houses were plentiful. A tourist trade had developed following the introduction of a regular steam packet service from London in 1815, bringing wealth and prosperity.[9] Two piers were erected during the 1830s to facilitate the landing of visitors and day-trippers, and amenities and attractions were established for their entertainment. In 1840 over a million day-trippers landed by boat, the year that the 'Directory of Watering Places' claimed that 'in point of view, health and pleasure, Gravesend will yield to none'.[10]

This period of Gravesend's success as a pleasure resort witnessed significant business and building booms. Property speculators 'cast covetous eyes' around the town, and new roads were cut, streets were widened and terraces of new houses built.[11] Bounded to the north by the river, the town expanded southwards, eastwards and westwards to cater for the growing permanent population and for the influx of visitors; the population increased from 4,539 to 18,782 inhabitants between 1801 and 1861. The arrival of the railway in North West Kent in 1849, however, which enabled visitors and holiday-makers from London to travel further afield, most notably to the Kent coastal resorts, signalled the decline of Gravesend's tourism. The local press in 1860 lamented the 'falling-off of Gravesend as a place of resort for Londoners, who are now carried away to other localities by railway'.[12] By the period of this study, therefore, Gravesend's heyday as a tourist destination was far behind it, leaving a sense of faded grandeur. The local economy was once again dominated by the town's role as a working river port.

Gravesend petty sessions minute books and local newspaper court reports recorded the locations of arrests for soliciting, the addresses of premises identified as brothels and prosecutions of publicans for 'harbouring prostitutes' on the premises. Taken together, these demonstrate that Gravesend's prostitution business was focused on two principal areas (see Map 4.1).

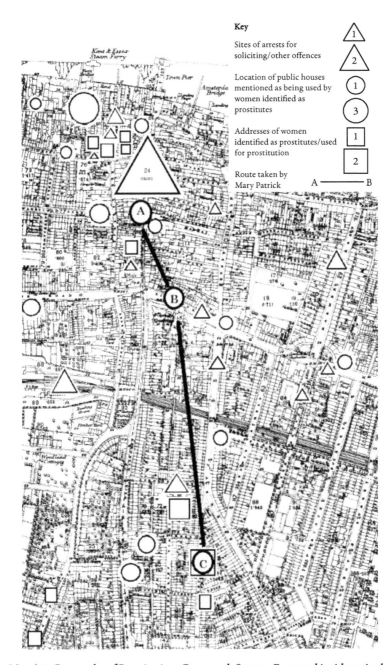

Key

Sites of arrests for
soliciting/other offences

Location of public houses
mentioned as being used by
women identified as
prostitutes

Addresses of women
identified as prostitutes/used
for prostitution

Route taken by
Mary Patrick   A ——————— B

Map 4.1: Geography of Prostitution, Gravesend. Source: Reported incidents in the
Gravesend and Dartford Reporter **for which locations can be established, 1856–79; map
based on Ordnance Survey 1874, 10-7, 1:10, 560.**

The first was the site of the town's pre-modern origins close to the pier and riverside, and the second was to the south of the railway line, close to the barracks. These were opened in 1863, and by the 1870s they accommodated over five hundred soldiers and marines. Intended originally as temporary accommodation for soldiers undertaking musket training at the rifle range at the canal basin, they were built to a high specification. This binary zoning of Gravesend's prostitution-related activity is exemplified in the case of Mary Patrick, with which this chapter opened. Having accosted her victim in High Street and taken him to drink in a public house in King Street, both of which were situated in the older part of the town, Patrick returned with him to her lodging in Clarence Street, situated on the other side of the railway line and closer to the military barracks. Similar patterns are reflected in comparable cases. The details of this pattern of differentiated zoning are individual to Gravesend, but, as will be seen, there are parallels to those elsewhere.

Dover's associations with the military date from the eighteenth century. Best known for its eponymous straights and as one of the historic Cinque Ports, Dover was garrisoned against the threat of invasion during the Napoleonic wars. As a major port and seafaring town, industries such as ship-building, boat repairing, rope-making and sail-making contributed to Dover's economy. The demand created by the military gave rise to industries such as watch-making (established to provide ships' chronometers and officers' dress watches) and leather working (to provide boots and belts to the navy and army), whilst milling and brewing activity also expanded to cater for the military centre, providing the ships and garrisons with flour, bread and ale. Other industrial enterprise such as the Buckland Paper Mill, timber and oil mills were less obviously dependent on the military, which during the 1870s represented 12 per cent of the town's total population.

Dover developed as a resort during the nineteenth century, when two railway lines, a steam boat service from Ramsgate, cross-channel boat services (three boats a day each to Ostend and Calais in the 1880s) and 'peculiar facilities' for sea-bathing all combined to attract visitors for 'health and recreation'.[13] These visitors, according to one contemporary, tended to 'keep to their parades and their esplanades, their green verandas, and their Bath-chairs' and away from the town centre and the other residents, described as the 'rout of engineers, contractors, quarry-men, masons, divers and navvies' on the one hand, and the 'sailors and pilots and mail-agents, and steamboat-captains' on the other.[14] This observation suggests significant geographical and social zoning within the urban landscape, which was replicated in the town's patterns of prostitution. Dover's prostitution trade, as measured using the same criteria as used for Gravesend, can be located to three main focal points; the town centre, the pier area, and Snargate Street, a busy thoroughfare that linked the two together (see Map 4.2).

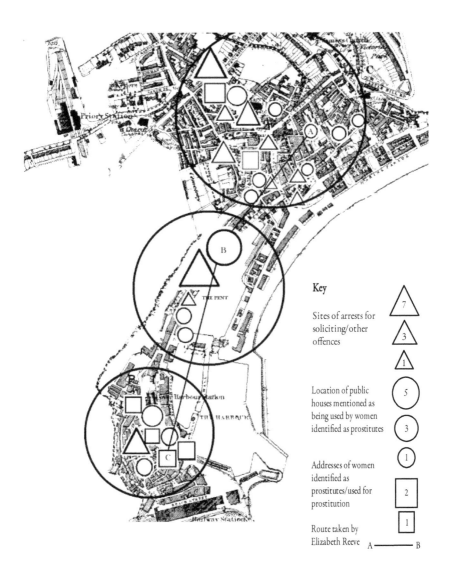

Key

Sites of arrests for
soliciting/other
offences

⟨7⟩

⟨3⟩

⟨1⟩

Location of public
houses mentioned as
being used by women
identified as prostitutes

⟨5⟩

⟨3⟩

⟨1⟩

Addresses of women
identified as
prostitutes/used for
prostitution

⟨2⟩

⟨1⟩

Route taken by
Elizabeth Reeve   A ——————— B

Map 4.2: Geography of Prostitution, Dover. Source: Reported incidents in the *Dover Express* for which locations can be established, 1860s–70s; map based on Ordnance Survey 1876, 068, 1:10, 560.

Public space in Gravesend and Dover was negotiated and contested between competing groups of users. The urban zones most frequently associated with prostitution were sites of high levels of social mixing and a diversity of usage. In both localities, whilst certain districts experienced higher levels of prostitution-related activity than others, to define these areas in terms of conventional 'red-light' districts risks overlooking the fluidity and flexibility of spatial and temporal boundaries.

Unlike Dover and Gravesend, Sheerness developed as a result of its long-established military installations, and during the period of this study the dockyard provided the principal source of employment. The site, on the north corner of the Isle of Sheppey at the mouth of the River Thames, was selected for the site of the Royal Naval dockyard in the seventeenth century as its deep water made it suitable for the building and repairing of ships. This location was isolated and inhospitable, and initially dockyard workers lived in hulks sunk into the mud on the foreshores.[15] In the nineteenth century, a shanty town was constructed around the dockyard boundaries, characterized by narrow streets and alleyways. Housing was assembled from rough wood taken from the dockyard and painted in grey-blue naval paint, as a result of which it came to be known as Blue Town. In the latter half of the eighteenth century, population expansion necessitated the building of additional housing, and a stipulation that workers should live no further away than one mile from the dockyard gates led to the new district being called Mile Town. Further dockyard expansion in the 1850s had drawn craftsmen from other dockyards, for example Chatham and Woolwich. Mains water and drainage were not initiated until the 1860s, thus both housing and sanitary conditions were poor. An unnamed magistrate described Sheerness as a 'dirty, low, demoralising little Chatham'.[16] Following the arrival of the railways in the 1860s Sheerness began to prosper, and by the 1870s was beginning to lose its reputation as, in the words of one local historian, 'an unhealthy, neglected, slow and generally undesirable locality'. At this time there were 1,900 resident military personnel, around one-eighth of the total population.

The geography of prostitution in Sheerness, as measured by the same indicators used to plot those of Gravesend and Dover, was concentrated on the narrow streets, alleyways and public houses of Blue Town (see Map 4.3). Arrests of women for soliciting, and of those identified as prostitutes for offences related to drunkenness, were most frequently made in the small triangular district bounded to the north by the dockyard wall and by West Street, thus supporting the contemporary testimony of one resident, who observed that 'Jack ashore' enlivened the area's public houses.[17] Most recorded arrests (over three-quarters of the total recorded between 1869 and 1879 in the Sheerness police court Registers) took place either in High Street, West Street or King's Head Alley. A representative example was the 1871 arrest of Eliza Cooper by PC Alfred Skinner. Recorded according to a formulaic wording, the offence consisted of Cooper, a 'rogue and vagabond', having been 'a common prostitute wandering in West Street, Blue Town' and behaving in 'a riotous manner'.[18]

Map 4.3: Geography of the Policing of Prostitution, Sheerness. Source: Sheerness police court records, 1867–79; MSS Census data, 1861–81; map based on Ordnance Survey 1896, 1:10, 000.

Key

Sites of arrests for soliciting and other incidents involving women identified as prostitutes, where the location can be established

Police officers' residences

Thus, Sheerness's cartography of prostitution was of a markedly different character from those of Gravesend and Dover. The town's origins as a garrisoned dockyard, which resulted in a more narrowly defined social profile, also produced a more restricted footprint of prostitution. Public space was contested, not between different classes of users, but between with the forces of moral order as represented by the local police force.

Temporal Boundaries

A range of temporal, permeable and moral boundaries served to differentiate between usages of public space within urban landscapes. The competing interests of users of West Street in Gravesend, for example, were managed by the erection of social and spatial boundaries that were temporal in nature. West Street was a major provisioning district, an area of poor housing stock and, at the same time, an area with strong links to prostitution. By daytime, middle classes from the outskirts of the town brought their custom to the area's butchers, fishmongers, greengrocers and grocers. Fish was a speciality, especially locally gathered shrimps. The north side of the street, running parallel with the river, was packed with wharfs, warehouses and provision merchants backing onto the piers and causeway on the river frontage, amongst which a labouring waterfront community lived in small, crowded courts. The area was also characterized by an abundance of public houses; the north side of West Street had more licensed premises in its 400-yard length than any other location in the town. Amongst these was the Old Falcon, where the Mayor gave a Christmas supper to the Borough Police, and the New Falcon Hotel, with its glass-fronted dining room looking out over the river, which was renowned for its whitebait suppers and was the venue for mayoral banquets. A nineteenth-century observer noted West Street's 'eating taverns and eating houses, some good hotels especially the New Falcon'.[19] This, therefore, was an area of dense pedestrian traffic between the piers, landing places and numerous public houses.

The presence of so many licensed premises accounts for the high levels of arrest on drunk and disorderly charges and of violence and assault that occurred here at night after the middle-class shoppers had returned to their homes on the outskirts of town. In 1879 Ellen Lane, described in court as 'a prostitute of West Street', was arrested there by Superintendent George Berry, who came across her some time after eleven at night in the middle of a large crowd of people, using, as he described, the 'most filthy and obscene language'.[20] The police claimed to have received complaints from the residents about the 'disorderly' behaviour of women known locally as prostitutes, but the complainants were seemingly unwilling to testify publicly against their neighbours or to put their grievances in writing, suggesting a reluctance to disrupt community relations. The onus was put upon the police to apprehend women in the act of soliciting, and thus they were frequent visitors to the area and well acquainted with its inhabitants.

By day this was the site of extensive commercial activity, attracting middle-class customers who lived on the outskirts of town. During the hours of darkness the area's character changed, and boundaries appeared to break down as it became colonized by a population with a different profile. In a manner reminiscent of the description offered by Simon Gunn, the inhabitants of slums and workers' districts 'spilled' on to the main street at night and during weekends.[21] In the case of a small town like Gravesend, the slums and workers districts were literally only yards away from the main thoroughfare, thus these boundaries were of a fragile nature. The tradesmen's outlets on West Street's south side were interspersed with fishermen's and watermen's homes. Described by a local historian as a neighbourhood in which the working-class and watermen's families lived, Sutties Alley, St John's Place, Pump Alley, Mermaid Court, Caroline Place and Passengers Court were predominantly composed of cheaply built wooden or lathe and plaster houses.[22] Casual labourers, itinerants and hawkers lived and lodged there alongside watermen and fishermen. Cesspool drainage, shared WCs and a standpipe water supply made these unhealthy and unsanitary courts, subject to frequent cholera outbreaks in the early and middle years of the century. As late as 1878, water from Pump Alley, along with that from houses in West Street, High Street and Bath Street, was analysed for the Town Council and condemned.[23] The area was finally cleared in a programme of slum clearance in the 1920s. Pump Alley was characterized by poverty, overcrowding and high levels of prostitution, as evidenced by the mention of several different addresses in the press in connection with prostitution-related incidents during the 1850s, 60s and 70s.[24] Three women publicly identified as prostitutes lived at number 7, whilst James Goodyer, the tenant of number 9½ which was nominally run as a lodging house, was linked to prostitution over many years. The 1851 census, unusually, records the occupation of three of Goodyer's lodgers as 'streetwalker'.

Evidently, given the material conditions amongst which the residents of Pump Alley lived, prostitution as practised in this environment was very much at the lower end of the scale. The alley comprised eighteen dwellings, four of which were described in 1852 sales literature as brick-built and consisting of three rooms and a cellar, commanding a rent of nine pounds per year which included the use of communal pump and privy. On census night 1851, ninety-nine people had been crowded into fourteen houses, three of which housed fifteen people each. A press report highlighting levels of poverty in Gravesend in 1879 described one family as living in one room described as 'very scantily furnished and as having no light'. The children had eaten no food that day.[25] The police were regular visitors to Pump Alley, and its residents were so frequently prosecuted for public order offences and breaches of the peace that it was mentioned during proceedings at petty sessions. Superintendent White was of the opinion that 'the whole of the houses in the court had pretty much of a much-ness about them; they were let out in lodgings to various characters'.[26] Cases of assault included the altercation between neighbours Mary Murphy and John Sowter, which resulted from Murphy having remonstrated with Sowter because he was 'beating the young woman he lived with', upon which he struck Murphy several times as well. The defendant's mother alleged that the complainant had been drunk. The Sowter family was back before the bench within a few months, on a separate charge of assault.[27] The *Gravesend Reporter*, commenting on such disputes, pontificated that 'the fetid atmosphere of these localities (is) so dis-graceful to the town – the acrid exhalations from which invariably affect the temperaments of the denizens'.[28] This comment reflected the influence of the 'miasmatic' theory, which held that disease was caused by the inhalation of air infected through exposure to rotting matter. This belief prevailed for much of the nineteenth century amongst the medical profession, shaping, as in this case, popular contemporary discourse. The disorderly and unsocial behaviour of the residents of Pump Alley was attributed to the foul air which they inhaled, thus symbolically associating them with of dirt, miasma and disease. Similar condi-tions applied in nearby Passengers Court, where in the late 1870s ten families were housed in one tenement, most of them living in a single room. In one of these, a husband and wife and four children shared a space reportedly measuring fourteen feet by ten, and in another a recently confined woman and her unem-ployed husband lived with seven children.[29]

The strong associations between prostitution and this area's public houses are reflected in prosecution rates of publicans at petty sessions. The India Arms retained a reputation for harbouring prostitutes over many years, and the landlord Jacob Beard was successfully prosecuted twice for this offence in the mid-1870s. The Privateer had a similarly long-established reputation. In 1856 the then land-lord, David Whiffen, received a caution from the magistrates after several local women, euphemistically described by the local press as 'members of the fair sex', residents of 'Pump Alley and its adjuncts', had gained entrance to the pub one Sunday morning by a side door left open for domestic purposes, and refused to leave until they had been served.[30] Several complaints had been received of the conduct of women understood to be prostitutes, but the residents, according to the Police Superintendent, would not make a formal complaint. The pub's reputa-tion continued undiminished for at least another twenty years. In 1876 landlord William Cox was convicted following a fight at the premises, part of the allega-tion being that he himself had been discovered lying on the counter of the bar talking to prostitutes. One of the women, Mary Ann Loft of Back Garden Row, was well known in the magistrates' court, having appeared there on at least three previous occasions charged with a variety of prostitution-related offences.[31]

Contested Sites

Contests for respectability were played out in main shopping streets between different groups of users, as was demonstrated in Gravesend's High Street and Dover's Snargate Street. These sites were significant mercantile and administrative thoroughfares and at the same time popular with soliciting women. Gravesend High Street climbed southwards away from the town pier, the river and West Street. The town hall, magistrates' court and police station were all located here, together with banks, provision merchants and retail outlets. The High Street's pre-modern origins were evident both in the crowded rookeries that were packed in behind it and in its extreme narrowness; being only eight feet wide in parts, it was described by a contemporary observer as 'highly inconvenient, especially in this "age of crinolines"'.[32] A series of fires in the eighteenth and early nineteenth centuries had destroyed many timber-built shops and houses; one such in 1850 razed twenty-four houses, together with many more in the adjoining courts and back yards. The opportunity was consequently taken to cut the first narrow streets running to the east and west, prior to which pedestrian pathways had provided the only outlet.

Unlike West Street, whose retail outlets were predominantly basic provision merchants, the premises in High Street included those of the principal retailers in the town. These, according to the testimony of a contemporary visitor, bore comparison with those of a similar class in London providing 'various lines of stationery and bookselling, drapery, fancywork, confectionary, glass and cutlery'.[33] An 1875 street directory confirms this impression, listing specialist outlets such as Frederick Burdock's pianoforte emporium, Hall's China and Glass Warehouse and the premises of Bryant and Rackstraw, draper and silk merchant, alongside more everyday butchery, grocery, bakery, tobacconist and fishmonger's outlets.[34] Amongst the retailers who kept shops in the High Street were several who had risen to local public office. These included Thomas Troughton, a magistrate and alderman who was a wax and tallow chandler, Charles Startup, tailor and outfitter and member of the Watch Committee, and grocer William Winnett, member of the town council who was elected mayor in 1864. This location was also the centre of Gravesend's business and administrative activity, and the London and Provincial and London and Liverpool Banks both had premises here.

This was therefore a vibrant and crowded environment in which soliciting women competed with a range of other users over the physically restricted and central territory, which was the site of dense traffic and bustling activity. This contest for space was facilitated, at a logistical level, by the district's urban geography. To the rear of the business and retail premises on High Street, in marked contrast to its respectable, prosperous and bustling main aspect, crowded courts and alleys could be reached on both sides by a series of narrow passageways. This area typified a common pattern of urban development in which small urban communities, consisting of no more than courts or rookeries, were squeezed in behind the main streets of a central business district.[35] Many of High Street's courtyards and alleys had been developed by the subsequent in-filling of the long narrow gardens behind narrow-fronted shops and houses. Early-nineteenth-century developers built workshops and houses down both boundaries along the length of these plots, creating inner courts of houses facing each other.[36] The double-fronted shop at number 17, for example, located next to the London and Provincial Bank, which in 1870 was the property of distiller Robert Sowter, was twenty-three feet wide but fifty-two feet deep, with a kitchen, scullery stores and a yard behind. The effect, as was experienced in Gravesend, was to produce 'a teeming warren of courts ... as many of these courts had back access; the town acquired a network of pedestrian ways leading through courts up and down the steep hills'.[37] The district was the site of the town's oldest housing stock, which had deteriorated to the level of slum dwelling by this period. The neighbourhood experienced a high level of social mixing and residential integration, and the casual poor competed for space with tradesmen and their employees, middle-class shoppers and administrative functions, including the police station. This competition for space, and the apparent fragility of the boundaries between the respectable High Street and the slums behind it, contributed to concerns about crime and violence, and about immorality.

This urban landscape had a direct bearing on the high levels of streetwalking and public prostitution practised in and around the High Street during the 1850s, 60s and 70s. This location was the site of the largest number of arrests both for soliciting and other street disorder offences. Street prostitution was facilitated by a convenient location with a high density of pedestrian traffic flow round the town pier and the railway terminus and by the facilities offered by the numerous licensed and other refreshment houses. These provided the opportunity to meet potential clients, who could then be swiftly taken through the many narrow courts and alleyways to one of the many houses that operated as brothels. Dark, narrow alleyways facilitated movement and the avoidance of the patrolling constable. One contemporary commentator observed of this area that 'The alleys and courts of the town swarm with "unfortunates", whose obloquy and shame are manifest'.[38]

The large number of licensed premises on High Street contributed to high levels of prostitution-related activity in this area, and provided temporary refuge from pursuing policemen or from aggrieved clients. The landlord of the Hole-in-the-Wall, which was situated literally at the end of a long passageway leading from the High Street, was charged with harbouring prostitutes in 1865, and prostitute Emma Jones was found drunk and riotous there in 1864.[39] The White Hart was the scene of several incidents of theft and assault, and was the address given to the authorities by Lydia Cripps and Mary Ann Smith when they were arrested and charged with 'disorderly and indecent behaviour, being prostitutes'. This incident earned for the area an ironic reference in the local press as 'one of the congeries of alleys at the back of White Hart Yard, in which charming locality both parties dwell'.[40]

A similar pattern of diversity of use is evident in Dover's Snargate Street, which served a strategic function in connecting the growing port area with the town centre. This, too, was a major shopping area and site of the town's foremost retail premises, including those of H. W. Newcomb (hosier, glover and hatter), J. Green and Son (cutler, engraver and optician), C. Gardiner (stationer and bookseller) and P. Thomson (French and English trimming, hosiery, haberdashery and glove warehouse). Snargate Street was also home to the offices of the *Dover Express*, the headquarters of the Salvation Army and to the Wesleyan Chapel. This was also the site of Wellington Arcade, a musical and fancy repository stocking pianos, harmoniums, games and perambulators. Established in 1811 under the name 'Squier's Bazaar', the arcade had been renamed following visits by the Duke of Wellington earlier in the century, when he was staying nearby at Walmer Castle.[41] Evidently, this was a vibrant and busy district during the daytime, attracting numerous shoppers and heavy pedestrian traffic.

Simultaneously, Snargate Street was the Dover location most often mentioned in petty sessions in connection with the prosecution of offences related to prostitution. In November 1869, Sgt Geddes of the Dover Borough Police informed magistrates that between fifty and sixty 'light women of the town' might frequently be seen between the top and bottom of Snargate Street. One such offender was Emma Ransley, arrested in 1870 for being drunk and disorderly and causing an obstruction. Ransley had allegedly been discovered 'stopping every person who passed', an offence apparently exacerbated by being committed before three o'clock on Sunday afternoon, when 'people were passing through the public thoroughfares on their way to different places of worship'.[42]

Snargate Street's status as a focal point for street solicitation is further reflected in levels of prosecution of publicans for the offence of 'harbouring prostitutes' on their premises. Between 1870 and 1872, Richard Burch of the Military Arms, George Tutt of the Bricklayers Arms and George Eastman of the Bee Hive were all brought to the attention of magistrates for this offence. The Bee Hive, it will be remembered, also featured in the episode involving Elizabeth Reeve, with which this chapter opened, and the bench considered withholding Eastman's license on the basis of evidence about the way in which the house was run. Police Sergeant Stevens testified to having watched 'prostitutes go in and out of the house'.[43] The Old Post Office, another Snargate Street public house, was also the subject of intense scrutiny during the prosecution of Mary Ann Godden on a charge related to the CD Acts in 1870. Inspector Capon's case was based on the fact that he had visited the Old Post Office at eleven forty-five one night to discover what he described as 'fifteen prostitutes, including the defendant, and several man-o-wars men, some dancing'.[44] Thus the street most populated by shoppers in the daytime and by concert goers in the evening was also the preferred haunt of women who solicited in the street and used its public houses in the pursuit of clients for prostitution.

The topographical restrictions of Snargate Street's location did not allow for the same level of development of crowded tenements in its back yards, as in High Street Gravesend. The cliff rose 'almost perpendicularly' to the rear, whilst the eastern, seaward side had once, according to an 1861 guide, been 'much closer to the proximity of the sea than at present'.[45] Nevertheless, a number of courts and yards had been in-filled behind Snargate Street's main aspect, with which they provided contrast. Chapel Court and Cliff Court housed mariners, labourers, laundresses and railway employees. Paris Yard, which was likewise home to working-class families, was the site of an 1861 disturbance perpetrated by Emma Richardson, described as an 'unfortunate'. In a state of 'intoxication', Richardson was arrested for 'abusing' other women. Whilst the superintendent of police, on being asked about Richardson' general conduct, was able to reassure the bench that she was 'generally well behaved', he added that 'the frail sisterhood in general wanted a great deal of keeping in order', and had of late grown very impudent to the police constables'.[46]

Nineteenth-century developments in retailing had also impacted on the contest for public space that took place between different users of these urban landscapes. Improvements in glass production, the introduction of gaslight, the development of a wholesale system and enhanced window-dressing techniques had all brought about a revolution in the experience of high street shopping. These developments enabled the development of fixed, lighted specialist shops with display windows that remained open all week and almost all hours.[47] Shoppers lingered longer than the minimum necessary to make their purchases, adding to the volume of pedestrian traffic on the streets. The establishment of restaurants and tea-shops provided the opportunity for rest, and paved and lighted streets further enhanced the experience and enjoyment of shopping for those who could afford it. This usage of public space by the more prosperous residents of provincial towns, and their movement to and from the centre, which Simon Gunn has referred to in terms of stylized 'ritual', necessitated differentiation from other groups of users.[48]

Many shops were still residential during the 1860s and 70s, and in most cases the proprietor and his or her family themselves lived on site. The gradual introduction of the lock-up shop that took place over the second half of the nineteenth century, which enabled owners to live in the suburbs, was still in process in our case study towns at this date. Live-in apprentices were still much in evidence, particularly in sectors such as drapery and grocery, as evidenced by the

1871 census. Draper George Littlewood at 55 High Street Gravesend, for example, was resident on census night with his wife, five children, three shop men and two domestic servants. Close by, eating house keeper John Sidby lived on the premises at number 60 with a wife, a niece, one assistant, one eating house servant, one waitress and a domestic servant. William Winnett, however, mentioned above, was absent on census night, but his premises were inhabited by two grocer's assistants and a housekeeper. Likewise, four draper's assistants, a draper's apprentice, a milliner, a dressmaker and a housekeeper spent census night on the premises of draper and silk mercer Harry Rose at number 61, though the owner was not resident. A similar picture of residence on retail premises is evident in Snargate Street, Dover. Nine assistants and three servants spent census night on the premises of draper James Greenfield, together with himself and his family. The premises of William Graves, also a draper, housed four 'shop-men', two 'shop-women' and three servants as well as Graves and his family.

Thus resident shop owners, their families and employees lived and worked amidst solicitation and other public evidence of prostitution, and public space was negotiated amongst competing users. When it came to light that according to a 'very respectable' source, a young alleged prostitute of fourteen years old was living at the Black Horse Inn in Gravesend High Street, for example, the public house in question was situated amidst a community comprising the families and employees of a butcher, a master boot-maker, a hatter and a fishmonger.[49] Only one of these premises had fewer than four people resident on census night in 1871.

Residence on working premises on the scale practised in these cases suggests that these commercial streets did not acquire a different character at night, nor were they abandoned or deserted. These districts were sites of activity and movement long into the evening. Thus the frequent incidents of soliciting and arrests of women identified as prostitutes took place in full view of passers-by. Ann Jones, for example, was arrested for soliciting at five o'clock in the afternoon.[50] A contest for public space was therefore entered into between all those who had a vested interest in maintaining the appearance of public 'respectability' such as shop-keepers on the one hand, and those women who needed to maintain a presence on the street for economic survival, on the other. As Croll has observed, the advantages for what he calls the rate-paying 'shopocracy', who depended on the free passage of goods carriers and customers, of a clean, passable and well-regulated High Street are clear.[51] An un-named Gravesend High Street shopkeeper, for example, made an official complaint in 1862 about 'the conduct of the girls residing in the courts and alleys' abutting onto the High Street, as a result of which a number of arrests were made for obstructing the pavement.[52] In Dover, too, retailers demonstrated a low threshold of tolerance towards women with the reputation of prostitute. Mr Haseldine, silk mercer of

Snargate Street, pursued the prosecution of Clara Edwards for ringing his door-bell, a case that was dismissed by Dover magistrates.[53]

Permeable Boundaries

Some of the districts most frequently associated with activity related to pros-titution were characterized by levels of residential and occupational mixing, which suggests that women who lived by prostitution were fully integrated into the surrounding poor and working communities. Reflecting a wider pattern of decline rather than increase in residential segregation in the three decades up to 1871, at district level the centres of Gravesend and Dover were socially mixed.[54] However, smaller-scale analysis reveals residential differentiation at the level of individual courts and alleys which were occupied by members of the casual and labouring poor. Certain small-scale urban zones had acquired the reputation as notorious slums. The courts and yards behind Gravesend High Street were asso-ciated with the residuum and which, the evidence of the local press suggests, conjured up images of dirt, criminality and depravity.

The Three Tuns public house was backed by Three Tun Yard, a closely packed court of crowded common lodging houses whose extremely narrow entrance consisted of an alleyway running alongside the pub. The close proximity of Three Tun Yard to the High Street made it a convenient location for the practice of lower-class prostitution. This was the scene of frequent incidents of drunken-ness, disorder and quarrels and fights between residents that frequently resulted in a summons to the magistrates' court. On census night 1861, sixty-seven peo-ple were crowded into nine addresses here, at least four of which were prosecuted as brothels during the 1860s and 70s. The local press considered Three Tun Yard 'a locality, we regret to say, which is familiar to scenes of outrage both of speech and conduct'.[55] Women solicited on the pavement of High Street near the nar-row entrance to the yard, from which position they could take advantage of the flow of pedestrian traffic up and down the street that was the main thoroughfare leading to and from the waterside, and between the numerous public houses. From here they could quickly and easily retreat into the yard with customers, or to avoid the patrolling constable when necessary. The newspaper report of the 1863 prosecution of Ann Swift for soliciting suggests that police officers would not follow loitering prostitutes into the alley unless they were in breach of the peace, so long as the High Street was kept clear and passable. On this occasion PC Jayne warned Ann to move on and she obligingly retreated inside the alley-way, only to return 'as soon as he turned his back'.[56] Jayne's colleague PC George Martin similarly cautioned a group of women who were standing talking on the pavement here, thus allegedly obstructing the way. The women, the court was told, 'paid no attention but only ran away and laughed when he passed'.[57]

That there was a good deal of traffic between Three Tun Yard and the public houses on the High Street is evidenced by the high number of incidents of drunken and disorderly or riotous behaviour by prostitute women and others reported to have taken place there. Louisa Turner, a young girl who described her own occupation as an 'unfortunate', was convicted of being drunk and using foul language in the yard; other examples include Louisa Collins and Margaret Groves, fellow lodgers at one of the houses who were brought before the bench, identified as prostitutes and charged with fighting as a result of an argument.[58] When four women were charged together as prostitutes with disorderly and indecent conduct in June 1874, three out of the four gave addresses in Three Tun Yard. Hannah Abbott, described in court as an 'unfortunate', stole a purse from Joseph Arnold at one of the houses there, after he had gone there with her after meeting her in the King's Head.[59]

Several residents of Three Tun Yard were convicted of running their premises as brothels. Thomas Day and Sarah Day, who herself had convictions as a prostitute, were convicted of the offence in 1869 and again in 1874. On the first occasion, the charge was prompted by complaints by High Street residents and the police were thus able to persuade magistrates that the house 'was resorted to by bad characters, and frequently there was disorderly conduct'. Margaret Green, one of the Days' lodgers who was identified in court as a prostitute, gave evidence for the prosecution.[60]

In a case of assault brought before the magistrates by Three Tun Yard resident Julia Callaghan against neighbour Margaret Marchant, the defendant claimed that her sister had been 'encouraged' by Mrs Callaghan to her house, which was run as a common lodging house, for immoral purposes.[61] This incident may have served to focus the attention of the police on the activities in the Yard, since shortly afterwards coal porter Thomas Smith and fish hawker John Mazar, residents of numbers 9 and number 10 respectively, were each charged with keeping brothels at their addresses. The charge against Smith resulted from an incident in which his wife had called the police after a fight had broken out at the premises between several prostitutes and a man, presumably a client. Smith was charged for a second time a few months later, following which he moved away from Three Tun Yard. Mazar was imprisoned for three months in Maidstone Gaol in default of being able to find two people to pay sureties of ten pounds each, or paying twenty pounds himself.[62]

In this district the local police were active in the maintenance of the boundaries of respectability that separated the main thoroughfares from the back alleys, and used local knowledge to differentiate between women with reputations for living by prostitution and others in the street for shopping and recreation. The location of the police station in the heart of the district contributed to high levels of surveillance.

This area typifies the 'promiscuous' urban environment described by Martin Daunton, who has written of the self-contained and mutually dependent worlds created by enclosed courts and alleys.[63] The social profile of this district is mirrored in Blue Town in Sheerness, which had the local reputation that one in two of its buildings was a public house and one in three a brothel. Whilst this unattributed saying may have owed something to exaggeration, it is partially borne out by census evidence. In 1861 thirty-two public houses and thirty beer halls catered for a population of 16,000; numbers 10, 13, 16 and 20 West Street, for example, all operated as public houses in 1861.[64] This was an over-crowded mixed urban environment, in which the families of the dockyard workers, the original inhabitants of Blue Town, lived amongst the ships' crews, members of the military, itinerants and the poor. Throughout the period of this study, the neighbourhood was home to a seafaring and transient community, and the numerous lodging houses were populated by sailors, dockyard labourers, hawkers and travellers. The lodging houses at numbers 6 and 13 West Street housed forty-three people and seventeen people respectively on census night 1871.[65] The shopkeepers and merchants of High Street Blue Town provided basic supplies rather than consumer or luxury items, comprising a butcher, baker, grocer and tea dealer, tallow chandler and furniture dealer.

In this milieu, women involved in prostitution lived in private lodgings or in public houses alongside the mixed itinerant and labouring communities. Margaret Cowl, who was named as a prostitute in court when she was twice convicted of being drunk and disorderly, gave her address as the Eagle Tavern in November 1865 and the Oddfellows Arms in January 1866, suggesting that she took lodgings where she could.[66] Elizabeth Tremain and Sarah Charlesworth, who were both mentioned in Chapter 2, were boarding in one of the three households that occupied number 9 West Street in 1871. Both were frequent visitors to the police court during the early 1870s, prosecuted on a number of charges related to prostitution. A charge of drunkenness against Charlesworth was dismissed after it emerged that at the time the offence was committed, she had been in the custody of a police inspector responsible for the operation of the CD Acts.[67] The association of this address with prostitution was long-lived. Emma Williams, who was living there ten years later, was unusually recorded in the census as 'prostitute'.[68] The neighbour on one side was a grocer and on the other a fruiterer, suggesting, once more, that women who lived by prostitution were integrated into the poor, labouring and trading communities that surrounded them.

The publicans of the district were frequently convicted of the offence of 'harbouring' prostitutes for longer than was necessary for them to take refreshment. Thomas Pell of the Swan, Richard Spencliff of the Anchor and Hope, William Goatham of the Lord Nelson and Isaac Mason Coody of the Mitre were all fined between five and ten pounds plus costs at various times for this offence.[69]

Coody, convicted in 1874 and again in 1876, appears to have moved between premises, since the 1861 census records him at the King's Head in West Street.[70] The Anchor and Hope was a favoured haunt of Elizabeth Tremain, mentioned above, who took a Royal Marine there, having asked him to 'liquid up' her and a friend. From the evidence given in court, when he returned with her to her lodging, she informed him that he could only stay the night if he had money.[71]

Arrests of women for ill-defined street disorder offences were frequent in this district. The wording of these charges invariably included the phrase 'being a prostitute', which appears to have secured conviction. Emily Brooks, a recidivist with numerous convictions to her name, incurred custodial sentences of between six weeks and three months in the late 1870s and early 1880s after being charged with 'being a riotous prostitute'. When she was once again admitted to Maidstone Gaol on 21 June 1883, the admission register noted that she had forty-two previous convictions despite only being twenty-three years of age.[72]

The pier district of Dover was similarly characterized by a mixed labouring community amongst which some women lived by prostitution, which may have been facilitated by the heavy traffic resulting from moored shipping. Disembarking mariners such as William Mortimer, master of the brig Providence, provided easy pickings to women such as the two 'unfortunates' who 'fell in' with him at the harbourside and asked him to buy them drinks before allegedly relieving him of his watch.[73] In this district, land reclaimed from the draining of Paradise Pent resulted in the construction of housing in Oxenden Street which, by the 1860s, was home to a mixed working community of pilots, labourers, mariners and customs officials and their families. Here, too, was the Duke of Cornwall public house, where an 1859 prosecution case against the landlord for harbouring prostitutes had failed on a technicality after police mishandled it.[74] Limekiln Street, which connected with Oxenden Street, was named after the limekilns that had previously burned chalk for lime at the base of the cliff. This was another mixed working-class neighbourhood inhabited by mariners' and labourers' families, many with resident lodgers. The large family group at number 36, comprising fourteen family members and one visitor, suggests overcrowded housing conditions. One resident was a shoemaker, a trade that experienced considerable depression at this date.[75] These residents, together with an oil seed crushing company, a general shop and ship's chandler, all rubbed shoulders with the premises of Susannah Tolney, an 'elderly' woman, who was prosecuted at Quarter Sessions in January 1862 for keeping a disreputable house at her home at number 20, next door to the Plume of Feathers public house.[76] Witnesses were called to prove that 'women of ill fame' resided in the house, one of whom was apparently Tolney's own daughter. According to this evidence, the house was the 'constant resort of soldiers and sailors who frequented the place at all hours and in various stages of inebriety'. The previous year's census had captured Tolney living in a household consisting of her husband and four children, with four unrelated single women aged between twenty and thirty-two also resident, one described as a dressmaker, one as a stay-maker, and two with no occupation recorded.[77] Nearby, Elizabeth White and Emma Richardson, mentioned previously in relation to an incident in Paris Yard, were also captured by the census living in Limekiln Street. White, described as a dressmaker, had been identified in court as an 'unfortunate' eighteen months previously, when she had been charged with breaking a window at a lodging house where she spent the night with a foreign sailor.[78] Richardson was recorded on the census as a needlewoman. Charlotte Oliver, described as an 'unfortunate', who lived in a room at 4 Medway Cottages in Limekiln Street, attracted attention to the neighbourhood after stealing from a man she had brought back there for the night.

Nearby Round Tower Street also featured in the hearings of prosecution cases at petty sessions. Jane Williams, mentioned in Chapter 2, who used a room at the Lord Warden public house for the purposes of prostitution, lived here. This was also the location of the Little Phoenix public house, which was brought to the attention of magistrates in 1873 when the landlord was charged with keeping a disorderly house. This incident resulted in the dismissal of PC Delph of the Dover Borough Police force after he was allegedly found in bed there with a woman named in court as a prostitute.[79]

The pier district of Dover, like Blue Town on Sheppey and Three Tun Yard in Gravesend, were mixed labouring and itinerant neighbourhoods, in which women who lived by prostitution were integrated into their immediate communities. These districts did not feature on the itineraries of the middle classes, and thus the contest for public space that was played out here was not between groups of users but with the police.

Women in Public and Public Women

The threat caused by the breakdown of moral boundaries between pure and fallen women is most clearly reflected in debates relating to the presence of 'respectable' women on the streets. Direct evidence relating to middle-class women's presence on the streets of Gravesend is scarce, but inference may be drawn from the busy calendar of religious, philanthropic and cultural events that took place in the town. The Assembly Halls (otherwise known as the Grand Theatre) in Harmer Street hosted a wide range of secular, sacred and comic concerts and performances, including those given by the Gravesend Philharmonic Society, the Gravesend Glee and Madrigal Society and the Gravesend and Milton Amateur Dramatic Club. The Gravesend and Milton Church Union met at the Assembly Halls, whilst Rev. William Guest gave historical lectures at the Congregational Church.

In Dover, this impression is also suggested by the presence of middle-class entertainment venues. Snargate Street was home to a variety of venues which ensured that it remained busy and populous into the evening. The Clarence Saloon produced concerts and ballets, and the Apollonian Hall (built in 1839) offered a mixed programme of theatrical performances, public and private balls, lectures and concerts. Amongst the features of the 1873 summer season, for example, were Miss Rebecca Isaac's ballad concerts.[80] The Apollonian Hall also served as the winter home to the Dover Catch Club, established since the early 1800s, and offered 'amusement to the lovers of music and song' weekly from November to March, at a cost of ten shillings for a season ticket for residents, or one shilling per evening. Wellington Hall, attached to the arcade, hosted concerts, balls, entertainments, lectures and meetings. A February 1873 entertainment given by the Dover Amateurs here was received by a large audience.[81]

These, taken together with the evidence regarding patterns of retailing and shopping, suggests that it is too simplistic to assume that middle-class women were restricted to the home other than when buying provisions. Historical accounts of the nineteenth-century middle-class woman's restriction to the domestic sphere, which ignored her presence in public places, has recently been challenged and described as the 'writing-out of middle-class women from the spaces of the city'.[82] Mary Ryan has reminded us that, on the contrary, women of all classes took to public spaces over the last quarter of the nineteenth century for routine shopping and recreation. However, according to Ryan, middle-class women's presence in public spaces and in particular on the street was carefully monitored and strategies developed for their regulation and protection. Amongst these was the concept Ryan refers to as the 'cartography of gender', by which women adhered to their own 'mental maps' of the town and avoided certain areas.[83] Croll has likewise referred to the 'mental maps that late Victorians may have taken with them as they stepped into the highways and byways of the town'.[84] These 'mental maps' would not have taken middle-class women to certain sites in the evening, but the programme of entertainment and improving activities in Gravesend and in Dover played a role in defining the public space where they could be expected to be found.

Working-class women, it could be argued, ran a greater risk of being mistaken for a prostitute. Field labourer Ellen Hartley, for example, fell foul of the pressure put on the police to suppress streetwalking and obstruction of the pavement when she was arrested having gone out to buy sugar and tea at eight-thirty in the evening after returning from work, when she stopped to chat with friends on the street. The case against Ellen was dropped, although she was warned by the bench 'to inform her friends that they must not assemble on the footpaths'.[85] The inference is that for magistrates and police it was not women's presence on the street in itself that created the possibility of being mistaken for a prostitute, but specific behaviour such as loitering that was easily mistaken for soliciting. As part of the civic project to keep public space respectable, free and passable, increasing emphasis was placed on speed and movement through the streets over the course of the nineteenth century, and arguably this applied especially to women.[86] It is noteworthy that Ellen was not arrested whilst on her journey to or from her place of work but having stopped to chat with friends.

As this study has shown, women who earned money from prostitution in Gravesend and Dover often lived and worked in close proximity to the very centre of middle-class commercial and administrative life. They did not therefore inhabit 'a different world, both morally and geographically' from the rest of the local community, but instead they shared geographical territories with the so-called respectable classes.[87]

Moral Boundaries

Footprints of prostitution can be brought into sharper relief when compared in juxtaposition with local geographies of policing. In Gravesend, the premises occupied by the Town Hall, magistrates' courts and police station with police cells were located in the High Street, which, as has been seen, was the site of the highest number of arrests for soliciting and of women identified as prostitutes for other offences. Residential accommodation was provided next door to the police station for the head constable and his family. Thus, the head constable, together with the police officer undertaking the role of gaoler and the sergeant-at-mace, a corporation official were all resident on site. Superintendent Frederick White, head constable from 1851 until his sudden death in service in 1873, brought up a family of four children in this accommodation, including one son who went on to become assistant police clerk. The location of the police station and magistrates' court in the midst of the area of highest levels of street disorder suggests constant surveillance and the maintenance of moral boundaries.

In Sheppey's Blue Town the courthouse and the police station were also situated in the heart of the area most strongly associated with prostitution. The former stood next to the Red Lion public house on High Street, Blue Town. The latter, situated on Station Road, was built in the mid-1860s and consisted of three suites of residential apartments, one each for the sergeant and the 'lock-up keeper', and one for the unmarried officers.[88] The 1871 census captures Sergeant Edward Coppinger resident with a wife and four children, Police Constable Benjamin Jessup with a wife and four children, together with PCs Job Paine, Alfred Skinner, Alfred Hollands and Henry Lane all living on site.[89] These officers' names feature frequently in the minute books of the police court around this time, in connection with prosecutions brought against women for prostitution-related offences. The arrests and prosecutions of Jane Pollard by Paine, Lucy

Williams by Lane, Mary Bennett and Eliza Bentley by Skinner, Sarah Hart by Hollands and Elizabeth Cecilia day by Jessup, each on a charge of 'being a prostitute, wandering and riotous', all related to offences that had taken place in the immediate neighbourhood surrounding the police station where the men lived and worked in the early 1870s.[90]

Local knowledge and experience were therefore central to the processes of surveillance and policing brought to bear on women who lived by prostitution and the networks surrounding them. This knowledge is reflected in the detail of the testimony given in court by officers who were called upon to support prosecutions. It is likely that what individual officers 'knew' about individual women was that they were identified as prostitutes by reputation and outward behaviour judged against contemporary agreed norms, rather than by any specific knowledge of a cash exchange for sex. Nevertheless, this knowledge was applied in the surveillance and policing of immorality. Gravesend publican William Cox, landlord of the Privateer on West Street, was indignant to be charged with the offence of harbouring prostitutes in 1876. Protesting against police tactics in prosecuting a charge that his house had been the 'habitual resort of prostitutes for some months past', Cox challenged the police officers' 'somewhat superhuman knowledge' in alleging that five of his customers were prostitutes. Cox may well have been surprised when the officers responded by identifying each of the five women by name in court.[91] At the time of the incident, four of the five police officers involved in prosecuting the case, John Jayne, Henry Dartnaill, George Bevan and John Fitch, had a combined total of forty-two years' experience patrolling the streets of Gravesend.

Serving police officers' own residential patterns offer additional insight into the accumulation of this local knowledge, and shed light on another facet of individual towns' geographies of prostitution. It will be remembered that the second focal point of Gravesend's prostitution was a district of working-class housing situated to the south of the town centre, close to the barracks. In this district, centred on Peppercroft Street and Clarence Street, women who lived by prostitution lived amongst a diverse cross section of the working classes, including police officers and their families. This district was located less than half a mile south of the old town centre close to the barracks, between two of the three principal thoroughfares leading southwards out of central Gravesend. Along these principal arteries a variety of housing types had been built, which included, at the further ends, the villa residences of a number of the town's small middle class and holders of public office. The space between the main roads had been infilled with streets of terraced working-class and artisan's dwellings, and these, unlike the town's old quarter discussed previously, are revealed on contemporary maps to have been regular and even, suggesting early-nineteenth-century development. Peppercroft Street was a cul-de-sac running north to south. The houses here were owned by private landlords who often purchased in multiple for letting, as evidenced in reports of property sales and auctions.[92] These suggest that properties changed hands frequently and usually with sitting tenants.

A detailed description of number 62 is provided by the publicity material drawn up when the house was advertised for sale in 1884. The house contained a basement consisting of a breakfast room with range, and a kitchen with sink and copper. On the ground floor there was a front parlour with stove and a back parlour, and on the first floor front and back bedrooms. Thus these houses, if number 62 is typical, contained front and back rooms on each of three floors. The garden at the rear contained a wash house and wood shed. The houses had alleyways running behind, thus facilitating movement through the network of streets. It was in one of these that a man called Benjamin Rouse was discovered in 1868 with a woman called Eliza Andrews; both were drunk and lying on the ground, and were charged with indecency.[93]

This neighbourhood was home to a mixed working-class community, and most tenants rented rooms rather than whole houses. Residents during the early 1860s included a baker, a blacksmith, two bricklayers and two carpenters, a carman and a glazier. The 1861 census lists only one labourer, with no hawkers nor anyone recorded as unemployed.[94] There are, on the other hand, several customs house officers and one fundholder. Thus this area appears to have a markedly different socio-economic profile from the West Street /Pump Alley area. This profile did not, however, mean that all inhabitants were prosperous or even comfortable. The 1858 inquest into the death of an infant called Charles Thomas, child of a shoemaker who lived at number 23, concluded that the death was caused by starvation resulting from poverty.[95]

Peppercroft Street's association with prostitution pre-dated the barracks, since magistrate Robert Oakes made reference in court in 1856 to a previous campaign to indict a man called Lane for brothel-keeping.[96] The association appears to have been reinforced by the establishment of the barracks in the early sixties. Mary Ann Westlake was convicted in 1873 for running her home, number 46, as a brothel.[97] William Elvidge, who lived at number 44 in 1870, was described in the street directory as a gardener. Whilst there is no evidence to confirm that he ran this address as a brothel, he was subsequently convicted for this offence at his new address in nearby Clarence Street, so it remains a possibility. On that occasion the charge was that he harboured prostitutes to the annoyance of neighbours. In 1871 Harriet Herrington, described as a prostitute twice during magistrates' court hearings, lived at number 18 Peppercroft Street. Harriet was described on the 1871 census as nurse to labourer Frederick Patten and his family, with whom she was boarding. Ten years later Sarah Darge, whose life story was related in Chapter 1, was a lodger at this house, thus continuing the association between the address and prostitution. Numbers 58 and 71 Peppercroft Street were both licensed premises; the Prince Regent at number 71 appears to have been used by prostitutes who lived in the area. Elizabeth Mitchell and another unnamed 'unfortunate' met a sailor named Daniel Austin there and took him to the brothel at North Cottage.[98] This area was also the scene of drunk and disorderly incidents involving prostitutes, such as the one involving Elizabeth Miller in 1864 and the fight between Sarah Darge and Mary Ann Street in 1873.[99]

Somewhat paradoxically, this district was also home to members of the Gravesend Borough police force at the period of this study. It is not certain why some streets should have had a disproportionately high number of police officers among its residents, but scholars cite the constraints of disposable income, the geography of the town, access to employment and the socio-economic structure of the community as likely influences on residential choices.[100] What is known about the socio-economic status of police officers at this period makes it likely that they would live in working-class neighbourhoods. It is additionally possible that notification of vacant properties was passed by word of mouth through co-workers' networks. PS John Jayne lived at at numbers 19 and 43 in the 1860s, PC William Barfield lived variously at numbers 32, 28 and 27 Peppercroft Street in the early 1870s and PC John Marshall at number 64 in the early 1880s.[101] These strong local ties throw up interesting questions when it comes to the examination of evidence related to the surveillance and policing of offences related to prostitution. At the 1873 hearing of the case against Mary Ann Westlake, mentioned above, for brothel-keeping, several police constables were in attendance to prove the charge. It is not clear whether any of her previous or current neighbours were amongst these witnesses, but they could be presumed to be aware of both the activities at the address and the attitudes of other neighbours.

Clarence Street ran parallel with Peppercroft Street and was described by a contemporary visitor as containing a number of 'small eating houses, convenient to the humbler classes, where coffee, tea and shrimps are supplied at small expense'.[102] Clarence Street also had well-established connections with prostitution. The 'notorious' North Cottage, mentioned earlier, had a long-standing reputation as a brothel. Successive residents of this address were convicted of brothel-keeping in the period between 1856 and 1873. The childhood home of Sarah Darge, who has been mentioned previously, was 35 Clarence Street, and number 34 was run as a brothel by William Elvidge for which offence he was convicted in 1874.

The pattern of arrests for soliciting clearly shows that the prostitution footprint of the Peppercroft Street/Clarence Street district was of a different character from that of the town centre. This was a mixed working-class residential area without the same degree of pedestrian traffic as the town centre, thus there were therefore fewer reported arrests for soliciting. However women who plied for trade in the streets and public houses of the central district often brought men the short distance back to the Peppercroft Street and Clarence

Street area, either to their own lodgings or to one of the houses that operated as a brothel. Women named as prostitutes were regularly arrested for drunkenness and for fighting in the street here, and the district's brothels and numerous public houses were mentioned in prosecutions of publicans and of brothel-keepers. Taken together, the evidence about this district reveals close spatial relationships between women who lived by prostitution, brothel-keepers and individual police officers over a long time period (see Map 3). The social mix of the area, which included the respectable working classes and the poor, was distinct from that in the town centre, since on the whole the middle classes had no reason to come here. These findings have implications for the question of mistaken identity, since less reliance could be put on signals such as dress as a means of distinguishing prostitutes from other women. In these circumstances it is likely that policemen relied less on visual indicators than on personal knowledge of the local women with reputations as prostitutes, and that this was enhanced by community networks of extended family, residence and shared housing.

In Sheerness, historical urban development had resulted in different residential patterns amongst its police officers. As has been seen, accommodation was provided for a number of men at the police station in the centre of Blue Town, the focal point of the district's prostitution-related activity. Arrests in High Street, West Street and the alleyways between them were made almost within sight of where these officers lived over the 'shop'. The area most popular amongst officers living in their own accommodation, however, was the grid formed by Hope Street, Alma Street and Rose Street in Mile Town. PCs William Rosier, Edward Sale, William Scott and Richard Topsom all lived in Alma Street in the early 1880s. PC Henry Brown moved between various addresses in Rose Street and Hope Street between the early 1860s and 1890s. These officers lived in a working neighbourhood whose inhabitants were principally employed in the skilled crafts and trades associated with the dockyard: joiners, blacksmiths, riggers and shipwrights. Labourers were also represented, together with heads of labouring gangs, which suggests identification with labour aristocracy. Unlike in Blue Town, most of the male residents had employment. It is notable that the public houses in this district, such as the British Queen and the Bricklayers Arms, both in Rose Street, were not amongst those most often prosecuted for the offence of 'harbouring' prostitutes. Arrests of women for soliciting or for other disorderly behaviour were also minimal. Amongst the Sheerness women named as prostitutes during prosecution hearings at the police court, Hannah Clasper had grown up in this district in James Street and Carrie Pardew in Alma Street. Their arrests, however, took place in Blue Town, as did most of those recorded in petty sessions for soliciting or drunken and riotous behaviour. Thus when PC William Empson, for example, arrested Mary Bennett and Sarah Hart for 'being a prostitute, wandering' in High Street, Blue Town in the early 1870s, he was less than a mile from his own home in Hope Street at the time.[103]

This ground-level approach to the study of the geographies of prostitution sheds light on the questions of identity and mistaken identity that lay at the heart of CD Acts repeal campaign discourse. In many locations, women who lived by prostitution, brothel-keepers and the police officers charged with the surveillance and control of their activity lived and worked in close proximity to one another in districts characterized by varying levels of social mixing. Whether in the packed courts and alleys behind the premises of middle-class tradesmen in the heart of the central commercial district, or amongst the inhabitants of working-class neighbourhoods, these women appear to have been assimilated into their immediate communities. Analysis of patterns of urban development facilitate the construction of geographies of prostitution which additionally cast light on the debate on mistaken identity in relation to the CD Acts. This combination of evidence casts doubt on the realistic likelihood of working-class women being mistaken for prostitutes on the streets on a wide scale, and less likelihood of a middle-class woman being so mistaken. The question is begged, therefore, why this question attained such prominence within the abolitionist discourse, such that it was investigated by the Select Committee in 1882.[104] One possible answer is that the repeal movement bought the support of the respectable working classes for its cause by overstating the threat posed to them by the operation of the CD Acts. Respectability was a positive moral force which, as Zedner argues, the urban poor themselves strove to maintain, and thus appeals for support for a cause based on sympathy for the plight of admitted prostitutes would have met with limited success.[105] In investigating the issue of mistaken identity, this case study raises a number of questions relating to the routine policing of prostitution. The discussion is taken a step further in the following chapter, with a more fully developed investigation of the policing regimes brought to bear on street prostitutes in the subjected ports and garrisons of Kent, exclusive of the CD Acts.

5 POLICING PROSTITUTION

Sitting in petty sessions in Gravesend in 1856, magistrate Henry Ditchburn presided over the prosecution of eighteen-year-old Sarah London, who had been discovered 'noisy and drunk' in West Street between eleven and twelve the previous evening. London had allegedly become abusive when instructed to move on by the attending officer, which resulted in her arrest, and had then been violent on arrival at the police station.[1] In sentencing London to one month's imprisonment in Maidstone Gaol, Ditchburn expressed himself of the view that it was 'lamentable and disgraceful' that someone of her age was leading 'such a life', adding, for good measure, that to his knowledge her mother lived 'by the wages of prostitution'. Turning to make some more general remarks to the assembled courtroom, he announced that he and his colleagues 'were trying to redeem the character of the town, so that respectable persons should not be annoyed'. They were determined, he said, 'to completely rid the town of prostitutes'.

Ditchburn's words reflect the lowering threshold of tolerance brought to bear on street prostitution by the mid-century. Entering into the increasingly moralistic discourse that characterized public discussion of the subject at this time, Ditchburn justified the campaign to 'rid the town' of the alleged nuisance caused by women who lived by prostitution by appealing to the cause of public decency. This campaign, waged by the justices of Gravesend in the name of respectable townspeople, epitomized the extension of civic responsibility in the second half of the nineteenth century beyond the maintenance of peace and order to the implementation of raised standards of public behaviour.

Clearly the policy that operated in Gravesend was one of suppression rather than the regulation or containment of street prostitution, whereas, as this chapter will show, approaches adopted by other authorities in Kent lay elsewhere on this continuum. This positioning was dictated by the particular combination of practical and administrative circumstances in each location, such as policing arrangements, local governance and legislative provision. Historians of crime have shown how from the late eighteenth century onwards, social disorder and crime, certain levels of which had previously been accepted as inevitable, began increasingly to be felt to be a serious threat to the social order and a growing problem in need of a solution. Previously tolerated public transgressions were redefined as unacceptable in urbanized environments, and punitive measures applied.

The Kentish evidence, as exemplified by the words of Henry Ditchburn, challenges the notion that the Contagious Diseases Prevention Act of 1864 represented the first serious attempt at the control of prostitution. Judith Walkowitz is amongst those who have argued that prior to this date 'the constable's formal control over streetwalkers was limited', and that there was a general 'policy of inaction and toleration'.[2] According to this view, the regulatory regime introduced under the CD Acts represented exceptional repression precisely because it contrasted so markedly with previous practice. In Kent, street prostitution was policed progressively more strictly in the years following the introduction of the 'new' police in the second quarter of the century, thus the surveillance and control of street prostitution formed part of a wider regulation of the casual poor. The previously tolerated public behaviours of this group, which also included beggars and vagrants and drunks, began to be redefined as unacceptable in line with new notions of respectability and raised expectations of public order. This approach locates the policing of street prostitution within a much wider narrative of urban control and the regulation of the day-to-day activities of the poor and working classes in the name of middle-class respectability, to which sexual morality was central. Historians of policing do not generally subscribe to the thesis of a policy of inaction towards street prostitution in the years before the CD Acts. Where there was such tolerance, as Clive Emsley observes, it was more likely to apply at the more discreet, less visible upper-class end of the market rather than to the streetwalkers and the habitués of 'the less salubrious houses of ill-fame' who are the subjects of this study.[3]

Analyses that frame the policing of prostitution within narratives either of monolithic repression on the one hand, or of widespread toleration on the other, run the risk of creating an over-simplistic dichotomy. They also obscure the variations in policy and practice, both from one place to another and over time, that are revealed by the documentary evidence, and the practical difficulties faced in some locations by those who wished to meet increasing expectations of public order. Therefore, a local perspective is required to allow for an exploration of these distinctions. Such an examination of the workings of the policing and criminal justice systems in the third quarter of the nineteenth century is dependent on the survival rate of petty sessions records for the period. In the case of the districts under examination here, this survival rate is variable, as is the degree of detail contained in them. For the purposes of this discussion, therefore, these have been supplemented with the reportage of the same hearings in the local press, which, as has been seen in Chapter 3, was a regular feature of local coverage. Clearly, the selection of cases for publication from each day's proceedings was not a value-free process, and it may be assumed, as has been seen, that this was done on the basis of a combination of entertainment value and didactic purpose. Where it is possible to do so, a comparison between the official records relating to a case and the corresponding press coverage of the same case allows some measure of understanding of the degree of embellishment added by the court journalist. Where newspaper coverage comes into its own, however, is in its reporting of additional detail, which remained below the radar of interest of the clerk to the court and would otherwise remain unknown. In the case of Sarah London, the newspaper coverage reported Magistrate Ditchburn's asides to the courtroom, including his claims to additional acquaintance with the background of the defendant, which were not otherwise recorded. For the historian using this newspaper reportage for analysis of contemporary attitudes to the regulation and surveillance of prostitution, therefore, this coverage opens a window onto more than the outline facts of the case. Approached critically and interpreted cautiously, this source material adds qualitatively to our understanding of the range of attitudes and regulatory, surveillance and policing measures applied to women living by, and on the margins of, prostitution in the third quarter of the nineteenth century. This discussion turns firstly to a consideration of changes in policing policy and practice in Kent, before considering the implications of these changes to the way in which policing was experienced at street level.

Policing in Kent

The growing intolerance of public behaviour deemed to be disorderly that is reflected in Henry Ditchburn's remarks to Sarah London was converted into social reality on the streets of Gravesend by the town's police force, established in 1836. This resource provided the magistrates, who were determined to 'rid the town of prostitutes', with the practical means of translating ideology into realized policy. This individual example constitutes one thread within a wider narrative of the development of policed communities during the nineteenth century. This long and evolutionary legislative process saw traditional, part-time, parish-based, reactive policing systems transformed into mandatory, preventative, professionalized and identifiably modern ones.[4] The increased manpower and greater visibility of what is often termed the 'new' police (that is, full-time, institutionalized police forces) resulted in the widening of their remit beyond the apprehension of criminals to the containment of petty street misdemeanours and the imposition of raised standards of public behaviour. The formation of professional full-time police forces in the regions of England and Wales did not take place in a uniform fashion, either geographically or temporally. This variation had a direct bearing on the differing levels of stringency with which prostitution and other street disorder were controlled at any given time, and accounts for the wide discrepancies between one place and another that are thrown up by the evidence. It also provides an alternative reading of situations that have been interpreted in terms of tolerance of streetwalking and of public prostitution.

In the years following the creation of the Metropolitan Police in 1829, a raft of legislative measures had launched the long road to nationwide institutionalized policing that was taken over the course of the century. That this process was a protracted one is reflected in the complex patchwork of co-existent policing models in place in Kent at the time of the enactment of the first CD legislation in 1864. Of the districts that would eventually be affected by the CD Acts, Gravesend, Dover, Deal, Canterbury and Maidstone were incorporated boroughs with their own police forces. Maidstone, the county town, housed the headquarters of the County Constabulary after its establishment in 1857, in addition to having its own borough force. Greenwich and Woolwich, being part of Kentish London, were policed by the R division of the Metropolitan Police. The civilian populations of Chatham and Sheerness were policed by divisions of the Kent County Constabulary, whilst their military dockyards were policed, from 1860 onwards, by the newly established Metropolitan Police Dockyard Division (MPDD). On the hand-over of dockyard policing to the MPDD in Chatham, the *Chatham News* reported that 'much regret' had been expressed locally at the change, the 'mild firmness of the old local police having given general satisfaction'.[5] The situation in Chatham was further complicated in that the geographical area made subject to the CD Acts included the adjacent city of Rochester, which had its own police force. Shorncliffe Military Camp was policed by a special division of the County Constabulary with extra officers supplied from the Metropolitan Police at central government expense, whilst the surrounding neighbourhood was policed by the Folkestone Borough Police.

Borough police forces had been introduced under the Municipal Corporations Act of 1835. They were answerable to the Watch Committees of Town Councils and responsible for a strictly defined territory within borough boundaries. Whilst the head constables of these forces could make recommendations regarding operational and personnel matters, all decisions, even the most routine, were taken by the committee, which comprised locally elected town councillors and was often chaired by the mayor.[6] Thus, in the boroughs, the same relatively small group of people was responsible both for directing the police force and for administering justice.

The response of borough councils to the requirement to set up an efficient police force was patchy, but within two years thirteen had been established in Kent, seven of which were in areas that would eventually be affected by the CD Acts. These forces initially experienced problems of indiscipline and high turnover in manpower that persisted into the 1860s and beyond. Watch committee minutes expose frequent breaches of discipline, for example being found on licensed premises, being missing from the beat or being found asleep or drunk on duty. William Downing, a constable in Folkestone, was dismissed in September 1842 after being 'continually drunk on duty'. His replacement Richard Morford only lasted three months before resigning.[7] Two Dover constables were dismissed for insubordination in 1864, and four were found drunk in December 1868.[8] In Gravesend, one constable committed sixteen disciplinary offences and was fined a total of fifty-six shillings during three years' service whilst another was demoted after 'questionable conduct' with a prostitute at the Maidstone Assizes.[9] These patterns were repeated across the county.

However, over time the forces became more organized and expectations were raised. The surviving rulebooks for Gravesend and Maidstone, for instance, document the expectation that the streets should be kept free and passable and nuisance tightly controlled. Beggars and drunks were to be removed, and constables given the power to apprehend 'every common prostitute wandering in the public streets ... and behaving in a riotous or indecent manner'.[10] Newspaper reportage of petty sessions hearings notes that head constables attended in person to provide the bench with supplementary information (for example regarding previous convictions) where necessary. Gravesend and Maidstone were two of only three borough forces in Kent to pass the mandatory central government inspection (introduced in 1856 and providing for a central government grant) at the first attempt. The successful 1860 inspection at Maidstone was noted in somewhat of a self-congratulatory tone in the local press; Captain Willis (central government Inspector of Police) had met with the Watch Committee at the Town Hall where the police force was assembled, and the 'cleanliness and general order' of the station house had, apparently, attracted particular remark.[11]

In Dover, by contrast, the road to efficient policing had followed a less smooth trajectory. By 1858 the Home Office police inspector was still unable to grant the certificate testifying to the borough force's efficiency. Recommendations of an increase in manpower, made in 1857 and again in 1858, were rejected by the Watch Committee, which repudiated what its members considered to be an 'interference' by central government as an attempted 'infringement of rights and privileges', thus reflecting the battle for local accountability which characterized the wider development of policing.[12] In early 1860, however, the committee finally made the decision to appoint an additional sergeant and eight constables, thus bringing the Dover force closer to optimal manpower levels.[13]

Local accountability is also reflected in the willingness of rate-payers and opinion formers to criticize policing methods, either by way of a direct complaint to the Watch Committee or, more frequently, of public complaints made through the vehicle of the local newspaper. A Folkestone resident observed that the police were not to be found in the High Street after eight in the evening, 'or if they are, they are very negligent in not stopping the disgraceful scenes that nightly take place in the principal thoroughfare of the town. Soldiers and prostitutes assemble around the doors of two notorious beerhouses'.[14] When three Gravesend churches were broken into within a fortnight in 1869, the *Gravesend and Dartford Reporter* ran an editorial criticizing the Watch Committee for 'ridiculous red-tapism', and explicitly commenting on operational procedure.[15] On other occasions complaints were made directly by the public to the police, such as the reports about prostitutes soliciting in Somerset Street, Gravesend, as a result of which a sergeant was placed there in plain clothes and subsequent arrests made.[16] The power of local opinion is reflected in the request made by the Dover borough force to the Watch Committee in 1864 requesting that committee proceedings should not be reported in the local press. The Committee, the *Dover Express* noted, 'declined to entertain' the request.[17]

By the early 1870s, however, most Kentish borough forces had overcome initial problems of manpower retention and resourcing and were moving towards stability and professionalism. Most had achieved or exceeded the benchmark manpower level of one officer per 1,000 head of population considered necessary for efficiency by this date.[18] The Gravesend force stood at a total strength of twenty-six officers for a population of 24,000, Canterbury at twenty-one officers (20,000), twenty-eight in Dover (28,000), fourteen in Folkestone (13,000) and thirty in Maidstone (26,000).

Outside of the boroughs, in contrast, rural Kent had continued to be policed by an improved version of the old system of largely unpaid and part-time parish constables. Finally, in 1856 the County and Borough Police Act legislated for a mandatory county constabulary but left the borough police forces in place. The Kent County Constabulary was established in 1857, comprising twelve divisions directly responsible to Captain John Ruxton, the chief constable, who answered to the Kentish justices in quarter sessions.[19] Ruxton's role as chief constable of the county force allowed for more operational discretion than his borough counterparts, and he had more say in all manpower issues. Thus there was no equivalent immediate, local accountability in areas policed by the county force as there was in the boroughs.

Not surprisingly, this pluralized policing arrangement led to operational conflicts. An 1870 case of sheep stealing resulted in the superintendent of the Boxley division of the county force calling the Maidstone Borough superintendent a 'donkey', and in Maidstone being described as a 'harbour for county thieves'.[20] Borderlines also threw up difficulties in places. Maidstone experienced a particular problem in that boundary arrangements left a narrow un-policed no-man's land between the jurisdictions of the borough and the county forces, to the dissatisfaction of the rate-payers who lived within it. The arrangement also created specific problems for the policing of rapidly expanding urban areas, such as Chatham, which were not incorporated boroughs. The control of street disorder proved problematic here because the county force operated according to a model designed for rural areas.[21] In towns, population density relative to policing manpower dictated preventative policing strategies, whereby officers' physical presence on the street constituted an effective deterrent against potential crime and street disorder. In rural areas where population was spread over a much wider geographical area, this approach was clearly not efficient and rural constabularies therefore put more emphasis on detection. Additionally, the county constabulary provided Chatham with less than half of the policing manpower than that deployed in the neighbouring boroughs. Police Superintendent Everist of the Kent County Constabulary told magistrates that the police manpower (one officer per 2,175 head of population) could not 'contend with the 27,000 inhabitants out of which number about 2,000 were in the streets at a late hour on Saturday nights'.[22]

This situation met with a good deal of dissatisfaction, and the *Chatham News* was amongst those voices calling for improved policing provision. In 1861 a member of the military wrote to the editor complaining that it was not possible for an officer in uniform to walk down 'one of the principal roads in Chatham garrison, at twelve o'clock in the middle of the day, without being yelled at and bawled after by three or four drunken prostitutes'.[23] Yet despite these strong feelings, local rate-payers were unwilling to pay to provide for a more effective police presence. In the early 1860s Chatham residents paid about two pence in the pound for policing, compared with seven pence in Gravesend.[24] Between 1859 and 1885 the town's policing needs and the apparent lawlessness on the streets were the subjects of numerous discussions between Captain Ruxton and Chatham officials. After more than twenty years, following numerous riots and the public humiliation of Chatham's reputation for lawlessness being mentioned in the columns of *The Times* ('In the town of Chatham ... the streets offer temptation unsurpassed in all the squalid loathsomeness of vice'), Ruxton finally capitulated and provided the extra manpower required from county resources at no additional cost to Chatham's rate-payers.[25]

Policing policy and manpower provision was therefore a significant factor in any town's ability to maintain order on the streets. The process that created policed societies was a lengthy one, and some forces were better placed than others effectively to enforce public order at an earlier date. Thus there was a variation from place to place in the efficiency with which street prostitution was policed. Local policing was not the only factor in the successful regulation of street disorder, however, but was one means by which the strategy decisions of local magistrates, as was seen in the case of Henry Ditchburn, with whom this chapter opened, were translated into practice on the street. Variations in local judicial policy and organization constituted a significant additional dimension to the policing of prostitution in Kent.

The Judiciary

County and borough justices of the peace (JPs) had traditionally been unpaid and untrained members of the local establishment, predominantly drawn from the landed gentry. The Municipal Corporations Act of 1835, however, gave elected municipal councils an influence over the appointment of borough magistrates. Thus the borough benches, whilst they continued to be composed of the most prominent citizens, became increasingly more representative of the middle and mercantile classes.[26] In addition, the wide variety of borough magistrates' additional roles and responsibilities, such as the appointment of parish officers, the ex-officio membership of the poor law guardians, the settlement of local disputes and membership of other committees, immersed them in the everyday life of their local community. The example of William Mowll, a Dover coal merchant who was both a member of the Town Council and sat on the bench of magistrates throughout the 1870s, is illustrative. Records of Mowll's public duties undertaken during the week commencing 13 June 1870 provide a snapshot of his involvement in and exposure to life in the local community. A special meeting of the Town Council on Thursday 16 June addressed itself to breaches of the Public House Closing Acts of 1864 and 1866, which stipulated that public houses should be closed between one and four o'clock in the morning. This detailed discussion made reference to several named local establishments. On the same day Mowll attended a meeting of the Local Board which discussed numerous matters under the remit of the Inspector of Nuisances, such as street watering, drains, paving and asphalting, together with reports of shop awnings that were below the stipulated height. The same week, in petty sessions, amongst the defendants passing before Mowll were those charged with drunkenness, stone-throwing, and desertion by a member of the militia.[27] This immersion into the affairs of the local community had a bearing on JPs' work on the bench. When, for example, a man called Henry Lintott was brought before the Gravesend bench in 1858 on a charge of keeping a ferocious dog, magistrate Robert Oakes took the opportunity to provide his colleagues on the bench with the seemingly unrelated information that the defendant had run his house as a brothel for a good many years.[28]

This local dimension became more significant during the period under study as summary justice was extended following the introduction of the 'new' police. A series of measures enacted in 1848 gave greater organization and formality to the summary courts (cases heard by JPs in petty sessions with no jury) and brought more cases within their remit.[29] By 1857, the justices in petty sessions were estimated to be handling twenty times the number of cases dealt with by all the other criminal courts combined.[30] Between 1857 and 1899 the annual number of prosecutions for non-indictable offences (that is, less serious offences such as soliciting that were dealt with in the summary courts) more than doubled from 329,019 to 761,322 nationally, in line with the growth in police numbers.[31]

A further significant development was the extension of the stipendiary magistrate system across the country during the nineteenth century. Introduced initially in London in 1792, stipendiary magistrates, unlike their amateur borough and county counterparts, were professional qualified barristers of at least seven years' standing. The Chatham and Sheerness Stipendiary Magistrates Act in 1867 provided for a paid professional magistrate to sit twice weekly at a police court in each of these districts. The new Sheerness magistrate, appointed at a salary of £700 per annum, sat for the first time on Tuesday, 27 August 1867, and the local newspaper commented, 'We hope our Local Authorities will heartily cooperate with the Police powers to make a speedy end of a host of local nuisances and street offences, which have hitherto been let alone as not worth the trouble of seeking the aid of the law in'.[32] Previously, offenders on the Isle of Sheppey had been taken to petty sessions hearings on the mainland at Sittingbourne, where it was felt that magistrates were unaware of the specific problems of street disorder facing Sheerness. In reporting a local drunk and disorderly case, for example, the *Sheerness Guardian* had commented, 'The worthy magistrate, who is evidently in entire ignorance of the increasing prevalence of this sort of nuisance in Sheerness, mildly admonished the prisoner and let him off with paying the costs'.[33]

The new legislation made it easier and cheaper for Sheerness residents to prosecute petty offences and removed the necessity for witnesses to travel to petty sessions on the mainland. Additionally it would appear that Sittingbourne borough magistrates had previously insisted that prosecutions be made by a member of the public. At the 1865 hearing of the case against prostitute Susan Maddocks for being drunk and causing a disturbance, for example, the magistrate told the prosecuting constable that it would be better if complainants attended to corroborate the evidence of the constable. They could not be compelled to attend, but 'if the inhabitants wish to keep the town quiet, they ought to attend and prosecute'.[34] Given that this had involved a journey to the mainland to attend petty sessions, it is little surprise that few were prepared to do so, particularly tradesmen, who might, according to the *Sheerness Guardian*, lose time and risk expense by attending to prosecute. As the nineteenth century wore on, police officers assumed a wider role in the prosecution of minor offences, leading to an increased number of arrests.[35]

The appointment of the Stipendiary Magistrate in Chatham facilitated a markedly more stringent approach to the suppression of public nuisance. Prior to the new legislation, cases of Chatham street disorder had been heard by magistrates in neighbouring Rochester, in a 'mean room, about as big as two Hackney carriages'.[36] Within weeks of the new arrangement, a Chatham woman named Mary Ann Wallis was convicted and sentenced to one month's imprisonment with hard labour for using 'foul and disgusting language', and the following year a Chatham prostitute named Jane Dunbar, described as 'incorrigible', was sentenced to two months with hard labour for being drunk and acting indecently.[37]

An additional dimension of JPs' roles in the effective policing of prostitution is the considerable variation in conviction and sentencing practice from place to place, highlighting once more the campaign waged in Gravesend in the late 1850s with which this chapter opened. The case of Sarah London demonstrated the policy of Gravesend magistrates in not tolerating streetwalking at all, which resulted in prosecution rates of women identified as prostitutes that were consistently the highest in the county over a twenty-year period. In Dover, by contrast, magistrates often demonstrated a more lenient attitude than their Gravesend counterparts, as demonstrated by their discharge of Elizabeth King, a young girl identified as a prostitute ('whose girlish appearance', the court reporter observed, 'appeared to excite the compassion of the bench'), on a drunkenness and disorderly conduct charge on her promise not to offend again.[38] Dover magistrates' instructions to the police appear to have emphasized the maintenance of order rather than the outright suppression of soliciting. Evidently, therefore, there was a wide margin for discretion and a variation in sentencing policy between magistrates from one town to another with regard to the punishment of women convicted as prostitutes. This judicial disparity reinforced the variation in policing manpower and policy.

Local Governance

The difficulties experienced in maintaining public order in Chatham that have already been outlined were further exacerbated because the town was not an incorporated borough. Instead the town was governed by a traditional system of medieval manorial government with a high constable and court leet. With no town council able to pass by-laws, there was no mechanism in place for a swift and efficient response to the problem of street nuisance. Following calls for stricter policing, Chatham authorities discovered in 1859 that the local Board of Health was the appropriate body to act in the suppression of street nuisance.[39] A Chatham committee was appointed in 1859 to draw up local regulations based on a selection of measures from the 1847 Town Police Clauses Act, which is discussed in greater detail below. Amongst these were restrictions on dangerous dogs, the 'wanton' ringing of doorbells, and obstruction of the footpath with goods for sale. Offenders were 'liable to a fine of forty shillings, or fourteen days imprisonment, and any constable may, without warrant, take them into custody and convey them before a justice of the peace'.[40] Although one clause specifically stipulated that prostitutes must not annoy pedestrians, as has been seen, police manpower was not sufficient in Chatham to enforce the regulations consistently, and so street disorder continued to be perceived as a problem by residents. In 1866 two church wardens attended magistrates' sessions to ask the bench to direct the attention of the police to the great nuisance caused every Saturday night by a crowd assembling on the streets at closing time. The 'swearing, fighting and shouting was most intolerable and being at a late hour, about twelve o'clock at night it was a source of great annoyance to the inhabitants'.[41] The press report of this incident – which quotes the magistrates' clerk as saying 'There is no by-law in Chatham to punish persons for using obscene language' and the police superintendent as saying that unless they (the police) found persons in a drunken state or creating a disturbance, they could not interfere with them – clearly underlines the wide variation in practice from place to place. In the adjacent incorporated City of Rochester, by contrast, there was a by-law specifically relating to 'indecent words or conduct' in the public streets, enabling police to prosecute such offenders.[42] In the same year as the Chatham church wardens' appeal to the magistrates, a woman named Mary Ann Frazer was convicted in Rochester of 'having made use of filthy and obscene language to the annoyance of the inhabitants contrary to the by-laws of the city' and fined twenty shillings plus six shillings costs, or in default one month in gaol.[43]

Incorporated boroughs were in a much better position to respond quickly and effectively to complaints about public nuisance. When, for example, the Dover Watch Committee received a letter of complaint from a member of the public regarding the obstruction caused by crowds gathering to hear a public preacher, they responded instantly by drawing up a set of guidelines to be issued to police with immediate effect.[44] In addition to variations in magistrates' sentencing policies, therefore, differences in local governance influenced the rigour with which standards of public order were maintained. This was done with reference to a legislative framework that was amended over the course of the nineteenth century to enable raised expectations and standards of public behaviour to be realized. It is to the consideration of this legislative structure that this discussion now turns.

Legislation

Street nuisance was regulated with reference to a range of national and local statutory mechanisms, often enacted to coincide with the establishment of a professional police force in an area. The 1824 Vagrancy Act, an 'Act for the Punishment of Idle and Disorderly Persons, and Rogues and Vagabonds', had been enacted against a background of growing middle-class fears of the riotous masses. It targeted a wide range of offending behaviour and provided for custodial sentences of up to three months with hard labour for a range of petty public order offences, including begging, sleeping out of doors and peddling without a licence.[45] Vagrancy was still felt to be a particular problem in Kent as late as the 1860s, and severe penalties were frequently strictly applied to offenders unfortunate enough to be in the wrong place at the wrong time.[46] Petty sessions minute books and the newspaper coverage of the court hearings reflect the fate of those who found themselves on the margins of local communities. Examples include William Lindsay, who was convicted of begging, and John Callaghan, who was committed to the house of correction for obstructing the footway in Dover.[47] Anne Smith and Mary Ann White were convicted as vagrants and sentenced to seven days' imprisonment with hard labour each, whilst Henry Kitchen of Sheerness, who 'did wander abroad to beg and gather alms', was sentenced to twenty-one days with hard labour.[48] In Chatham Elizabeth Thompson and William Edmunds were convicted of sleeping in the open air and having 'no visible means of existence' and were accordingly sentenced to fourteen days with hard labour, whilst Frances Maria Bailey was sentenced to one month with hard labour for 'sleeping in a closet and not having any visible means of support' in Dover.[49] Old age or infirmity do not appear to have constituted mitigating factors, since William Turner, 'an elderly man', and eighty-three-year-old Margaret Walton, both of Gravesend, were sentenced to ten and fourteen days with hard labour respectively for begging.[50] Jane Seamark, a young girl, was sentenced to fourteen days with hard labour for 'lodging in the open air and having no visible means of support'.[51]

The Vagrancy Act was the first piece of legislation to coin the phrase 'common prostitute', which was applied to women found wandering in public and behaving noisily, indecently or boisterously.[52] It employed the word 'riotous' in its literal connotation of civil unrest, but as this chapter will show, this word came to be interpreted increasingly liberally by police and magistrates over succeeding decades, and its inclusion in the 1824 statute enabled magistrates to convict for a range of noisy or raucous behaviour. Despite minor amendments, almost sixty years after the enactment of this piece of legislation, its use in the policing of prostitution was still widespread. Of the seventy-five admissions of women whose occupation was recorded as 'prostitute' into Maidstone Gaol during 1883, thirty-two were convicted on charges related to the Vagrancy Act.[53]

In addition to providing for the establishment of borough police forces, the Municipal Corporations Act (1835) had contained a clause enabling officers 'to apprehend all idle and disorderly Persons whom he shall find disturbing the public Peace' and to take them before a Magistrate.[54] As the threshold of tolerance towards perceived disturbance of the public peace was lowered, interpretations of 'idle' and 'disorderly' brought the street life of the poor and marginal increasingly within the jurisdiction of the new police.

Additionally, as has been seen, the 1847 Town Police Clauses Act consolidated guidance to police with regard to the regulation of towns and 'populous districts'. Provision was made for the suppression of all activity that impeded free and easy movement through the public thoroughfare or which annoyed or caused offence to fellow residents, as well as the regulation of public safety. Offending behaviour, catalogued in a list of 'obstructions and nuisances', included exposing goods for sale on the pavement, wantonly ringing door bells, singing obscene songs, indecent exposure, flying kites and beating rugs or carpets after eight o'clock in the morning.[55] Dover police broke up a running match because the road and pathway were blocked by spectators, the magistrates commenting that 'it had better be understood that running matches would not be allowed on the highway'.[56]

In addition, local by-laws, described by historian David Taylor as part of a 'complex puzzle facing the constable on the beat', were also brought into play against offending public behaviour.[57] Gravesend by-laws for example were enacted in 1836, the year of the establishment of the borough police force, to prohibit obstruction and 'annoying any person' as well as swearing and gambling on the street.[58] A handbill dated 1849 cautions 'idle and disorderly persons' against 'making a noise and disturbance in the vicinity of the pier' and against 'using obscene language and swearing'.[59] In Maidstone, printed 1836 instructions issued to police prohibited the flying of kites and the trundling of hoops on any public street.[60] It is clear from Maidstone petty sessions records that there, obscene language and drunkenness offenders were prosecuted under local by-laws, whilst the Vagrancy Act was used in the case of beggars or 'disorderly' prostitutes.

Policing the Streets

Discussions of the control of prostitution that define the subject exclusively in terms of the repression of dangerous sexuality and gendered power relations risk overlooking the impact of the mid-century zeal to clean up the streets of other marginal and socially disadvantaged groups. These included the homeless and vagrant, unsupported mothers and the elderly poor. As was seen in Chapter 1, the distinctions between these groups were often fluid ones, and the category 'prostitute' was a constructed one. Those at the margins fell prey to the raised expectations of public order and decorum that accompanied the introduction of the 'new' police in any area, and arrest and conviction rates for petty street disorder offences escalated accordingly.[61] Public behaviours that had previously been contained and tolerated were redefined as unacceptable, and the working classes in particular were subjected to what has been called an 'unprecedented degree of scrutiny and control'.[62] Scholars of policing are generally agreed that from the late eighteenth century onwards social disorder and crime, a certain level of which had previously been accepted as inevitable or, in historian Clive Emsley's words, as 'social phenomena', began increasingly to be seen as a serious threat to the social order and a growing problem in need of a solution, an effect that was exacerbated by the process of rapid urbanization. The street life of the casual poor was controlled ever more strictly in line with rising expectations of public order and decency. Previously tolerated public misdemeanours were redefined as unacceptable in urbanized environments. This approach to the policing of street prostitution therefore locates it within a wider discussion of the imposition of new standards of order on the streets, and the assertion of control over the day-to-day activities of the poor and working classes in the name of public morality and respectability.

Women identified as street prostitutes, beggars, gamblers and those wandering with no visible means of sustenance or unable to give a good account of themselves were liable to arrest and prosecution. The regulation of public order occupied the majority of police time and the number of petty offences prosecuted far outweighed the number of serious crimes.[63] This trend has been attributed to the combined effects of the influence of moral reform movements, increased manpower, the fact that offending activities such as soliciting conducted in the street were easily observable by the patrolling constable, and because the control of petty offences was a relatively simple and productive task when compared with the detection of crime.[64]

Punishments for the transgression of new codes of acceptable public behaviour started with fines, such as the one shilling plus ten shillings costs imposed on George Brett, a Canterbury lad, for sliding on the pavement, the eleven shillings on three Sheerness youths convicted of throwing snowballs, and the fifteen shillings on George Marsh of Maidstone for playing Pitch and Toss on Easter Sunday.[65] Thomas Smith, convicted of sitting on a windowsill at the Nelson Inn in Gravesend, was fined one shilling plus costs, whilst in Chatham 'wandering minstrels' Robert and Elizabeth Highmore were fined seven shillings for creating a disturbance.[66]

The use of 'foul' or 'obscene' language was considered to be an offence against public decency and punished harshly in most locations; for example, Mary Ann Lewis of Maidstone, landlady of the Jolly Sailor public house, was fined one pound and ten shillings, plus another eleven shillings to be paid to Mary Burrage, for calling the latter a "bloody whore" to the annoyance of residents', and two Canterbury lads were fined 'for singing obscene songs in Watling Street'.[67] In addition to the use of bad language, 'disorderly behaviour' also appears to have been defined in terms of making unnecessary and indecorous noise in public places, or within earshot of public places. Clearly any argument carried out in public could, in this sense, be defined as disrupting the public peace. Elizabeth Allum of Gravesend, for example, was convicted of noisy and disorderly conduct and fined five shillings for quarrelling with her husband, albeit that she was standing at her own front door at the time.[68]

All fines carried a default custodial sentence for those unable to pay. Mary Ann Probin and Emma Smith for example, arrested as 'common prostitutes' for being riotous and quarrelling with each other in the Anchor and Crown, were sent to Maidstone Gaol for fourteen and twenty-eight days with hard labour respectively, being unable to pay fines of ten and twenty shillings.[69] Penalties escalated to mandatory custodial sentences for more serious offences and for recidivists. Martha Burgess was sentenced to seven days' imprisonment for disorderly conduct, her offence having been 'standing on the pavement and refusing to move'.[70] William Marsh, who was arrested for 'loitering on the streets and not being able to give a satisfactory account of himself' in Sheerness, was sentenced to twenty-one days, the same sentence awarded to Mary O'Donald of Chatham, identified as a prostitute and convicted of 'sleeping in an outhouse and wandering about without any visible means of existence'.[71]

Public drunkenness was a persistent problem, and authorities in all locations appear to have been prepared to deal with it severely. An elderly Canterbury woman for example was imprisoned for fourteen days with hard labour for being drunk and using obscene language, whilst eighty-year-old Sarah Knight served a seven-day custodial sentence for drunkenness in Dover.[72] Maidstone justices saw more than their fair share of cases of drunkenness, because prisoners from the county gaol were given a sum of money on discharge to enable them to return to their place of settlement. Often this money was spent at one of the local public houses. At the hearing of a drunk and disorderly charge against Catherine Smith, who by 1874 had at least twenty-four previous similar convictions, Police Inspector Gifford explained to the bench that Catherine 'never turned up' in Maidstone except when sent from elsewhere to the prison, and the police generally came into contact with her after her discharge.[73]

The desire for public order was not a simplistic matter of the imposition of one class's value system on another. When Gravesend solicitor Charles Voules was found drunk and annoying persons in the public street after dining with friends, he was fined twenty shillings plus costs in line with his income. At the hearing of another case of public middle-class drunkenness, magistrate Henry Ditchburn, with whom this chapter opened, took the opportunity to inform the court that 'it would be most unjust to the poor people, who were being continually fined for drunkenness and disturbing the public peace, if they allowed gentleman-like defendants, whose position in society ought to teach them better, to offend with impunity'.[74]

Thus by the period of this study there was a general raised expectation of order, respectability and decorum on the streets and in other public places. Street prostitution was not unique in being targeted in the drive to keep public thoroughfares free, passable and decorous. In many locations the elderly poor, the destitute, the homeless and vagrants were equally vulnerable to persistent harassment at the hands of local police and likely to be punished with custodial sentences, old age and infirmity notwithstanding. The policing of street prostitution can therefore be located within a wider narrative of the regulation and control of the casual poor and the imposition of raised standards of respectable public behaviour. This focus of discussion now turns specifically to the routine, everyday policing of prostitution in the ports and garrison towns of Kent, in the years prior to and during the enforcement of the CD Acts.

Policing Prostitution

Prostitution per se was not prohibited by the law, though it was an offence to run a 'house of ill-fame' or for a woman to solicit on the street.[75] Government judicial statistics record that women classified by the police as prostitutes were prosecuted for a wide variety of offences consistently over the period with which this discussion is concerned.[76] In 1857, the first year for which national statistics were compiled following the introduction of mandatory nationwide policing, and seven years before the first Contagious Diseases Act was introduced to the statute book, 21,798 women so categorized were prosecuted nationally. This figure represents 28 per cent of the total number of women proceeded against summarily and by indictment. By 1883, the year that the Contagious Diseases Acts were suspended, this figure had risen slightly to 24,704, which represented 18 per cent of the total number of women proceeded against.

In the Kentish ports, garrisons and dockyards the general trend of this national picture was reflected. However, the local focus of this study throws up a good deal of variation that is lost from the national perspective. In some towns, women faced regular arrest by local police as prostitutes for a wide range of street disorder offences, and the number of summonses by local police, using a range of legislative instruments, was consistently significantly higher than those brought under the CD Acts. Streetwalking and soliciting were controlled in Kent with reference to a combination of the national and local statutory instruments discussed earlier, formulated to impose standards of behaviour in the streets and public highways. Streetwalkers were liable to be so arrested, and they often appear to have been liable to harsher penalties than other offenders convicted of committing the same offence.

Additionally, licensing laws were used to control prostitution since it was an offence for a licensee to allow prostitutes on the premises for longer than was necessary to take refreshment, a clause designed to prevent licensed premises being used for prostitutes' liaisons. John and Fanny Ware, proprietors of the Devonshire Arms public house in Chatham, were amongst the landlords in that town who were able to circumvent the law against using licensed premises as brothels. Many adopted the enterprising practice of constructing what were euphemistically called 'cottages', but often appear to have been no more than huts, at the far ends of their gardens on land that technically lay outside the boundary of their property, and could therefore be argued to be separate from the main premises and thus not subject to the law.[77]

Prosecutions of women named as prostitutes, under local policing and using the range of legislative measures outlines above, were consistently higher in all Kentish locations (outside of Kentish London) than under the CD Acts.[78] Moreover in some of the Kentish subjected districts local policing and suppression mechanisms appear to have represented a far more common and far more punitive hazard in the lives of women who lived on prostitution than the apparently haphazard and exceptional CD Acts policing measures. Many women faced regular and repeated arrest and custodial sentencing in addition to the material privations that were outlined in Chapter 1. When balanced against these factors, the relative impact of the CD Acts appears less uniquely and distinctively repressive than has sometimes been perceived.

The public acts of soliciting and streetwalking appear to have caused more offence in the Kentish port and garrison towns than prostitution in itself, thus suggesting that visibility was a central concern.[79] Protest was articulated by local residents, for example the complaint by a Sheerness resident of prostitutes walking the streets and offending public decency.[80] Evidently local officialdom also perceived streetwalking and soliciting to be matters of public nuisance and disorder as much as ones purely of morality, and dealt with them as such. Maidstone Police Superintendent Barnes, for example, described Ann Chatfield as a 'complete pest' to the bench at the hearing of the case against her of being drunk and disorderly, and Clara Greenstreet of Dover was described by PC Campany as 'one of the biggest nuisances walking the streets' before she was sentenced to fourteen days' imprisonment.[81]

Practice varied from location to location with regard to the statutory instruments used to control street prostitution. In many Kentish locations the Vagrancy Act appears to have been the preferred option, its advantage being that it enabled the police to arrest on suspicion and thus placed the onus with the arrested party to prove their good intent.[82] The wording of the statute, 'unlicensed pedlars, prostitutes, and beggars shall be deemed idle and disorderly persons, and may be imprisoned for one month with hard labour', was frequently incorporated into the charge, as recorded in court minutes. In Maidstone in the early 1870s, for example, it appears to have been the preferred practice to charge prostitutes under the Vagrancy Act for being riotous, the conviction being as an 'idle and disorderly person'.[83]

The Town Police Clauses Act of 1847 provided for 'Every common Prostitute or Nightwalker loitering and importuning passengers for the Purpose of Prostitution' to be taken into custody by a police officer without warrant and to be 'conveyed before a Justice'.[84] The penalty on conviction was a fine not exceeding forty shillings or, at the discretion of the JP, a custodial sentence not exceeding fourteen days. This statute also provided for a fine of up to forty shillings or a custodial sentence of up to seven days for 'Every person drunk in the street, and guilty of any riotous or indecent behaviour therein'.[85] Elsewhere local by-laws were used to charge prostitutes with soliciting.[86]

No matter which piece of legislation was used, the effect on women who worked the streets was punitive. Police manpower permitting, evidence suggests that many local authorities attempted to clamp down on street prostitution and that local police in many locations stuck to their instructions to control it strictly. Gravesend police, for example, were given discretionary powers of arrest over any prostitute loitering 'to the annoyance of the inhabitants' and any 'loose, idle or disorderly person whom he had reason to suspect might be about to commit misdemeanour'.[87] For a combination of reasons Gravesend consistently prosecuted more alleged prostitutes than other location in Kent, a total of 710 prosecutions under summary justice over an eighteen-year period.[88]

Kentish evidence suggests that police officers were allowed a degree of operational discretion in the interpretation of 'riotous' and 'indecent' behaviour on the part of women alleged to be prostitutes, and that magistrates were easily persuaded of the intent of women brought before them accused of such offences. A member of the Dover bench stated in 1862 that 'police had described them as streetwalkers, and that was sufficient'.[89] In Gravesend PC Kissock was able to persuade magistrates that Annie Burch had been in the market place 'for the purposes of prostitution', and PC Lock that Frances Bond had been 'importuning persons for the purpose of prostitution'.[90] On other occasions, there was apparently less room for doubt; Mary Jane Brown was convicted for 'endeavouring to persuade a man to accompany her' and Ellen Mudge for 'unlawfully decoying a seaman' in Sheerness.[91] The case of streetwalker Rose Brown, who was arrested with a man called William Robinson, illustrates the liberal interpretation of the term 'riotous'. Both were convicted of drunken and riotous conduct, but as the incident was described in the press it transpires that their 'riotous' behaviour had consisted of dancing and singing in the street, 'hallooing' and calling after each other.[92] In this context, therefore, the word 'riotous' was used to describe a range of noisy and boisterous behaviour.

In the first instance most women found soliciting or loitering appear to have been requested by the police officer to move on, the primary objective being to prevent obstruction and annoyance to passers-by. It is clearly not possible to estimate the percentage of cases that were dealt with in this informal way and which were taken no further. Press reports of the Gravesend charges brought against Kate Trew, Sarah Rouse, Sarah London and Emily Butler, for example, together with that of Sarah London with whom this chapter opened, state that in the first instance the arresting policemen asked them to go away or to go home, and the arrest ensued after they refused or were abusive in response.[93] As was seen in the previous chapter, police officers were sometimes forced into a cat and mouse game with women who disappeared only to return when their back was turned.

By definition, streetwalkers, whose livelihood depended on their being able to elicit business in public places, were unable to permanently vacate the streets. This group, as the evidence suggests and as has been discussed previously, made up the majority of the women who lived by prostitution in the ports and garrison towns of Kent.

Soliciting

This charge appears to have been applied to a wide range of offending activity, from the overt solicitation of passing men to loitering, obstructing the footpath and refusing to move. Magistrates in some Kentish locations appear to have been prepared to deal strictly with women arrested for this category of offence, particularly if it was supported by a complaint from a member of the public. Kate Douglas of Gravesend, for instance, described as 'a notorious prostitute', was found in the street between one and two in the morning by PC George Goodwin, who cautioned her and gave her the option of going home. She declined, was arrested and convicted, and ordered to be imprisoned for twenty-one days.[94] When Ellen Gladstone and Dinah Butcher were arrested in Chatham, PC Hibbard told the bench that their conduct had been of the 'most indecent kind'. This, it transpired, consisted of 'calling to gentlemen as they passed down the street'. One of the gentlemen 'insulted' by the women in this way was a clergyman. Gladstone was sentenced to fourteen days' imprisonment and Butcher to ten days.[95]

The press reportage of over 500 prosecutions brought against prostitutes in Gravesend in the twenty-four years between 1856 and 1879 shed some considerable light on the way in which convictions were brought for this category of offence. A comparison with the total number of cases for part of this period as recorded in parliamentary Returns of Judicial Statistics suggests that these 500 reported cases represent some two-thirds of the total. The first category consists of offences that relate directly to prostitution. These were variously described as 'soliciting', 'loitering for the purposes of prostitution', 'importuning passers-by' and 'obstructing the footpath'. Of the total number of reported cases, 25 per cent come into this category. In forty-three cases the option of a fine was offered, though the records do not always note whether this option was taken. However, it is clear that whereas in some cases the fine was set at a level where it might serve as a deterrent (for example, one shilling plus costs imposed on four women in 1874), on other occasions it was set at a level which might reasonably be supposed that the woman would be unable to pay, and that the default custodial sentence was imposed in default. Catherine Rawlinson and Elizabeth Tovey, for example, served twenty-one days and fourteen days in default of fines of ten shillings plus four shillings and six pence costs and ten shillings respectively.[96]

Since it is not always possible to determine from the records whether a fine was paid or whether a custodial sentence was served instead, for the purposes of the following analysis fines have been divided into those above and those below ten shillings, an arbitrary figure, but one above which it seems reasonable to assume that in most cases the default custodial sentence was likely to have been served. Thus the total figures given here for custodial sentences are, if anything, likely to be severely understated. The most common sentence imposed for soliciting in Gravesend was fourteen days with hard labour (31 per cent of cases). In 9 per cent of cases a sentence of seven days was served, and in an additional 15 per cent of cases a custodial sentence of longer than fourteen days was imposed. Thus 56 per cent of the Gravesend women who were convicted of soliciting, loitering or obstructing the passage served a mandatory custodial sentence. Examples include Selina Calver, a 'young girl' discussed in Chapter 1, who was charged with 'being about the streets for the purposes of prostitution' having been found sleeping in Market Place by Constable Robert Flinn. He told the bench that he had frequently seen her there in the company of men. She was sentenced to fourteen days' imprisonment.[97] Emma Preston, Ellen Baker and Ann Newman were each summoned for 'obstructing the footpath, being prostitutes' in January 1865 and sentenced to between fourteen and twenty-one days with hard labour.[98] Elizabeth Miller and Sarah Day were charged with loitering at the rear of Harmer Street for the purposes of prostitution and were sentenced to two months with hard labour each. During one single week in 1870 five women were prosecuted on the charge that being prostitutes they either obstructed the footpath or were found loitering for the purposes of prostitution. Sentences ranged between fourteen days and one month. Similarly, in the first week of June 1874 seven Gravesend women were brought before the magistrates on charges of 'obstructing the footpath and causing an inconvenience'. Sentences ranged between seven and fourteen days.[99] Sophia Stibbs was charged in 1874 with 'being a disorderly prostitute' without any specific offence being mentioned. She was found guilty and sentenced to twenty-one days with hard labour.[100] In an unusual 1863 case, Ann Harper was charged under statute 'Edward lll 34' with 'being a person of ill and evil fame and a common prostitute', having been heard using abusive and obscene language from inside a known brothel. Ann was sentenced to two months' imprisonment in default of sureties of forty pounds from herself and two of twenty pounds, which it might reasonably be supposed she was unable to find.[101]

The largest group of prosecutions against Gravesend women identified as prostitutes was for misdemeanours related to drunkenness. These include charges of being 'drunk and disorderly', 'drunk and riotous' and 'drunk and causing a disturbance'. Over 200 of such cases were reported in the press during the period under examination, representing 40 per cent of all cases reported. In these cases, as in that of Sarah London with which the chapter opened, the charge was often worded in such a way that the woman's occupation was recorded and inferred to be of relevance, even when unconnected to the specific offence. Jane Barber, for instance, was charged with being drunk and incapable and lying down in the roadway, but was actually convicted as a disorderly prostitute and sentenced to fourteen days. This category of offence was more likely to be punished by a fine than those previously discussed, but default custodial sentences were on average more severe. Examples include Emily Boswell, sentenced to twenty-eight days with hard labour in April 1869 for being drunk and soliciting prostitution in the High Street, and Eliza Jackson, twenty-eight days for being a prostitute, being drunk and abusing PC Pemberton in Stone Street.[102] In January 1870 Elizabeth Bond and Mary Ann Willoughby were each sentenced to twenty-eight days with hard labour for being 'drunk and disorderly prostitutes'. In a rare display of compassion, Rosetta Groves was escorted back home having been charged with being a prostitute, being in a state of intoxication with three men on the canal bank and attempting to commit suicide by jumping into the water. Two weeks later, however, she was back in court on a charge of drunk and disorderly conduct, being a prostitute and causing a disturbance in High Street. This time Rosetta was sentenced to twenty-eight days with hard labour. An additional 7 per cent of the Gravesend charges were for 'disorderly behaviour' when alcohol was not mentioned, 2 per cent for 'indecent behaviour' or 'indecent exposure' and 5 per cent for verbal abuse or foul language. Thus, 52 per cent of the charges brought against women named as prostitutes in Gravesend were for public order offences, in addition to the 25 per cent for soliciting.

Practice appears to have been somewhat different in Sheerness, where the majority of prosecutions against women named as prostitutes were brought under the Vagrancy Act. Charges typically read that 'she, then and there being a common prostitute wandering in a certain public street called (West Street, Blue Town), did then and there behave in a riotous manner'.[103] The surviving police court registers document over 160 of such charges brought against women publicly named as prostitutes between 1869 and 1879, following the appointment of the stipendiary magistrate.[104] It is clear from these records that prosecutions brought against alleged prostitutes in Sheerness were one of the few categories of charge where a mandatory custodial sentence was the norm and the option of a fine was not offered to the defendant. Sentences for prostitution alone with no additional offence were on average harsher than in Gravesend. Analysis of the prosecutions of prostitutes in the period 1869 to 1879 show that in cases where there was no supplementary charge such as drunkenness involved, 52 per cent of custodial sentences were for one calendar month or longer and 23 per cent were for three calendar months. Examples include Emma Cable and Eliza Dann, both arrested for 'wandering in High St., Blue Town and being prostitutes behaving in a riotous manner' on 17 August 1869.[105] They were both sent to Maidstone

Gaol to serve fourteen-day sentences with hard labour. The Sheerness prosecution of Sarah Charlesworth in May 1870 once again illustrates the process by which police incorporated the allegation of being 'riotous' into the charge. The arresting officer, PC Henry Lane, alleged that Sarah had been 'shouting, halloing and swearing in a very loud tone of voice', thus securing a conviction under the Vagrancy Act. This episode earned Sarah a sentence of fourteen days with hard labour.[106] Sarah's companion, Mary Ann Payne, arrested on a similar charge on the same day, was sentenced to twenty-one days with hard labour. The 1871 convictions of Fanny Pearce and Eliza Mudge were secured without even an allegation of riotous behaviour. They were each convicted of 'being a prostitute, wandering'.[107] In 1871 in Sheerness, a woman was prosecuted by local police on average once every three-and-a-half weeks on the charge of 'wandering and behaving in a riotous manner, being a disorderly prostitute'. By 1878 the rate had risen to one every two-and-three-quarter weeks.

In Maidstone fewer women were prosecuted on charges directly mentioning prostitution than in Gravesend or Sheerness, and when they were, penalties were less severe. Clare Lucas, for example, was convicted as 'an idle and disorderly person' for an 'offence against the Vagrant Act (disorderly prostitute)' and sentenced to seven days with hard labour in December 1871, as were Jane Boorman and Matilda Mordant in July 1872.[108] On passing sentence in the latter case, the chairman of the bench said he hoped 'they would be careful in future'. He trusted 'this would be a warning to their unfortunate class, for if any more came there the magistrates would go to the extent of the law, and they would be more severely dealt with', suggesting that he was consciously not inflicting the maximum sentence.[109] There is evidence that some charges against women under the Vagrancy Act for being disorderly prostitutes were dismissed altogether in Maidstone, such as those against Leonora Lucas and Catherine Collings. However, identified prostitutes were penalized heavily for a range of other public order offences, suggesting that Maidstone typifies what has been said relating to magistrates' use of a wide variety of offences to punish prostitutes.[110] Charlotte Smith was sentenced to fourteen days for using obscene language and fourteen days on another occasion for being drunk and disorderly.[111] Louisa Gardener was sentenced to two months in Maidstone for 'abusing a woman named Smith and using abusive language in the public streets' because she had previous convictions.[112]

In Chatham, according to Metropolitan Police figures, the scale of prostitution was much higher than in most other Kentish subjected districts.[113] This impression is based on a calculation of the number of women registered as prostitutes under the CD Acts in 1871 relative to the number of single and widowed women between the ages of fifteen and forty-five as recorded by the census of the same year.[114] The resulting ratio for Chatham (including the neighbouring districts of Rochester and Strood) is 1:30. Comparable figures for Canterbury,

Dover, Gravesend and Maidstone are 1:52, 1:54, 1:80 and 1:134.[115] Prosecutions in Chatham of offences related to prostitution during the 1860s were not reflective of the scale of prostitution suggested by this evidence, which implies that police were successfully controlling only recidivists and the most blatant breaches of the peace. Those women found drunk or creating a public disturbance appear to have been specifically targeted, and on conviction had severe penalties imposed, for example the one month with hard labour awarded each to Mary Macguire and Margaret Foley for this offence.[116] Caroline Pierce, arrested after being found by police 'behaving in a riotous and indecent manner' but not charged with drunkenness, was sentenced to twenty-one days with hard labour after the arresting constable 'informed the bench of the nature of the language used by the prisoner'.[117] Mary Scutts and Isabella Thompson were each sentenced to twenty-one days with hard labour in February 1865, Scutts for being drunk and indecent, and Thompson for being drunk and using foul language.[118] The notorious Eliza O'Malley was sentenced to one month with hard labour for being drunk and riotous, her appearance before the bench in June 1863 being her fiftieth, and having only been released from Maidstone the week before having completed a one-month sentence for the same offence.[119]

The situation appears to have changed markedly following the implementation of the 1867 Chatham and Sheerness Stipendiary Magistrates Act. By the mid-1870s, newspaper reportage of Chatham police court hearings suggests that practice had been brought in line with that elsewhere in Kent, and that the policing of prostitution was carried out increasingly more stringently. A conviction on a charge of 'riotous' conduct on the part of a woman named as a street prostitute could attract a punitive custodial sentence. The *Chatham News* columns for the end of 1975, for example, record sentences of between eighteen days and one month with hard labour imposed on four women convicted on charges of being 'an unfortunate' and behaving in 'a riotous manner', the precise nature of which was not defined.[120] The *Chatham News* edition of 2 September 1876 alone noted the convictions of five women in a police court item entitled 'Disorderly Prostitutes'. Custodial sentences of between fourteen days and one month were imposed.[121] By 1883, fifty-four of the seventy-five women admitted to Maidstone Gaol whose occupation was recorded as 'prostitute' during the twelve-month period were sent from Chatham.

In Dover, while general street disorder was policed in line with procedure elsewhere, it is clear that magistrates took a more lenient view of soliciting if practised without threat to public order. Whilst statistics demonstrate that arrests of prostitutes in Dover were consistently the second highest in the county after Gravesend, local press reports of police court proceedings indicate that few of these arrests were solely for soliciting. According to PS Geddes, women were arrested only if they were disorderly or became abusive to the police.[122] As in

Chatham, however, the Dover authorities appear to have taken an increasingly intolerant view over time. By the early 1870s punishments were more stringent in line with other locations. Custodial sentences of between fourteen and twenty-one days were imposed on three women in August 1873 on conviction of the offences of being drunk and disorderly, and causing an obstruction.[123]

Women identified as prostitutes were punished more severely than other offenders prosecuted for the same transgression, indicating that the judiciary was making use of a wide range of street nuisance offences, over and above those directly related to prostitution, to curtail the activities of streetwalkers. This is particularly the case when charges of drunkenness are taken into consideration. When Julia Swift and Sophia Winn were arrested together for being drunk and disorderly, Swift, described as an unfortunate, was sentenced to twenty-one days with hard labour, whereas Winn, whose occupation was not mentioned, was fined five shillings.[124] Similarly when John Hayes and notorious prostitute Eliza O'Malley were prosecuted together in Chatham for being drunk and disorderly, Hayes was discharged on promising not to offend again, whilst O'Malley was convicted and sentenced to two months.[125] Chatham magistrates heard two unconnected cases of drunkenness on the same day in December 1861. Elizabeth Brown, named in court as a 'common prostitute', was sentenced to fourteen days with hard labour, whilst an un-named 'young man from the country', who had been found drunk and incapable, was discharged.[126]

Magistrates in some locations appear to have taken every opportunity to impose punishment on women named as prostitutes. Mary Jane Harriet Brown, for example, was charged in Gravesend in 1863 with stealing a purse of money from a would-be client who had agreed to 'go for a walk' with her. There was insufficient evidence to prove the theft charge and so the case was dismissed, but Mary Jane was convicted instead 'as a prostitute' and sentenced to one month's imprisonment.[127] Martha Bereman and Rose Jackson, young girls identified in court as prostitutes, appear to have been particularly unfortunate after they had picked some sprigs of lavender that were trailing over the wall of the grounds of Trinity Church in Gravesend. They were convicted on charges of 'wilfully destroying shrubs', and sentenced to fourteen days' imprisonment each.[128]

These sentencing patterns are, of course, likely to reflect the effect of recidivism, which was specifically targeted. Hetty Nash of Sheerness was charged with being riotous and being a prostitute in February 1877 only six months after having served twenty-one days for a similar offence, and was sentenced to three calendar months after pleading guilty on both occasions.[129] Elizabeth Tremain of Sheerness was arrested for being a riotous prostitute three times between January 1876 and May 1877; she received escalating sentences of fourteen days, six weeks and two calendar months. Maria Gales appeared before magistrates in April, June and September 1872 in Sheerness on charges of 'wandering, being a riotous prostitute' and was sentenced to twenty-one days, one month and three months respectively. She therefore spent a total of twenty weeks out of the fifty-two that year in Maidstone Gaol. Emily Huntley spent a total of fifteen months there in the fifty-month period between 30 November 1874 and 3 February 1879 on seven separate charges relating to prostitution.[130]

In summary, therefore, in some locations and at certain points in time it may be true to say that the police 'entered into some accommodation with streetwalkers', permitting them to ply their trade as long as they were not public nuisances, as Walkowitz has suggested.[131] However, the type of behaviour that was defined as a public nuisance requires close scrutiny. For many women in the ports, garrisons and dockyards of Kent it seems to have consisted of 'wandering up and down', 'being in the street day and night' or even standing for too long on the pavement. A wide range of public nuisance offences was successfully used to get round that fact that prostitution was not in itself against the law. Charges of 'riotous' and 'disorderly' behaviour were brought against women identified as prostitutes for a range of behaviour that contravened notions of public decency, enabling them to be convicted under statutes that carried heavy penalties.

Policing Houses of Ill-Fame

Whilst prostitution was not in itself against the law, running what was known as a 'house of ill-fame' was. The 'street cleaning' approach to the control of prostitution was therefore supplemented by prosecutions for brothel-keeping brought against the keepers of those public houses, coffee houses and refreshment houses used by women known to be practising prostitution. This was most often done when disorder threatened to spill on to the streets, or in response to complaints made by the public. A range of legislative measures provided for the regulation of prostitution on licensed premises and other places of refreshment. The 1847 Town Police Clauses Act provided for a fine of up to five pounds for the keeper of any refreshment house who 'knowingly suffers common Prostitutes or reputed thieves to assemble and continue in his Premises'.[132] Licensing laws forbade permitting prostitutes to remain on licensed premises for longer than was necessary to take refreshment. The 1872 Licensing Act provided for a fine not exceeding twenty pounds and the loss of license for 'any licensed person convicted of permitting his premises to be a brothel'.[133] The wording of the statute put the onus on the police to prove that that the landlord 'knowingly harboured' prostitutes, but there appears to have been some variation between local authorities in the application of the law in this regard.[134] When Maidstone eating-house keeper George Ripley was prosecuted for allowing 'prostitutes and drunken persons to assemble at his house' in January 1876, Police Sergeant William Waghorne explained to the court that he was instructed to enter disorderly premises only in response to specific complaints, but that if the disorder spilled onto the street, as was the case on this occasion, the police had powers of arrest.[135] Ripley's lawyer argued that it could not be proved that the proprietor knew that the women were prostitutes and knowingly allowed them to remain on the premises, or that the premises were 'the habitual resort of prostitutes'. The case was accordingly dismissed.

Evidently it was common practice for Dover magistrates to be provided with proof that police officers had previously informed the landlord that women on his or her premises were prostitutes. The constable would then return to the premises several hours after having given the warning, and if the women remained, the case could then be proved on the basis that the prostitutes were 'knowingly harboured'.[136] In an 1859 case, PS Scutt was admonished by the Watch Committee after an incident in which he had prosecuted the keeper of a public house for harbouring prostitutes without firstly having warned the defendant that the women were, in fact prostitutes, thus jeopardizing the success of the prosecution case.[137]

Elsewhere, it would appear that convictions were successfully made on the basis that police officers testified to women being prostitutes. Gravesend licensees were fined between ten shillings and two pounds plus costs for this offence, and fines escalated sharply for a repeat offence. Thomas Treherne of the Royal Sovereign was fined ten pounds plus costs for a subsequent offence. The ultimate penalty against landlords was to be refused renewal of their licence. Mr Mitchell of the Admiral Duncan in Gravesend was warned that his house would be closely observed in the future, because 'young lads and prostitutes met there for dancing', and the renewal of the license of Jacob Beard of the India Arms was postponed following two such convictions. When John Davis applied to magistrates to re-open the Black Horse Inn in the High Street, he was reminded that the license had previously been removed because of 'alleged immoralities' there, and he assured the bench that he would conduct business in a respectable manner in the future. Within three months, however, trouble had arisen again after a fight broke out and Police Sergeant John Jayne testified to seeing seventeen prostitutes leave the house, and a 'very respectable person' had informed the bench that a young girl of fourteen years of age was 'harboured' there. Davis was found guilty and fined twenty shillings.[138] Maidstone magistrates fined publican William Towns twenty shillings plus seventeen shillings costs because prostitutes were known to have attended a Boxing Night party at his premises, albeit that Towns himself had not been present at the time. During the case against Edward Russell, keeper of the Swan Inn in Gravesend, it was alleged that several neighbours had complained of the disorderly conduct of the house, which was the habitual rendezvous of prostitutes, by sending notes to the police.[139]

The prosecution of three Gravesend residents for running brothels within a three-week period in 1870 suggests that periodic crackdowns took place. The penalty in these cases was to be bound over to keep the peace on payment of 'sureties' paid by the defendant and two others. John Mazar failed to find sureties of twenty pounds for himself and two others of ten pounds each in such a case, and was imprisoned for three months. He was brought before the bench again eighteen months later charged with the same offence, clearly not having been deterred by his stay in Maidstone Gaol.[140] Magistrates' powers extended further than the imposition of fines or custodial sentences. When Sarah Goodger was convicted of keeping a disorderly house in John's Place Gravesend, it was decided by the bench that her landlord should be instructed to cease her tenancy of the property.

Clearly, the indirect suppression of prostitution as described here, which restricted women's ability to use licensed and other premises for meeting clients and practising their trade, was not experienced as punitive to the women themselves in the same way as the repeated custodial sentences for streetwalking described previously. Nevertheless, these measures served to force prostitution back onto the streets where the police had greater powers of arrest.

Punishment

As the foregoing discussion has demonstrated, for many of the women identified by this study, custodial sentences appear to have been a routine and integral part of a life on the streets quite irrespective of the CD Acts. This was likewise the case for the many other members of the casual poor who, as has been seen, were regularly arrested on a variety of street misdemeanour charges. In the first instance and where appropriate, perpetrators of minor public nuisance offences such as causing an obstruction appear to have been requested to move along, as demonstrated by the example of Sarah London, with whom this chapter opened. If they refused or were abusive to the constable, or as in the case of many drunks they were incapable of moving on, offenders were arrested. Defendants were detained in police cells before being brought before one or more local magistrates in petty sessions and tried summarily without a jury. Nationally, women categorized as prostitutes represented 13.3 per cent of all female offenders dealt with summarily in 1857.[141]

Police cell accommodation at the period under study was variable. In Gravesend after 1850, prisoners were accommodated in new police cells measuring eight feet by nine feet by nine feet high, and were kept to rations of a pint of coffee and two ounces of cheese twice a day and a pound of bread three times a day.[142] The cells had the advantage of a water closet, but there was a persistent problem with vermin eating the straw mattress stuffing thus leaving only hard boards on which to sleep.[143] In Sheerness it was not until 1866 that accommodation for prisoners was improved, when four large, airy, well-lighted cells heated with hot water pipes were provided.[144] Chatham prisoners, prior to the 1867

Chatham and Sheerness Stipendiary Magistrates Act provided for magistrates to sit in the town, were walked through the streets to the magistrates' court at Rochester. It was evidently customary for a mob to gather around the police station to witness this spectacle. In May 1863, for example, the local press reported that a 'mob of fifty boys and girls collected round the police station to see the prisoners conveyed away'.[145]

Open to the public, petty sessions allowed for the accused to enter a plea and to produce witnesses. The magistrate then pronounced verdict and sentence, which with rare exceptions for summary offences was a maximum of three months. This category of prisoner was sent to a local prison, which in the case of Kent was one of the two county gaols, Maidstone and St Augustine's at Canterbury. These prisons came under the jurisdiction of local magistrates and were managed by boards of visiting justices, thus their regime, size and standards of accommodation varied according to local conditions and the attitudes of the local magistracy. Maidstone was the older of the two Kentish county gaols, having been built in 1819. Whilst the total prison population declined substantially during the period under study, the proportion of that total represented by women inmates remained constant. In 1861, eighty-six of a total of 496 were women (17 per cent), in 1871 ninety-five of 449 (21 per cent), in 1881 fifty-six of 287 (19.5 per cent) and in 1891 twenty-one of 138 (15 per cent).[146] Nearly half of these were women categorized as prostitutes.[147] This proportion had fallen by the early 1880s. The admissions registers show that of the 500 women admitted during 1883, seventy-five had their occupation recorded as 'prostitute'.[148]

In the 1860s concerns about the conditions and the restricted diet to which the Maidstone prisoners were kept attracted comment. Doctors believed that the inmates were inadequately fed for the scale of labour to which they were kept, with the result that 'weakness and hunger are very visible on all convicted prisoners'.[149] One prisoner lost thirty pounds in weight during a nine-day stay. The regime at Maidstone was based on the principle of physical isolation; communication between prisoners was forbidden and the rules stipulated that a female prisoner 'when out of her cell shall not approach within five paces of any other prisoner'.[150] Locked into unheated and unventilated cells at six each evening, the female prisoners had lights turned out at eight o'clock. Cells were unlocked again at six the following morning before the first session of hard labour that lasted until breakfast at eight. By the 1860s women prisoners kept to hard labour were no longer put on the tread-wheel as were their male counterparts, but were employed in scrubbing and cleaning the prison and in laundry work for a daily total of ten hours. This was the regime experienced by all those who served custodial sentences for the range of street disorder offences that have been discussed thus far, and by all women named as prostitutes charged by local police and convicted of a variety of misdemeanours, including soliciting, obstructing the footpath, using bad language and being drunk or riotous. These prosecutions were brought and these sentences imposed and served exclusive of the CD legislation.

Despite the severity of this prison regime, some women convicted of offences related to prostitution, together with other members of the casual poor, not only appear to have become hardened to it but used it as part of their economies of makeshift. Indeed, according to historian Lucia Zedner, 'women deliberately sought access to their local prison as a welfare agency, preferable even to the workhouse'.[151] Evidently this was the case with Ellen Higgens, a Gravesend woman who was arrested for breaking a pane of glass. She said in her defence that she did it so that she might be 'taken up', as she was destitute.[152] Kate Vance of Dover clearly operated a similar negotiation strategy as well as having a detailed knowledge of the system. On being sentenced to ten days' imprisonment for a 'drunk and disorderly' offence, eighty-two-year-old Vance requested that she might be given one month instead, because the food allowance was greater for tariffs of one month or longer.[153]

Certainly many of the Kentish streetwalkers identified by this study appear to have accepted sentences of imprisonment with indifference, if not outright defiance. Sarah Stapel 'impudently thanked their worships' on being sentenced to one month with hard labour on a conviction of being drunk, crying out 'murder' and clinging to a soldier at the top of Harmer Street.[154] In a similar vein, Martha Dell, on being sentenced to six weeks with hard labour for being on the street for the purposes of prostitution, being abusive to the arresting constable and then being 'abusive and impertinent to the bench', retorted that she would 'serve it like a brick'.[155] Mary Ann Simpson, meanwhile, on being sentenced to twenty-eight days with hard labour for causing an obstruction, admitted that she did not know how many times she had been in Maidstone Gaol.[156]

The records reveal that recidivists were frequently arrested again almost immediately after release from gaol. When sisters Hannah and Mary Ann Simpson were arrested for being drunk, 'being prostitutes' and causing a disturbance in the early hours of the morning, it emerged that they had only returned from Maidstone the previous week. They were sent back for one month with hard labour. It would appear to be true of the streetwalkers of Kent that, as Taylor has observed: 'It is a measure of the harshness of life for many working-class women that prison was seen as preferable to life outside'.[157]

Conclusion

The control of prostitution by local police forces forms part of a wider narrative of the regulation of the casual poor, which was enforced more rigorously in line with the establishment of the 'new' police from the second quarter of the nineteenth century onwards. The evidence from Kent paints a complex and variable picture, with a considerable degree of variation between locations and over time. This variation was influenced by a combination of factors that included the local police force, systems of local governance and the inclination of the local judiciary. However, in a considerable number of locations streetwalkers were liable to frequent and repeated arrest by local police forces and to imprisonment on conviction under a broad range of legislation. Levels of arrest, prosecution and conviction of women publicly identified as prostitutes by local police were consistently much higher in most Kentish locations than those brought by the Metropolitan Police under the CD Acts. Considered in this context, the additional relative impact of the CD Acts appears less uniquely draconian than it is usually considered. It is to this hypothesis that this discussion now turns.

6 THE CONTAGIOUS DISEASES ACTS IN KENT

On 21 March 1882 Frederick Wheeler was summoned to give evidence before the Parliamentary Select Committee on the Contagious Diseases Acts. The retired grocer, Quaker and philanthropist from Rochester, as has been seen, had been involved in local anti-CD Acts activism for many years by this date. Amongst the matters on which he was called to give evidence by the Committee was the case of a young woman called Caroline Wybrow, which had attained, by the date of the hearing, something of the status of cause célèbre.[1]

Wybrow's story, as told by Wheeler to the Committee and as recorded in her declaration (as appended to the Committee's final report), conflicted with the testimonies of the police officers and medical practitioners involved on a number of counts.[2] The uncontested facts of the case were that she was the daughter of 'a poor woman receiving parochial relief', the widow of a marine. Following the death of Caroline's father some years previously, the family had moved to Chatham, where they rented a room in a lodging house. The two women augmented the one shilling a week relief they received by charring and washing. When the lower floor of the same lodging house was subsequently rented by three other women, Caroline earned additional income from cleaning their rooms. In January 1875 a police constable visited the house to discharge his duties in accordance with the requirements of the CD Acts, a visit that set in motion a series of events with widespread consequences. His purpose was to give notice to Elizabeth Coppin, Alice Gilbert and Kate Simmonds to attend for medical examination, since they allegedly lived by prostitution.[3] Discovering Wybrow in one of the women's rooms, the officer assumed she was a prostitute, later describing the lodging house as a 'brothel'.

The details of subsequent events were energetically contested. The police case was based on the claim that in addition to having been found in an alleged brothel, Wybrow had been observed on numerous occasions and over a long period of time, both on the street and in the Golden Cross beer-house, in the company of soldiers and of women known to the police to be living by prostitution. By Wybrow's own account, she was accordingly ordered to attend for medical examination, which she repeatedly refused, was intimidated into putting her mark onto a form that she did not understand under threat of being sent to Maidstone Gaol, was threatened with physical force, detained illegally at the lock hospital on a reduced diet of bread and tea and finally coerced into being medically examined for venereal disease albeit that she stated that she was a virgin. Some time following these events, Wheeler made an official complaint to the Home Office with regard to Wybrow's treatment and the way in which the case had been handled. The resulting furore threw up allegations of malpractice and of the payment of 'hush money' by officials, following which the case was taken up enthusiastically by the anti-CD Acts publicity machine.[4]

An exploration of the contrasting accounts brings the arguments and the discourses of the pro- and anti-abolitionist camps into sharper relief. For the abolitionists, the Wybrow case constituted a compelling narrative, its appeal enhanced by the representation of its protagonists in terms of stock melodramatic stereotypes, for example the impoverished widowed mother, the villainous policeman figure and the imperilled virgin. These characteristics facilitated the narrative's adoption and longevity within repeal discourse. The case turned additionally on the question of mistaken identity, which was a popular and prevailing theme in repeal literature. For champions of the legislation, the case both rested on and reflected the set of gendered assumptions about women's public and private behaviour which not only underpinned the CD Acts, but permeated contemporary societal attitudes more generally.

Caroline Wybrow's trajectory through the machinery of the CD Acts system illuminates its workings at ground level in the subjected districts of Kent, casting light on the roles of the dockyard police, the medical establishment and local magistrates in petty sessions, as well as the activity of local repeal activists such as Wheeler himself. In charting Wybrow's progression through this system, the discussion that follows will consider what this particular case can reveal about the ground-level operation of the Acts in the localities more generally. This dual approach makes use of a range of sources, taking the official documentation of the machinery of the Acts, together with Parliamentary Papers, as a starting point and supplementing them with local records that provide a more narrowly focused perspective. The juxtaposition of the top-down with the bottom-up viewpoint has the advantage of bringing inconsistencies into sharper relief. Since Wybrow's journey began with the visit paid by the police to 7 Seaton Court, home to the Wybrows as well as to Elizabeth Coppin, Alice Gilbert and Kate Simmonds, a visit which was the catalyst in the chain of events that resulted in Wheeler's testimony before the Parliamentary Select Committee, it is to the policing of the CD Acts that this discussion firstly turns.

Policing the Contagious Diseases Acts

The CD Acts provided for a police officer to instruct any woman whom he 'had good cause to believe' to be involved in prostitution to be medically examined for signs of sexually transmitted disease. She would then be asked to sign the voluntary submission form by which she agreed to be bound by the terms of the legislation and to attend for future regular examination. These policing operations were carried out by small units of plain-clothed officers recruited from the MPDD rather than by local forces. The primary duties of this unit, operating within a fifteen-mile radius of the dockyard sites, related to the protection of government property, the apprehension of 'stragglers' and deserters, and the enforcement of regulations pertaining to 'drunken and disorderly' seamen and marines.[5] This principal responsibility appears to have remained in place even whilst officers were assigned to CD Acts duty. Police Inspector Charles Hallet, for example, whose name appears in the Sheerness Police Court registers as the prosecutor in cases of women charged for offences against the CD Acts throughout the 1870s, appeared before the stipendiary magistrate in 1871 on behalf of the Admiralty to prosecute a man for fraudulently 'passing' an altered baptism certificate, and again in 1872 to prosecute a man charged with the theft of a seaman's property.[6]

As was demonstrated previously, the introduction of the CD Acts into a district did not result in the cessation of routine, day-to-day policing of prostitution. Rather, the latter continued largely unaffected by CD Acts policing, which operated under an entirely separate mechanism. The police court records of each of the Kentish petty sessions districts made subject to the CD Acts, together with the police court columns of local newspapers, show that in these areas, for the duration of the period when the Acts were on the statute book, prostitution was being policed under two parallel systems. Maidstone petty sessions minute books for 1871, for example, record prosecutions of women before the same bench of magistrates in connection with offences under the CD Acts and for offences related to prostitution under other legislation. In the case of the former, prosecutions were supported by Inspector William Luscombe of the MPDD, whilst in the latter case by members of the Maidstone borough police force.[7] In some cases, such as that of Jane Boorman (who was introduced in Chapter 3 as 'Grecian Bend'), women were recorded as being brought before the same bench of magistrates, charged by Luscombe on a CD Acts-related offence, within just a short time of being charged by a member of the borough police force with an offence under the Vagrancy Act as a 'riotous prostitute'.[8]

The CD Acts policing regime attracted widespread censure from pro-repealers for its operational practices, the specific charge being that it was brutal and degrading ('a grievous, cruel, oppressive law') to the women made subject to it.[9] The dominance of this discourse is reflected in the reportage of the *Shield*, the Ladies National Association (LNA) publication, and was particularly influenced by the experience of Plymouth and Devonport, where Inspector Silas Anniss appears to have been especially zealous in the execution of his duties. Frequently vilified in the pages of the *Shield*, Anniss achieved no fewer than 189 mentions by name during the years of its publication, many of which were prefixed with the adjective 'notorious'. The most disparaging language, however, was reserved for a retrospective article published in 1900, fourteen years following the repeal of the CD Acts: 'there reigned a petty tyrant ... Mr. Anniss, whose name may still convey a thrill of horror to those few now living who remember his cruel methods'.[10] Whilst Anniss provided the repeal cause with ammunition with which to articulate a discourse of cruelty, what is less clear is the degree to which his working methods were entirely representative, how far they deviated from prescribed procedures, and thus what they might reveal about the policing of the Acts more generally.

Inspector William Capon, the senior officer involved in the Wybrow case, failed to live up to the exceptional notoriety of Anniss, warranting only twelve mentions in the *Shield* during the years of its publication. He was, however, amongst those named officers singled out for attack, having been involved in a number of other high-profile cases prior to Wybrow's. When he was named it was with a similar level of personal hostility as applied to Anniss: 'His name is Capon, and, like others of his calling, he does not like to part with his prey unless compelled to do so'.[11] Whether Capon was as predatory as this accusation suggests is difficult to ascertain from the available evidence. What the records do show is that he was the son of a gunner in the Royal Artillery, and had joined the MPDD in Woolwich where he was raised.[12] By the age of thirty-five he had risen to the rank of inspector, and over the course of the following decade he was seconded to oversee the operations of the CD Acts in Kent, firstly in Dover and subsequently in Chatham. Whilst in Dover he had been involved in the case of Susannah White, who had made a formal application to the magistrates to have her name removed from the CD Acts register, as she was about to be married.[13] Under cross-examination by the solicitor appointed to act for White, Capon explained that there was no mechanism in place for a formal de-registering of this type, suggesting a methodical approach to his duties. By the time of his involvement with Caroline Wybrow, therefore, Capon had accrued substantial experience overseeing the operations of the Acts. Subsequently he appears to have left the MPDD somewhat prematurely, since by the early 1880s, aged still only in his mid-forties, he had removed to Deptford where he worked as a time-keeper.

The police case against Wybrow was built upon the claim that she had been in the habit of keeping company with women alleged to be known prostitutes and soldiers, on the streets and in the Golden Cross beer-house. From this, it was inferred that she must also be living from prostitution. Thus the case turned on the question of mistaken identity, which was allocated a prominent place within repeal discourse. The alleged threat posed to all women in public by the legislation formed part of the abolitionist platform and permeated repeal literature. As early as 1863 Florence Nightingale had claimed that 'Any honest girl might be locked up all night by mistake by it', and Harriet Martineau, writing in the pro-repeal *Daily News* under the pseudonym 'An Englishwoman', argued similarly that 'A woman, chaste or unchaste, is charged by a policeman, rightly or wrongly, with being a prostitute. The law makes no distinctions of degree or kinds'. The focus on mistaken identity enabled abolitionists to oppose the legislation without appearing overtly to defend or support prostitution. However, it also served further to reinforce the overly simplistic dichotomy between the categories 'pure' and 'fallen'.

Cases of alleged mistaken identity, including several from Kent, filled the columns of the *Shield*. That of Eliza Southey from Dover was taken up by Alderman Rowland Rees, which led to it also being investigated in 1882 by the Parliamentary Select Committee. In this case the police attested to having seen Southey on the streets at different times with a number of different soldiers, but since she had no previous association with prostitution or brothels the identification was deemed to be suspect. In this instance the police were found to have served an order illegally, and eventually the Home Secretary was forced to issue a reprimand and to transfer the individual officers concerned.[14] In a second Dover case Elizabeth Burley was chased through the streets in 1881 by two policemen followed by a mob of boys, and threw herself into the harbour to escape. The pursuing police officer at this point, according to a passer-by, left her to her fate, to be rescued by members of the public. The incident prompted a considerable local public outcry, meetings were held and the Home Secretary eventually reprimanded and transferred the police officers responsible. The Woolwich case of Mary Ann Hart, like those of Wybrow and Southey, was based on police evidence that she had been seen in the streets and going into public houses in the company of known prostitutes, sailors and what the police termed as 'quashers', described as 'loafers, idle companions and attendants on prostitutes'.[15] Hart was imprisoned for one week in 1878 for refusing to be medically examined, claiming that she was 'not and never has been a prostitute'.[16] However, her sister-in-law Minnie Davis, who acknowledged herself a prostitute, did Mary Ann no favours by testifying against her, leading the magistrate to conclude that there was sufficient evidence to show that Mary Ann was 'in that state of life which either sooner or later would lead her to prostitution'.[17]

Thus the case of Caroline Wybrow, together with others amongst the Kentish cases, turned on questions of identity, reflecting the processes of labelling and 'othering' that were applied to women living at the margins, processes that were explored in Chapter 3. These cases do not support Martineau's contention that police allegations were levelled indiscriminately at all women walking the street, but rather they reflect the ambiguity and lack of precision in the law's wording, which created practical difficulties in its application. The interpretation of 'good cause to believe' was coloured by prevailing ideological expectations of women's respectable public behaviour and demeanour. Nevertheless, many of the cases were characterized by sufficient ambiguity to challenge a hypothesis of widespread mistaken identity. Indeed, the selection of the Wybrow and Southey cases for investigation by the Select Committee, some several years after the events, might suggest that far from being representative of 'hundreds' of cases as alleged by Wheeler, they were remarkable for being unusual. This reading is supported by the personal testimony of some local contemporary observers. Rev. Hugh Baker of Woolwich, whose missionary work brought him into contact with prostitute women, claimed never to have heard of 'virtuous women or quasi virtuous women hav[ing] been brought on the register'.[18]

An additional cause for the condemnation of the CD Acts policing regime was that it was carried out by officers in plain clothes. This factor became elaborated, within repeal discourse, into the claim that the officers were 'spies' and contributed to a 'spy system'. Alderman Rowland Rees of Dover's comment, made during a Watch Committee meeting, that he had misgivings about the employment of policemen in plain clothes and did not like 'the spy system as an institution' reflects this mode of thinking.[19] At a national level, correspondents to the *Shield* made similar reference to the 'employment of spies', for example Josephine Butler, who claimed with a rhetorical flourish that: 'our rulers have dared to put in force a law which authorizes the Government spy to enter every poor man's house and claim his wife and daughters for devil's uses'.[20] This antipathy to policing carried out in plain clothes echoes the reaction with which the Metropolitan Police's initial introduction of a detective unit in the 1840s had been met. For many, policing carried out by non-uniformed officers had represented an obstacle to individual freedoms and was thus indistinguishable from spying. The repeal campaign's use of the 'spy' idiom can therefore be located within a wider and pre-existing discourse. Older traditions of mistrust of covert policing methods were mobilized anew to articulate specific opposition to the CD Acts.

The MPDD units were additionally censured on the grounds that they were incomers deployed from London, as reflected in the *Chatham Observer's* 1875 assertion that 'The officers under the Acts were not our own police force whom, as a body, we honour and respect, but men who were sent down from London'.[21] As Chatham was home to an HM Navy dockyard, however, the MPDD unit had already been established there for several years at the commencement of operations of the CD Acts, as was also the case in Sheerness. The officers appointed for CD Acts duty were drawn from amongst its numbers, and in many instances they had been recruited locally. Local historian Brian Joyce has noted that the

MPDD officers employed in Chatham had local roots as strong, if not stronger than, those of the women they policed.[22] Census evidence corroborates this argument, demonstrating that Edward Green and George Weeks, for example, who each served in Chatham, were both born in Kent and thus had not been sent from London.[23] In neighbouring subjected garrison towns where there was no MPDD unit already in place, officers were seconded for CD Acts duty from military dockyards. Constable James Porter, for example, who was appointed to police the Acts in Gravesend at the age of twenty-five, was Hampshire-born and had previously lived at Plumstead, suggesting previous service at the Woolwich dockyard. His replacement in Gravesend, Joseph Stanlake, was Cornish and had previously seen MPDD service at the Sheerness Dockyard, where evidence suggests that he met his Kent-born wife. At the time of his posting to Gravesend, Stanlake had already been resident in Kent for upwards of seven years. For the most part, therefore, MPDD officers were not outsiders and the evidence, on the contrary, suggests considerable prior community integration. These men made their homes and raised their families amongst the communities they policed. Inspector Charles Hallett, who has already been mentioned, who was stationed at Sheerness Dockyard, spent over ten years there, living in the community amongst shipyard workers such as carpenters and shipwrights.[24]

The MPDD's policing operations were contrasted unfavourably, as was seen in the extract from the *Chatham Observer* above, to the established, uniformed policing carried out by 'our own police force whom, as a body, we honour and respect'. Frederick Wheeler, in his evidence before the Select Committee with which this chapter opened, laid emphasis on this distinction between the MPDD and the local Kent County Constabulary, to whose efficient operations he attributed an improvement in public order and in particular the public behaviour of prostitute women. This ideological construction of a clear demarcation between forces is not supported by the records, however, which point to joint working where it was mutually advantageous. Collaboration was dictated by official procedure, and the evidence that it occurred in practice questions the notion of unrestrained power on the part of officers of the MPDD. The evidence thrown up by an 1870 incident relating to an assault on a Maidstone policeman by a man called William Brown, for example, shines some light on these procedures. Brown, it appears, was acting to prevent the arrest of a woman called Anne Baker, who had refused to attend for medical examination under the CD Acts.[25] The press report of the incident relates that Sgt Charles Phipps, having called at Baker's lodgings with a warrant, was struck three times by Brown.[26] Local records reveal that Phipps was not employed by the MPDD but was an experienced and uniformed officer of the local borough force, who at the time of the incident had accrued seventeen years' service on the streets of Maidstone.[27] The 1871 census records Phipps, who was himself Maidstone-born, living with his wife in Perry Street in the centre of the town, some two-thirds of a mile from Anne Baker's own lodgings in Woollett Street.[28] In order to mobilize any power of enforcement over Baker, the MPDD had handed the case over to the local police force, which had applied to magistrates for a warrant before pursuing an arrest. This interpretation supports the statement made by Captain Harris of the Metropolitan Police before the 1871 Royal Commission, that once magistrates had issued a warrant for arrest, the matter became the responsibility of the local police force.[29] Reciprocity was given in the form of evidence given by members of the MPDD units in support of prosecution cases brought by local police forces against publicans on charges of harbouring prostitutes. It has been seen that convictions were secured if it could be proven that the defendant had 'knowingly' allowed the women on their premises. Numerous such convictions were secured in Kent using the testimony of MPDD officers that they had discussed the requirements of the CD Acts with prostitute women with the knowledge, and often within the hearing, of the women's landlords, whom, it was argued, must therefore have known how the women lived. Reportage of court hearings in Chatham, Rochester and Gravesend uncovers this process at work, by which MPDD officers attended to provide magistrates with the necessary evidence to secure convictions in prosecutions brought by local forces.[30]

Manpower and workload levels amongst the small MPDD units charged with overseeing the CD Acts cast some shadow of doubt over the notion of universally brutal and repressive policing measures. In Chatham, where this chapter opened and where the scale of prostitution was highest amongst the Kentish stations, one inspector and four constables were allocated to police the Acts.[31] During each year of the seventeen years of operations in Chatham, they procured an average of over 3,000 medical examinations, and an average of just over 200 women were processed for the first time through the register.[32] In Gravesend, during the first year of operations, PC James Porter procured 1,016 medical examinations and registered 117 individual women, of whom an average of fifty-nine was on the register at any one time. In Dover, the two police officers appointed at the commencement of operations in 1870 registered a total of 204 women (including re-registrations); they procured a total of 347 signatures on so-called voluntary submission forms and brought about 1,654 medical examinations.[33] At the height of operations in 1872 they registered a total of 269 women, including re-registrations. Between them they brought about a total of 3,239 medical examinations and procured 612 signatures on Voluntary Submission Forms.[34] In Maidstone, Inspector William Luscombe and PC William Griffiths, the two officers initially appointed to oversee operations, registered a total of 80 individual women during the first year of operation, during which time 697 examinations were carried out. This volume of work suggests that on the whole women cooperated with the requirement for registration and examination without widespread resistance. This allocation of resources did not provide the necessary manpower for coercive tactics on a widespread scale. The local evidence thrown up by these cases about the CD Acts policing regime paints a picture, therefore, of bureaucratic adherence to procedure rather than an unrestrained power wielded and abused by covert police.

Medical Examination

Following her encounter with the officers of the MPDD, Caroline Wybrow's route through the CD Acts system brought her to the Chatham Lock Hospital, where she was detained pending medical examination, which was one of the most controversial aspects of the CD legislation. As had been seen, Wybrow initially resisted but eventually capitulated. The legislation provided for the genital examination for the purposes of detecting venereal disease of women whom police 'had good cause' to believe were living by prostitution. Under the initial 1864 statute, this was to be carried out as and when instructed by a police officer, but the arrangement was formalized under the final 1869 amendment and increased to a routine once-fortnightly timetable. The examination soon attained symbolic status within the abolitionist movement and became the focus of fierce protest, particularly (and understandably) from the Ladies National Association, the women's branch. The examination featured widely in abolitionist discourse, and references to 'medical lust', 'instrumental rape', 'disgusting examination', 'legalized torture' and 'violent outrages' permeated repeal literature.[35] Frederick Wheeler considered that 'after the women have passed through the examination there, they give up all hope, all is lost, as to their character'.[36]

There is an inevitable paucity of first-hand testimony relating to the opinions and attitudes of the women made subject to this regime, and what survives is mediated through the attitudes and voices of the commentators on both sides of the fiercely contested debate surrounding the CD Acts. Whether women who practised prostitution in the Kentish dockyard and garrison towns found the prospect and experience of internal medical examination as abhorrent as the middle-class activists who purported to speak for them, or whether, on the other hand, they were quite as nonchalant about it as the legislation's proponents claimed, is difficult to determine. An alternative reading is that it represented, for many women of the marginal poor, one further obstacle to be negotiated in the furtherance of personal survival strategies, in addition to those outlined in earlier chapters. Clearly it is difficult to attribute motive or opinion to historical actors, and impossible to do so in relation to those who have left so little record. One strategy open to the historian is to examine what took place.

Statistical data suggest that the majority of women in Kent who were required to submit to regular medical inspection did so. Government statistics for the period when the Acts were in operation recorded the yearly number of medical examinations carried out at each station together with the actual and average numbers of women registered as prostitutes during each year. In the Kentish stations, 173,914 medical examinations were carried out on a combined yearly average of 718 registered women during the sixteen years of reported operations.[37] Expressed as a percentage of the maximum number of examinations possible (given that examinations were expected to be performed fortnightly after 1869 and taking into account the date on which operations commenced in each district), the following scenario emerges. In Sheerness, 85 per cent of the possible maximum number of examinations for the twelve-year period was carried out; 79 per cent in Chatham, 73 per cent in Shorncliffe, 72 per cent in each of Woolwich, Gravesend and Deal, 70 per cent in Dover, 69 per cent in Greenwich and Canterbury, and 68 per cent in Maidstone. Whilst clearly these figures are approximations since they are calculated from averages, they nevertheless reveal relatively high rates of compliance. Moreover, the evidence (as was discussed in the previous chapter) that many of the street prostitutes identified by this study served repeated sentences in the county gaol for street disorder offences (which would have removed them from the street for substantial periods of time) makes the figures for compliance with the requirement for medical examination all the more remarkable.

Anecdotal evidence supports these statistics in suggesting that opposition to the examination was not universal amongst the women directly affected. A young woman brought before Greenwich magistrates for refusing to attend the medical examination, for example, was offered an exemption from it as an inducement to enter a reformatory. She declined this offer and agreed to be examined instead, suggesting that she found the prospect of medical examination preferable to that of entering the reformatory system.[38] In another Greenwich case, that of Ellen Sandford, refusal to comply with the Acts appears to have been the demonstration of opposition to bureaucracy and authority rather than to the examination itself. Having been summoned before the bench for non-submission, Ellen told the court: 'I am willing to be examined, but I will not sign any paper. I am ready to be examined … now, if you like'.[39] In Maidstone, meanwhile, Stephen Rimbault, whose twenty-eight years' religious missionary work with the poor had given him a good working knowledge of the women involved with prostitution there, said that from his experience, 'the registered girls; they do not object to it, but they did very strongly at first'.[40]

The demeanour of women going to and from the medical examination was remarked upon by observers on both sides of the repeal debate. Much of this testimony undermines the proposition that women necessarily felt degraded and humiliated by the examination. In Chatham, for example, Frederick Wheeler himself testified to having observed 'much loud talking, laughing, and occasional screaming among themselves, and boys looked on. A number of the women, say a dozen or twenty, visited one or other of the drinking houses on the way up or down'.[41] Similar scenes were witnessed in Woolwich by William Krause, who observed women on the way to their examination 'dancing in a manner that is most disgusting'.[42] In Dover, similarly, an eyewitness described 'these "gay girls" … in parties of two and three, trooping down to the examination room dressed in all their best and generally very cleanly and smartly decked out for the occasion. Sometimes they are accompanied by male companions, who wait for them at a neighbouring public house and on re-joining them examine their papers and then march off with them'.[43] Similar incidents were witnessed in Canterbury by Ann Heritage, as women attended for examination.[44] Whilst it would be incautious to over-interpret these incidents (which might be argued to reflect little more than bravado under duress and defiance of authority echoing those discussed in Chapter 2), they nevertheless cast some doubt on the contention that the medical examination was universally experienced as brutal and degrading. It was demonstrated earlier in this study that the Kentish evidence points to heterogeneity amongst the women who were drawn into prostitution, thus eschewing overly simplistic attempts at categorization. The range of responses to the medical examination recorded by witnesses on both sides of the debate over the CD Acts reflected this heterogeneity. The diversity of women's individual circumstances in respect of age, health and degree of entrenchment into prostitution influenced their response. Caroline Wybrow was representative of those younger women caught up in the machinery of the CD Acts legislation by association. Her resistance to being examined is indicative of her individual situation, but caution should be used in using it to extrapolate more widely, given the range of privations and degree of oppression to which many of these women were already subjected.

Hospitalization

Wybrow's subsequent detention in the Chatham Lock Hospital, and her testament to having been kept on a reduced diet of bread and tea whilst there, introduces the role of government-certified lock hospitals within the CD Acts machinery into this discussion. The mandatory detention for treatment of all women who were found at the medical examination to have symptoms of venereal disease was a key component of the CD Acts' medical surveillance system, and from 1869 onwards, as has been seen, women could be detained compulsorily for up to nine months. The coercive nature of this medical regime earned the condemnation of abolitionists such as Chatham repeal activist Annie Young, who remarked 'how completely a government Lock Hospital resembles a prison'.[45] The Chatham Lock Hospital was purpose-built to accommodate 100 patients at a total cost to central government of around £10,000, and it opened its doors in 1870 for the treatment of women from the subjected districts of Chatham, Sheerness, Maidstone and Gravesend.[46] By March of that year, forty women were undergoing treatment. Previously, patients from these towns had been treated in the lock ward of St Bartholomew's Hospital in Chatham, as had voluntary patients prior to the passing of the first CD Act. With the enactment of the new legislation, the medical care of lock patients became funded by central government at the rate of thirty shillings per year per patient rather than from the local purse.[47]

The lock ward of St Bartholomew's was the site of frequent incidents of vandalism during the 1860s, which were perpetrated by patients in protest against their incarceration. Cited by the *Shield* as evidence of their opposition in principle to the CD Acts, reportage of these incidents was reproduced there in detail from the *Chatham News*. The opening of the new hospital did not bring about a cessation of these acts of protest, and the account of one such incident, the 1870 prosecution of Harriet Beasley, Rhoda Cooper, Elizabeth Cripps and Elizabeth Taylor, attracted much attention. The resulting publicity disclosed the reason for the episode, which was a difference of opinion between one of the women and the doctor as to whether she was cured and thus should be discharged. The four women broke twenty-six panes of glass in protest, to which they all pleaded guilty when charged, which earned them custodial sentences of two months each.[48]

Local sources enable the examination of these incidents over time and from a different perspective from that taken by the *Shield*. The incidents were commonplace by 1865 and generally consisted of hospital windows being broken. It is notable from the press reports in the *Chatham News* that most women did plead guilty once brought before magistrates, and many apologized to the bench on being convicted. Of a total of seventeen such incidents reported in the local press between 1865 and1870, in no case did the perpetrators ascribe their actions to a protest against the CD Acts per se. No convicted woman is reported as having voiced an objection to the law, or to the regime it introduced. Generally the protesting women cited either boredom or a difference of opinion with the doctor as to whether they were cured as reasons why they had carried out acts of vandalism. Fanny Goldsmith and Anne Crockford, for example, who pleaded guilty to breaking six panes of glass in February 1867, complained of dullness and said that they had protested because their confinement 'is very irksome' and because they needed amusement, 'something to relieve the tedium'.[49] Hospital trustees informed the court that patients had draught boards, dominos and a recreation ground, and that if they worked at shirt-making they could keep their earnings. According to a trustee representative, patients did not like the confinement and 'committed these outrages in the hope of sooner being set at liberty'. When Sarah Clarke and Sarah Boozer were convicted of breaking windows, it emerged in court that they had inflicted the damage by throwing a bible and a

prayer book, which may suggest a protest against the mandatory religious observance in which they were expected to participate whilst at the hospital.[50]

Other cases suggest that hospitalized women were initially prepared to cooperate with medical intervention because they perceived that there was a health
benefit to be had, but they generally believed themselves cured sooner than did
their medical practitioners. Emma Epps and Louisa Usher, for example, broke
nine panes of glass because they 'considered themselves fully recovered', and Matilda Anderson four panes 'because she thought she had been in the hospital long
enough'.[51] Mary Ann Turner, who broke two panes of glass, said it was because
she had wished to be discharged from hospital but the Medical Officer had
not agreed.[52] These women's cases suggest that, their primary sores having been
cured, they believed themselves free from infection. Enterprising Lydia Litchfield
adopted a less violent strategy: she simply falsified her medical records by forging
the doctor's signature in order to secure her early departure from the Lock ward.[53]
In a reflection of Caroline Wybrow's claim that she was kept to a restricted diet
in the hospital, the reason given by Fanny Smith and Sarah Cooper for breaking
four panes of glass was that they had not been adequately fed.[54]

Eventually, with hospital trustees growing increasingly frustrated with the
wave of vandalism, the court hearing of the case against Kate Parr uncovered
the loophole in the system that hospitalized patients had been exploiting. Parr
informed the bench that new inmates were advised by fellow patients that breaking windows ensured an earlier release from hospital.[55] On conviction, hospital
patients found guilty of vandalism had been sent to the county gaol at Maidstone to serve a fixed-term custodial sentence. It transpired, on investigation,
that there had been a procedural lack of communication between the gaol and
the administrators of the hospital. Instead of returning the gaoled women to
hospital to resume treatment on the completion of their fixed term sentences,
the prison authorities had been releasing them into the community. Therefore,
whereas women hospitalized for the treatment of venereal disease were required
to remain until declared free from disease by the medical officer (which could
be several months or longer to a maximum of nine months), fixed-term gaol
sentences were generally of no more than six or eight weeks' duration. Thus a
custodial sentence was in most cases of a far shorter duration than the average
period of hospitalization of venereal disease, and represented a guaranteed means
of securing an earlier overall release date. When the loophole was discovered, the
Chatham bench accordingly sent a communication to the governor of the county
gaol drawing his attention to the section of the Act of Parliament that specified
that prisoners committed from the lock hospital should be sent back on completion of their sentences. Other women appear to have taken advantage of the free
healthcare provided by the government lock hospital. Frederick Wheeler, elsewhere in his evidence before the Parliamentary Select Committee, argued that

many prostituted women believed the hospital to be a good thing. He told how, on one occasion, when he had been accosted in the street by a group of women he claimed to know were prostitutes, one of them had shouted 'That is the old — that wants to shut up the hospital', whereupon one of her companions called out after him 'If you shut up that hospital I hope you will drop down dead'.[56]

The Criminal Justice System

Caroline Wybrow's capitulation on the question of medical examination, as has been seen, was allegedly secured under threat of being sent to Maidstone Gaol, since conviction of an offence related to non-compliance with the CD Acts was punishable by a custodial sentence. Thus, the role played by the criminal justice system in the operation of the CD Acts is brought under the spotlight. The Kentish evidence, discussed earlier, of relatively high levels of compliance with the mandatory medical examination is substantiated by correspondingly low levels of prosecution for non-submission. During the sixteen years of reported operations up to 1881 when, as has been seen, a total of 173,914 medical examinations were performed, there were 1,017 prosecutions of women before Kentish magistrates for disobedience of the CD Acts.[57]

The legislation created three categories of offence, two of which are pertinent to the present discussion. The first category, described as 'non-submission to the Acts', consisted of outright non-compliance. Ninety-nine of the 1,017 Kentish cases fell into this category. Once brought before magistrates in response to this summons, in the event that this was her first appearance the defendant would be issued with an order to attend for medical examination. The second category of charge was brought against those women who, once having signed the voluntary submission form or who having previously been summoned before the court and having received a magistrate's order to be examined, subsequently failed to attend for examination. In the subjected districts of Kent, a consistently and notably higher number of prosecutions were brought for this second category of offence than for the first. This difference suggests that of the women brought before magistrates, most had complied with the law initially but had subsequently failed to attend for examination.

Imprisonment

At the discretion of magistrates, cases could be adjourned to allow women the opportunity to attend for examination if they indicated an inclination to do so at this stage, after which charges would be dropped. Alternatively, magistrates could convict and impose a custodial sentence. Relatively few prosecutions of women before magistrates in connection with the CD Acts resulted in imprisonment in Kent, despite the threat of Maidstone Gaol that was allegedly brandished at

Caroline Wybrow. Levels of custodial sentencing are difficult to measure across the whole period when the legislation was on the statute book, due to inconsistent recording practice. The information was, however, documented initially and when combined with local sources, throws some light on this question. Central government statistics show that thirty-seven of the total of 167 summonses (22 per cent) of women before Kentish magistrates for non-compliance during the twelve months ending 30 June 1871 resulted in a custodial sentence. This ratio is consistent with that for the imprisonment of twenty-two individual women in Dover between 1870 and 1881, which resulted from the prosecutions of seventy-nine women (28 per cent).[58]

Local records paint a similar picture. Forty-one out of the forty-four cases of women prosecuted before Maidstone magistrates in connection with the CD Acts between 1871 and 1876 as recorded in Metropolitan Police statistics can be traced in local petty sessions records. Of the forty-one identified summonses, fifteen (27 per cent) resulted in a custodial sentence. Ten of the cases were adjourned, eight resulted in an order for medical examination being issued, six were withdrawn, and the outcome of two is unclear from the records. Thus, it would appear to be the case that a minority of prosecutions resulted in a custodial sentence. Where cases were adjourned, evidence suggests that the most common reason was that the women declared themselves prepared to be examined once they were brought to court. The cases of Helen Holdsworth, Fanny de Vere, Jane Boorman and Emily Beech, for example, were all adjourned on 24 June 1871, though the court records do not specify a reason. The charge in each case was subsequently withdrawn at a hearing on 22 July. A similar picture is suggested by cases from other subjected districts. The summonses of three Dover women between October 1880 and August 1881 for failing to attend for medical examination, for example, were all adjourned 'to see if defendant attends'. In one of these cases, that of Mary Ann McNally, the defendant subsequently attended for medical examination, and so on 22 August 1881, according to Dover petty sessions records, the case against her was withdrawn. Of the thirteen women summoned before Dover magistrates during 1882 for CD Acts offences, the charges against eight were withdrawn because the defendant had attended for medical examination in the meantime.[59] Similarly, the case against Prudence Payton in Canterbury was adjourned for a week 'so that enquiries may be made into the truth of certain allegations as to her wish to abandon her evil courses and lead a virtuous life'.[60] Carrie Pardew of Sheerness was summoned before the magistrate in May 1878 by Inspector Charles Hallett, but the case was dismissed because she had been examined in the meantime. When she was brought back to court twelve months later, again for neglecting to submit to examination, she pleaded guilty and was sentenced to the apparently token sentence of one day with hard labour.[61]

This local evidence relating to the outcome of prosecutions before magistrates allows them to be examined from a different perspective from that of the bare statistics furnished by central government. Nominal record linkage allows the progress of individual women through the criminal justice system to be charted, and a more fully rounded understanding of the outcomes of their cases to be constructed. This picture suggests that many cases resulted in the withdrawal of charges because the women had been examined in the meantime, and again questions the thesis of women's widespread opposition to the machinery of the CD Acts in principle. The time-table of the charges brought against Fanny de Vere of Maidstone, mentioned above, suggests for example that the measures of the Acts were not always applied in the draconian fashion exemplified by the better known cases that attained public notoriety. De Vere was first brought before the bench on 1 April 1871 by Inspector William Luscombe of the Metropolitan Police, and an order made that she should attend for regular examination during the twelve months commencing 11 April. Seemingly Fanny did not attend that appointment, and so she was brought back before the bench on 6 May, at which point the hearing was adjourned for one week. She returned on 13 May when the case was further adjourned, and again on 20 May when the court heard an application by Fanny to be relieved from examination. This being refused, Fanny was finally convicted and sentenced to fourteen days. After her release, Fanny was once again summoned before the bench on 24 June, but this second charge, as has been seen, was subsequently withdrawn on 22 July.[62] The seeming lack of urgency in this schedule substantiates the claim of Mr Fraser, chaplain to Maidstone Gaol, that: 'The Acts are worked with great indulgence at Maidstone. The fortnightly examination is not strictly pressed'.[63]

The consistently high levels of compliance with requirements of the CD Acts in Kent may be explained in a number of ways. Possibly the fear imprisonment was sufficient inducement for some, as is illustrated by the case of Caroline Wybrow. Alternatively, as has been seen, some women were believed to have been coerced, bullied or tricked into attendance. Others may have complied in order to avoid a public appearance at the magistrates' court, which has been argued by some historians.[64] Each of these possibilities warrants consideration.

Fear of Imprisonment

It was seen in Chapter 5 that women convicted of offences related to prostitution, together with those women identified in court as prostitutes and convicted of unrelated offences, were subjected to an unremitting regimen of arrest and custodial sentence in the name of public respectability. In many districts, custodial sentences at the county gaol appear to have been a routine feature and regular occupational hazard in many streetwalkers' lifestyles. When considered in this wider context, the suggestion that women submitted to the medical examination imposed by the CD legislation out of a fear of imprisonment loses credence. Maria Gales of Sheerness, for example, as was mentioned previously, spent a total of twenty weeks out of fifty-two in 1872 in Maidstone Gaol, whilst Emily Huntley, also of Sheerness, spent a total of fifteen months there in the fifty-month period from November 1874 to February 1879 on seven separate charges relating to streetwalking.

In Gravesend, where more alleged prostitutes were consistently convicted under local policing than in any other location in Kent, 710 prosecutions of women on charges related to prostitution were dealt with under summary justice over an eighteen-year period. During the seventeen months between September 1873 and January 1875, a period when Metropolitan Police records and local records both show that only five prosecutions were brought for breaches of the CD legislation, thirty-five charges were brought against named women identified in court as prostitutes for alleged public order offences.[65] Similarly, Sheerness police court registers show that thirty-three women were awarded custodial sentences during the year 1876 for offences such as 'being a prostitute, rioting' or 'being a prostitute, wandering'. During the same period just one custodial sentence was imposed for neglecting to attend for medical examination. The woman concerned, Alice Robinson, served twenty-one days with hard labour, but this incident constituted but a small proportion of her contact with the Sheerness stipendiary magistrate and the criminal justice system that year. She had already served five days in March and one month in April before the prosecution under the CD Acts, and was subsequently sentenced to two months in August, all of which were for 'being a prostitute, and riotous'.[66] Lavinia Pearce, who was sentenced to fourteen days in 1871, was the only woman to receive a custodial sentence in Sheerness that year for not attending for medical examination, having previously signed the voluntary submission form. Pearce had previously served eighteen days for 'wandering and behaving riotously'.[67] The emotive *Shield* editorial that spoke of 'imprisonment for life with hard labour, in repeated doses from one to two months' and Josephine Butler's description of 'cells with grated windows and heavy doors where delicate girls are immured' omitted to mention that this was already a routine feature of many women's lifestyles, under a variety of regulatory legislative measures other than the CD Acts.[68] Of the seventy-six women admitted to Maidstone Gaol in 1883 where 'prostitute' was recorded as their occupation, only five were serving sentences for offences related to the CD Acts. The remaining seventy-one were convicted for a range of other offences, of which fifty-seven were related to the Vagrancy Act.[69]

Since Kentish streetwalkers already ran the continual risk of arrest and imprisonment, one might suppose that had they been as opposed to the internal examination as contemporary repeal activists frequently alleged, they had little to lose by defying the law and serving the appropriate custodial sentence. It would seem unlikely that the prospect of one further period in custody could have constituted a serious deterrent to women such as Selina Boswell, for example, who was arrested on five different occasions in eighteen months and sentenced on each occasion to up to month in custody, or to Ellen Bannister, who experienced three separate spells in the county gaol in a single year in 1870 for soliciting and being drunk. Nor to Ann Whiting of Folkestone, who when brought before magistrates for refusing to comply with the CD Acts, had 'recently on several occasions occupied the attention of the bench', according to the local press.[70] Had opposition and hostility to the legislation been widespread, the documentary evidence might be expected to record a far higher number of custodial sentences for non-compliance than was the case. There were none at all for offences against the CD Acts in Gravesend in 1870, which suggests that Boswell and Bannister, together with the majority of other registered women, all submitted to regular examination as required that year. Fanny Pearce, one of only three Gravesend women to be summoned for non-compliance in 1873, was no stranger to the court when she was sentenced by magistrates to fourteen days' imprisonment with hard labour for neglecting to attend for medical examination.[71] Pearce had been prosecuted on seven previous occasions in both Gravesend and in Sheerness on charges of a variety of non-indictable offences and had served numerous custodial sentences, including two of one month each, both for 'being a prostitute, wandering' and behaving in a 'riotous' manner.[72] Mary Ann Ridley, likewise, who served fourteen days for non-submission in 1873, had previously experienced imprisonment more than once, one of which occasions consisted of a three-month sentence.

When fully contextualized in this way, the imprisonment of women convicted for offences related to the CD Acts appear to have represented not so much an exceptional trauma but part of a much wider experience of sustained policing, surveillance and control, the majority of which was carried out with reference to other legislation. Moreover, the evidence relating to the serial imprisonment of women for public order offences such as soliciting and drunkenness, as was discussed in the previous chapter, suggests that custodial sentences did not necessarily represent a deterrent. As was also seen, many streetwalkers, together with other women of the casual poor, appear to have faced imprisonment with indifference and resignation, and many re-offended within a very short time of release.

Considered in context, therefore, fear of imprisonment alone seems an unlikely motive for wide-scale cooperation with the system. Whilst Frederick Wheeler, with whom this chapter opened, published the claim that 'Hundreds of terrified girls have signed this crafty form under the threat and terror of imprisonment', he was unable to substantiate it. The allegation was widely distributed in a leaflet called *An Authenticated and Shocking Illustration of the Working of the Contagious Diseases Acts*, but when challenged by members of the Parliamentary Select Committee to evidence his assertion, Wheeler was forced to admit that he had none. He was able to cite one case (that of Caroline Wybrow) rather than one hundred. However, the leaflet had already been widely circulated between 1876 and 1882, so that by the time the claim was shown to be unfounded, it had become a central piece of received wisdom in abolitionist discourse.[73]

It was seen in the Wybrow case that one of the key points of evidence was her allegation that she had been coerced into signing a form that she did not understand: '[he] filled up a printed paper and told me to sign it. He did not read it or explain its meaning. I did not know what it meant, but I put my mark to it as he told me'. This claim reflects one of the key charges made by repeal activists that lies, bullying and trickery on the part of police officers were routinely used to intimidate women into submitting to medical examination and to sign the voluntary submission form. The lawyer engaged by repeal activists to defend women prosecuted as prostitutes in Canterbury against charges of non-compliance, for example, told magistrates that the women to whom the CD Acts applied were 'of a very ignorant class and ... they signed the voluntary submission form without knowing what it said'. In a similar vein, Canterbury repeal activist Ann Heritage claimed that prostitutes had no idea what was meant by 'examination' when they signed the voluntary submission form. She told the 1871 Royal Commission that 'they thought the doctor would ask them a few questions. They did not know what they signed'.

Since these alleged incidents were on most occasions a matter of one person's word against that of another, it is difficult from the surviving evidence to evaluate the validity of the claims. However, coercion and trickery do not explain the consistently high rates of regular attendance for medical examination revealed by the statistics. Ann Heritage contended that regular pressure to attend was exerted, but that it was done by brothel-keepers 'who wish to stand well with the authorities' and were responsible for 'urging' prostitutes to attend for examination.

Avoidance of Public Appearance at the Magistrates' Court

The suggestion that large numbers of women underwent the alleged ordeal of medical examination to avoid a public appearance at the magistrates' court and consequent public identification as 'common prostitute', as suggested by historians Judith Walkowitz and Jeffrey Weeks, is somewhat at variance with the evidence from Kent.[74]

It has been seen already that women branded as prostitutes were most often brought before magistrates in connection with offences unconnected to the CD Acts. When a named prostitute was prosecuted in petty sessions, this identification was routinely made in court, no matter how unrelated it may have been to the alleged offence. It was then invariably repeated when the case was reported in the press. Women identified as prostitutes were publicly named as such when charged with offences not immediately related to their occupation or to the CD Acts, such as petty theft, drunkenness or petty vandalism. A comparison between police court records and newspaper reports for Sheerness in 1870, for example, suggests that in every case where a recognized prostitute was prosecuted before the stipendiary magistrate charged with a minor public order offence, this identification was mentioned in court. This was then repeated in the subsequent press report. The police court register entry for 1 February, for example, notes that Julia Gorman was 'convicted of being an idle and disorderly person, in that she, at Sheerness on 29 January 1870 then being a prostitute wandering in High Street Blue Town, did behave in a riotous manner'. The report of this incident, carried in the *Sheerness Times and General Advertiser* a couple of days later, notes that Julia Gorman was convicted of 'wandering abroad and behaving in a riotous manner, *she being a prostitute*' (my italics). The press reporter's phraseology so closely matches that used in the official minutes that it suggests that he was repeating, almost verbatim, the wording used in the public courtroom.[75] Women recognized as prostitutes were publicly identified as such, even during the hearing of cases in which they were the victim rather than the defendant. Thus when Thomas Simmonds, for example, was charged with stealing money from Charlotte Smith, the local newspaper reported the case describing Charlotte euphemistically as a 'nymph of the pave', albeit that she was the prosecutor in the case.[76]

In contrast, provision was made for CD Acts cases to be heard in private with the press refused entry, ostensibly to protect the woman's privacy. In theory the woman had the right to request the admittance of the press. It was in fact repeal campaigners who argued the case for public trials, as evidenced by an exchange of views on the subject in the columns of the *Maidstone Telegraph*. An un-named female correspondent, evidently with repeal sympathies and signing herself 'mother of a family', wrote to request that the editor 'diffuse the information that the class of women brought before them (the magistrates) *have a right to demand a public trial* [original emphasis] and that any one of them can be provided with counsel free of cost'.[77] There are no recorded incidences of a similar offer of free counsel being advanced to the same women who faced repeated prosecution for 'wandering', 'obstructing the path', soliciting and the broad range of charges discussed in the previous chapter.

The acts of disobedience and resistance to the CD legislation perpetrated by women identified as prostitutes have generally been interpreted through a lens of female agency, whilst cooperation and compliance have been seen as indicative of repression, exploitation and victimization. An alternative reading, as suggested by the Kentish evidence, is equally valid. The women identified by this study as having been drawn into prostitution in the Kentish ports and dockyards at this period were women of the labouring poor who employed a range of survival strategies within makeshift economies in order to subsist. In this context, the level of cooperation with the CD Acts uncovered from the Kentish evidence reflects marginal practice and negotiation of the system for personal ends as much as it does repression and exploitation. If it is possible to read a woman's initial move into prostitution as a 'rational choice, given the set of unpleasant alternatives' as Judith Walkowitz has done, then the same must hold true for compliance with the CD Acts in the furtherance of individual best interests.

Advantages of the Acts

The final possibility is that many women became registered as prostitutes and complied with the requirement for medical examination because it represented for them, in the context of the rest of their lives, less an exceptional trauma than one further hurdle to be negotiated in the pursuance of opportunistic survival strategies, such as were discussed in Chapter 1. The claim made by the *Lancet* in 1867 that 'the women readily acquiesce in the arrangement which they seem to understand is intended for their benefit' represented the dominant discourse of the medical profession and undoubtedly represented a gross over-statement of the case.[78]

Others appear to have actively welcomed the Acts for a combination of reasons and complied because they perceived that there was a material advantage to be had in doing so. The legislation provided for free medical treatment, and furthermore women's earning capacity from prostitution was enhanced by the infection-free status it conferred. Moreover, in some quarters the law was seen as having bestowed a measure of validation on women who had hitherto been regarded as members of the criminal classes. The *Shield* in December 1871 commented regrettably that prostitutes leaving the examination room at Canterbury had been heard to comment in relation to the examining surgeon that 'he is our servant, paid to wait upon us ... Government pays them to wait upon us!', which lends weight to the hypothesis that some women felt that their lifestyle was legitimated by the Acts.[79] Josephine Butler commented disappointedly that 'They call themselves "Queen's Women". They walk in silks and satins and assume an arrogant manner. When warned of the sin in which they are living by one of the National Association agents, they answer: "Oh, it's quite different now. We don't need to be ashamed".[80]

The suggestion that the CD Acts may have been viewed positively by some women is supported by anecdotal evidence from a number of local contemporary sources. Mr Krause, the missionary in Woolwich, claimed that prostitutes in his district called themselves 'Government girls', and considered themselves a 'privileged class'. 'They say the government ought to take care of them when they are ill and not suffer them to go on the parish', which had, as was seen in Chapter 1, been the case previously.[81] This testimony suggests that some women responded positively to the legislation for the same reasons that the LNA opposed it, namely because it legitimized prostitutes' status and conferred on them a novel sense of quasi-respectability. The LNA dismissed the evidence that some prostitutes responded positively to the Acts as a sign of deviance: 'This is simply another illustration of the fact that the more degraded of these women have learned to regard themselves as under the paternal care of the government as "Queen's Women" even as soldiers are "Queen's Men"'.[82]

Aside from the testimony of contemporary observers in the subjected districts, most of whom, as has been seen, were strongly partisan, the nearest evidence that remains of prostitutes' own attitudes to the CD Acts consists of the eleven petitions presented to Parliament in favour of the retention of the Acts from prostitutes in the subjected districts during the eleven years from 1871 to 1881.[83] These carried the signatures of a total of 1,233 'Fallen Women'. No evidence has been found to indicate whether any of the petitions originated in Kent; others came from Windsor and Plymouth, and one, presented in 1872, was signed by forty-eight prostitutes in Colchester, Essex. This was to the effect that 'the total repeal of the Acts would be a great calamity to themselves, and that it would be a terrible misfortune to the country at large'. These petitions have been called 'The most original use of femininity in the defence of the Acts', and they were roundly denounced in the pages of the *Shield*, their authenticity being called into question.[84] In response, John Henry Strange, overseer of Clewer parish near Windsor, site of a penitentiary for fallen women, wrote a letter to the *Shield* strongly refuting the accusation that the petition was a fake and attesting to its authenticity.[85]

Some registered women used the infection-free status bestowed upon them by their compliance, specifically the regular medical examination, as a marketing device. Edward Swales, examining surgeon at Sheerness, for example, told the Parliamentary Select Committee in 1869 that: 'I have often thought that they might use it (the medical certificate) as a clean bill of health'.[86] Similarly Richard Hanson, army scripture reader at Woolwich, reported that he had heard women calling out to each other after the examination 'I am alright today; I am clean today'.[87] Likewise Sarah Guest, Gravesend repeal supporter, observed the same effect at work in that town. 'Young women', she complained, 'with fine hats and gaudy feathers, flaunt up to every young man they meet, declaring the testimony of the medical examiner as reason why he may with impunity become the companion of a harlot'.[88] Ann Heritage, as has been seen, claimed to have seen men and boys loitering about the examination place in Canterbury, 'the girls would show them their papers and tell them they were free for another fortnight'.[89] Josephine Butler herself reported to have observed prostitutes in a public house in Chatham with their medical certificates pinned to their dresses by way of advertising their healthy status. 'The piece of paper signed by the surgeon, which each woman receives on leaving the examination house, is indeed a prize to a shameless woman'.[90]

Evidence suggests that one consequence of the operation of the CD Acts was that infection-free registered women acquired a larger share of the prostitution trade. Metropolitan Police statistics demonstrate that following an initial increase, numbers of registered prostitutes in the subjected districts declined over the lifetime of the Acts as a result of prostitutes leaving the district, becoming hospitalized or abandoning prostitution as a way of life. In the absence of any evidence that the opportunities for prostitution diminished accordingly, it must be concluded that the women who remained and were declared to be free from infection made a better living as a result. William Krause, town missionary with twelve years' experience in Woolwich, gave evidence to this effect, saying that registered women had no need to solicit on the streets, and claimed: 'I have heard of one woman who would boast that she had twenty four men in one night, and she boasted of this number in the open street'.[91] It was observed by some contemporary witnesses in the subjected districts that recognized prostitutes seemed better groomed and dressed since the introduction of the Acts, thus suggesting an improved standard of living. One such was Frederick Wheeler himself, who attested to the fact that 'they have more money and better dress'.[92] Clearly, therefore, some women appear to have taken advantage of the material benefits to be had by conforming to the requirements of the CD Acts in the pursuit of individual survival strategies.

Repeal Agitation

Of all the prosecutions of women for non-compliance, 824 (81 per cent) occurred during the first five years following the enactment of the final (1869) amendment to the CD legislation, when opposition to the Acts was strongest and levels of repeal activism at their height in most areas. Taken together with the pattern of initial compliance followed by subsequent disobedience that is revealed by the Kentish statistics, this evidence raises the question of to what degree repeal activism was a factor in stimulating disobedience.

As has been seen, active opposition to the CD legislation was mobilized following the enactment of the 1969 amendment, as awareness of its implications increased. Whilst feelings ran extremely high amongst opponents at a national level, active local repeal associations were formed in only four of the ten Kentish subjected districts, namely Canterbury, Dover, Maidstone and Chatham.[93] This is consistent with the wider pattern of repeal support in the subjected districts which was generally not strong, but which, where it did exist, was enthusiastic, vigorous, but often heavily reliant on the efforts and energies of a small number of activists.[94] Well-attended public meetings which produced the desired outcome were widely reported by the abolitionist publicity machine, but many others reflected apathy at best and at worst hostility. Of two meetings held in Deal, for example, the first, according to an observer, was fairly well attended but 'there did not seem any inclination to support the repeal', whilst the second 'was an utter failure'.[95]

The abolitionist movement aimed to mobilize public opinion against the Acts through a variety of strategies including local elections, lobbying, parliamentary debates, the press and other printed media. In addition, the National Association and LNA both employed a band of salaried agents who travelled the country visiting ministers and mustering support. At a local level, evidence suggests that repeal effort was largely aimed at encouraging women not to cooperate with the CD Acts system, since it was seen as obstructive of rescue and reform efforts.

In Canterbury, a repeal association was established within six months of a meeting convened in April 1870 at the Guildhall for the purpose of protesting against the Acts, during which a resolution to petition Parliament for repeal was carried. A subsequent letter published in the local press complained at the way in which the resolution, 'cut and dried for the purpose', had been carried at a meeting where 'about ninety people only are present out of an adult population of about 18,000 and sent up for presentation to the House of Commons in the name of the citizens'.[96] Nevertheless, in spite of a critical local press, the association was founded and Rev. A. W. and Mrs Ann Heritage appointed as its secretaries. Heritage's objections to the Acts were founded on, as he saw it, their immoral sanction of vice, their interference with individual liberty, and their obstruction of 'the rights of local self-government'. During the course of one public speech in 1870, Heritage urged prostitutes to resist the Acts and 'go to prison rather than submit'. That year, fifty-three prosecutions were brought against Canterbury women for non-compliance. This figure includes both those who refused to comply with the system from the outset, together with those who failed to attend for examination, having previously signed the voluntary submission form or having received a magistrate's order to do so. In the twelve months to June 1871, thirteen Canterbury women served custodial sentences for 'refusing to attend' and 'absenting themselves from' medical examination, including two who served more than one term each.[97] According to the chaplain to Maidstone Gaol, nineteen (59 per cent) of the total number of thirty-one female inmates in the county gaol for non-compliance as at March 1871 were from Canterbury.[98]

Canterbury activists supplemented their public speeches by encouraging women to break the law and risk imprisonment. Female association members personally visited brothels and other houses where prostitution was practised and, according to the evidence of one young woman, told them that they 'hoped *all* the girls in the house would be of one mind and not go up anymore to be examined'.[99] The chaplain to Maidstone Gaol claimed to have been told by prison inmates that 'there were ladies who go into their houses and advise them not to obey the law, and tell them that they will be supported in their resistance of the law, and that they have only got to club together, and in time the Act of Parliament will be altered'. Fraser said that in the course of his religious ministry amongst the prisoners at Maidstone, he made a point of asking the women sentenced for non-submission to the CD Acts as to why they had refused to be examined: 'I have enquired of every one of them without exception. The Canterbury girls, I may say without exception, answer that they have been put up to it'.[100] It is likely that Ann Heritage was one of the ladies in question, since she admitted to 'visiting girls' for the purpose of sending them to a refuge. Mrs Heritage claimed that brothel-keepers tried to prevent her from getting access to women to carry out her rescue work.[101] Although Ann Heritage denied that she and the 'ladies of the committee' were responsible for encouraging Canterbury prostitutes to break the law, Fraser's account corresponds to the evidence of the statistics relating to non-submission.[102] Of the fifty-three summonses of Canterbury prostitutes before the magistrates for non-compliance in 1870, thirty-eight (72 per cent) were cases where the woman in question had previously either signed a voluntary submission form or had been given a magistrate's order. Fraser's evidence, as given to the Royal Commission, coincides with that of the prison governor who wrote a long letter to the same effect to the *Kentish Gazette*. He claimed to have spoken to one young prostitute from Canterbury on the occasion of her release from gaol, who told him that 'she had been examined fortnightly since the law first came into force, and had never objected until she was persuaded by the lady to do so'.[103]

In the case of women who had already been convicted and imprisoned for non-compliance, Canterbury activists met them at the doors of Maidstone Gaol on the day they were released, and, according to the prison governor, would 'extort from her, if possible, the statement that she refused to be examined from modesty'.[104] The governor claimed that repeal activists on occasion 'have actually induced girls to break the law and suffer imprisonment in order that they may be able to make use of their cases to favour the cause of their petition'.[105] Ann Heritage again denied this accusation, though she did not deny being active in visiting prostitutes in brothels in connection with her rescue work, and in placing those who 'wished to return to a virtuous life' in permanent homes, in at least one case actually paying herself for the girl's board in the meantime whilst arrangements were being made.[106]

Having encouraged women to non-compliance, the next stage in repeal campaign strategy was to provide the women with free legal representation when they appeared before magistrates. Examples include the Canterbury cases of Sarah Waters, Jane Boodle and Eliza Bing in April 1870.[107] Thus, the Canterbury evidence points to a direct correlation between repeal activism and levels of non-compliance, in which sustained action during the first year of the operation of the Acts resulted in a high number of prosecutions. This pattern of resistance was not sustained, however. Rev. Heritage died in March 1871, before the CD Acts had been in operation a full year in the city. During the following recorded year the number of summonses in Canterbury dropped dramatically from fifty-three to two, in a year when 64 per cent more (747) examinations were performed.[108] Thereafter, aside from small increases in 1872 and 1873, the number of summonses remained very low for the remaining years of operation. Thus, of the seventy-five Canterbury prosecutions for non-compliance over a twelve-year period, fifty-three (71 per cent) occurred within the first year of operations, following which the total was never higher than eight in a single year.

In contrast, in Gravesend, which had a similar total population size and where the number of women registered as prostitutes was comparable to that in Canterbury, there was little appetite for sustained repeal activism, despite the Liberal MP Sir Charles Wingfield's stated preference for a voluntary system of regulation rather than a mandatory one.[109] Public meetings had mixed results and demonstrated a large degree of ambivalence, if not outright apathy, amongst the local residents. In 1868, two years prior to Gravesend's having been made a subjected district, a public meeting had passed a resolution in favour of the extension of the Acts, at which Lord Darnley, the local landowner, and the mayor had both supported the motion.[110] Two years later, following the commencement of operations, two separate meetings passed resolutions in favour of repeal, one of these being a meeting of women at which Josephine Butler spoke. The chief supporters of repeal activity in Gravesend were the Revd. William Guest, the minister of the Congregational Church, and his wife Sarah. Guest was active in a wide variety of religious activities and charitable causes, including being the driving force behind a project to build a new Congregational Church. He sat on the School Board, gave public lectures on the Old Testament, was vice president of directors of the London Missionary Society, and an associate of the Philosophical Society of Great Britain.[111] This breadth of interests and busy schedule may explain why, having given 'an able and most eloquent speech' in favour of repeal in 1870, Guest was not present and therefore unable to lend his support at a subsequent meeting only three years later, which had a conspicuously different outcome.[112]

On this occasion in January 1873, a deputation was sent to Gravesend by the National Association for the Repeal of the Contagious Diseases Acts to attend the meeting which attracted upwards of five hundred people. The press reporter dryly commented that 'the usual prevailing element in Gravesend public meetings was by no means wanting, the roughs mustering in strong force'.[113] Before long, showers of peas were being thrown about, two pigeons were released to fly about the hall and fireworks were set off, filling the room with smoke and sulphur.

Amidst the resulting mayhem, Mr W. Newman, who had held public office as borough treasurer and who was indignant that no Gravesend resident had been invited by the organizers to sit on the platform, proposed that Robert Sowter, a local businessman, should take the chair. The initiative having been seized away from the organizers from out of town, Newman offended Association officials by accusing them of being 'paid agents', and proposed a motion calling for the continuation of the Acts. This motion was carried amidst the general uproar, and the meeting broke up, according to the *Reporter*, 'in the most admired disorder'.[114] In a letter to the local press following the incident, Frederick Banks, the secretary to the National Association for Repeal, made the unsubstantiated claim that the 'ruffians' who had disrupted the meeting had been 'hired' to do so by the Association's opponents and attributed the meeting's passing of a resolution in favour of the Acts to the audience having been 'carried away by excitement or political feeling'.[115] By June 1880, when another Gravesend meeting was held at the Town Hall to hear a speaker condemn the Acts, organizers were able only to attract 'a very thin attendance including only a few ladies'. On this occasion the speaker, Miss Jessie Craigen, an LNA agent, took the opportunity whilst she held the platform 'of advocating the right of women to the Parliamentary franchise'.[116]

The outcomes of public meetings in Gravesend over a twelve-year period therefore suggest that there was no sustained public feeling against the CD Acts. Sporadic expressions of opposition were instigated by repeal activists from outside the town, and interspersed with occasions that had a very different outcome. Consequently, there were no prosecutions at all for non-compliance in Gravesend in either of the first two years of operations, when 1,860 examinations were carried out. There were no more than four prosecutions in any one single year (1875), and a total of only eighteen across the whole twelve-year period. The inference that levels of non-submission were linked to repeal activity, specifically in the light of the drop in levels of disobedience over time, was substantiated by the evidence of William Shaen, chairman of the National Association for the Repeal of the CD Acts, in a statement made to the Parliamentary Select Committee in 1881. 'In the early days', he explained, 'we rather searched for cases in order to ascertain the working of the Acts; of late years we have ceased to do that, and have only gone into cases that have been forced on our attention'.[117]

Elsewhere, levels of non-compliance varied widely from one subjected district to the next. In Sheerness, 11,520 medical examinations were carried out on an average yearly total of forty-three women registered as prostitutes over the seventeen-year period between 1865 and 1881. There was no active local repeal association during this time, and only nine summonses for negligence to attend for examination. Edward Swales, the Sheerness surgeon, gave evidence to the Parliamentary Select Committee in 1869 to the effect that in his experience prostitutes had initially looked upon the Act 'as a punishment' but had subsequently came to 'believe that it is for their own good'.[118] Whilst Swales's professional allegiance is likely to account for a good deal of partiality in his opinion, the fact that his testimony is supported by the statistics on medical examinations lends it some weight. In Chatham, 53,439 examinations were performed on a yearly average of 205 registered prostitutes, during which time there was a total of only forty-eight prosecutions for non-compliance.[119] In Dover, which saw 12,283 examinations and a relatively high figure of seventy-nine prosecutions for non-compliance, there was an active local repeal association, led by the Wesleyan alderman Rowland Rees, who has already been mentioned. The volume of signatures on petitions presented to Parliament for repeal, which were the third highest of all the subjected districts, suggests strongly that in Dover also there was a direct correlation between non-compliance and repeal agitation.[120]

Epilogue and Conclusion

Following the notorious events of early 1875, Caroline Wybrow married John Dunster, a soldier. The subsequent birthplaces of their children indicate that the couple moved frequently with Dunster's regiment (the seventy-sixth) between Dover, Aldershot, Shorncliffe and Ireland. By 1881 the family had returned to Chatham and were living once again at 7 Seaton Court, the scene of Caroline's alleged downfall. Rachel Wybrow, Caroline's mother, and prostitutes Elizabeth Coppin, Alice Gilbert and Kate Simmonds were all still living at the same address. This fact may have been the cause of Judge Advocate General Osborne Morgan's allegation, made during a Parliamentary debate, that Caroline Wybrow 'was now keeping a house of convenience at Chatham'.[121] John Dunster died in 1889 at the age of thirty-five, and the following year the couple's fifth child was born posthumously. The family remained in Chatham.

The Wybrow case has brought the workings of the machinery of the CD Acts at a local level into sharper focus, leading to a somewhat revised reading. The Kentish evidence suggests that for the most part the policing of the Acts was not carried out with excessive zeal nor brutality, but by a small number of officers with heavy workloads who adhered to administrative procedure and worked in collaboration with local police forces. Furthermore, there was a substantial level of cooperation with the requirements of the law on the part of women who lived by and on the margins of prostitution, suggesting that levels of defiance and disobedience experienced elsewhere were not matched in Kent. These findings enable a challenge to be made to the standard narrative of the Acts based on the experience of Plymouth and Southampton. It was seen in earlier chapters that the women who were drawn into prostitution in Kent were not a homogenous group, and responses to the CD legislation appear to have been governed by individual circumstances. Women's cooperation with the CD Acts as part of individual strategies of survival can therefore legitimately be interpreted through a lens of agency and marginalized practice, as much as through one of repression and victimization.

AFTERWORD

The CD Acts were suspended in 1883 and removed from the British statute book in 1886, though they remained in force across the British Empire. Britain's experiment with the state regulation of prostitution was briefly revisited during the First World War under the auspices of the Defence of the Realm Act, when women's deviant sexuality and the threat it was seen to pose to the military were brought together once again under the spotlight. The wider surveillance and policing of prostitution and the legislative framework upon which it rests, which has received attention from a number of historians, has come under periodic amendment in line with fluctuating political and social circumstances.[1] The discourses surrounding prostitution, too, have shifted in line with intervening wider cultural change.

Many of the themes and questions thrown up by nineteenth-century debates on prostitution do, however, remain evident in current public discussion and official policy making. In particular, the extent to which prostitution should be made subject to legislation continues to stir substantial controversy. The British government's 2006 policy document *A Coordinated Prostitution Strategy*, for example, called for a more proactive policing approach to 'commercial sexual exploitation'.[2] Proposing the increased regulation of prostitution and the criminalization of prostitutes' clients, it placed emphasis on providing women with exit routes from the lifestyle. Employing a discourse of victimization reminiscent of the nineteenth-century writers with whom this study began, it talked of 'exploitation and violence, serious drug addiction and poor health'. Thus, debates about the regulation of prostitution continue to be characterized by the victim/agent dichotomy that preoccupied nineteenth-century thinking.

Reaction to the proposals ranged widely. Joan Smith, writing in the *Independent*, made the comparison with the 1860s in representing liberal and feminist opinion, observing that 'misogyny is the theory, paying for sex the practice'.[3] The Rights of Women organization similarly welcomed the government's initiative and its acknowledgement that 'prostitution is a form of exploitation requiring a wide-ranging co-ordinated approach'.[4] The Scottish Prostitutes' Education Project by contrast responded by asserting that 'Banning the buying of sex on the grounds that prostitution is violence towards women, is invalid – this is fundamentalist feminist propaganda and untrue.'[5] The English Collective of Prostitutes, arguing for decriminalization in the best interests of the health and safety of working prostitutes, argued for the freedom for women to make choices regarding their own sexuality.

Twenty-first-century media offers a platform to those on all sides of the current debate. The voice of the nineteenth-century women who have been the subject of this study, by contrast, remains silent. How these women experienced the various regimes of surveillance and policing imposed upon them remains largely unknown, since what little record survives has been mediated through the discourses of those doing the recording. The ultimate success of the campaign for the repeal of the CD Acts, albeit that this was achieved only after what has been described as a 'long and often demoralizing slog', secured for the movement a deep and lasting influence on the historical record.[6] The movement left behind it by way of legacy a wealth of evidential material that has provided rich pickings for scholars, thus ensuring a permanent place for the voice of repeal activism and for narratives of the CD Acts in the history of prostitution in the period. The extent and scope of the policing of nineteenth-century prostitution before and alongside of the CD Acts, though it has received less attention in the historical literature, is recorded in the documentation of the developing criminal justice system. This, too, is highly coloured by the preoccupations and ideology of the period; Victorian positivist confidence in the power of science and statistics classified transgressors into neat and rigid categories that belied the complexities of life at the margins.

This study has taken a bottom-up approach to the evaluation of these complexities, one that has considered the material conditions amidst which women lived and practised prostitution as well as the multiple strands of the regimes of surveillance and policing to which they were subjected. It has attempted, as far as is possible, to see beyond the crude stereotypes created by Victorian ideology and perpetuated in the written record, to the diversity and multifariousness of human experience. In particular, it has sought to restore agency to those who are more usually portrayed through lenses either of victimization or of one-dimensional deviance, the 'sufferers' and the 'shameless women' of the extracts with which this study opened. The women identified by this study appear, as far as the evidence shows, to have marshalled a variety of responses to the regimes of regulation and control imposed upon them, from cooperation for personal advantage, to public defiance and bravado. Rather than view these different reactions as conflicting, they are more helpfully seen as different points on a continuum of marginalized practice.

It seems fitting, therefore, to close with the words of Catherine Rawlinson, who was brought before the Gravesend bench, described in court by PC Flinn as a prostitute, and charged with being drunk and riotous. In the nearest we have to a verbatim account of Rawlinson's words, she is recorded as having declared to the bench and assembled witnesses that the 'constable's evidence was all lies', and the 'only bit that was true was that she was drunk'.[7]

NOTES

Introduction

1. Letter to the Editor, *Folkestone Chronicle*, 26 November 1870.
2. 'Annual Meeting of the Friends of the Chatham House of Refuge', *Chatham News*, 1 March 1873.
3. Letter to the Editor, *Sheerness Guardian*, 20 May 1865; Letter to the Editor, *Kentish Gazette*, 9 May 1871.
4. *Dover Express and East Kent Intelligence* (hereafter *Dover Express*), 10 June 1870, p. 2.
5. 'The Social Evil: The House of Refuge', *Chatham News*, 17 March 1860.
6. Letter to the Editor, *Gravesend and Dartford Reporter*, 9 April 1864.
7. J. Harsin, *Policing Prostitution in Nineteenth-Century Paris* (Princeton, NJ: Princeton University Press, 1985).
8. Ibid., p. 59.
9. W. Acton, *Prostitution*, ed. P. Fryer (1857; London: Macgibbon & Kee, 1968).
10. P. Fryer, introduction to Acton, *Prostitution*, p. 12.
11. Logan, W. *The Great Social Evil: Its Causes, Extent, Results and Remedies* (London: Hodder and Stoughton, 1871), cited in E. Trudgill, *Madonnas and Magdalens: The Origins and Development of Victorian Sexual Attitudes* (London: Heinemann, 1976), p. 103.
12. W. R. Greg, 'Prostitution', *Westminster Review*, 53 (July 1850), pp. 238–68, on p. 241.
13. Ibid., p. 243.
14. Ibid., p. 261.
15. Trudgill, *Madonnas and Magdalens*, p. 277.
16. T. Henderson, *Disorderly Women in Eighteenth-Century London: Prostitution and Control in the Metropolis 1730–1830* (London: Pearson Education, 1999), p. 189.
17. See, for example, J. R. Walkowitz, *Prostitution and Victorian Society: Women, Class and the State* (Cambridge: Cambridge University Press, 1980), and F. Finnegan, *Poverty and Prostitution: A Study of Victorian Prostitutes in York* (Cambridge: Cambridge University Press, 1979).
18. 'Dover Home for Young Women', *Dover Express*, 26 July 1872; Letter to the Editor, *Sheerness Guardian*, 15 July 1865; J. K. A. Banks, 'Warning to Unfortunate Loiterers', *History of Dover*, at http://www.doverhistory.co.uk/warning-to-unfortunate-loiterers.html [accessed 30 May 2012].
19. 'Police Intelligence', *Chatham News*, 11 February 1865.
20. *Chatham News*, 24 September 1864.
21. P. Howell, *Geographies of Regulation: Policing Prostitution in Nineteenth-Century Britain and the Empire* (Cambridge: Cambridge University Press, 2009), p. 12.

22. Report from the Select Committee on the Administration and Operation of the Contagious Diseases Acts *PP* 1882 (340) IX (hereafter Select Committee 1882).

23. Report from the Select Committee on the Administration and Operation of the Contagious Diseases Act *PP* 1866 (306.1) VII.1 (hereafter Select Committee 1866), p. 57.

24. For example, *Shield*, 7 March 1870, p. 1.

25. 'The Contagious Diseases Act', *Chatham News*, 29 February 1868.

26. Editorial, *Gravesend and Dartford Reporter*, 29 January 1870.

27. Letter to the Editor, *Kentish Gazette*, 3 May 1870.

28. 'Dover Town Council', *Dover Express*, 17 June 1870, p. 3.

29. *Pike's Blue Book and Dover Directory* (Brighton: Robinson, Son and Pike, 1888–9), no pagination.

30. 'The Contagious Diseases Act Agitation', *Dover Express*, 27 May 1870, p. 4.

31. See P. McHugh, *Prostitution and Victorian Social Reform* (London: Croom Helm, 1980), p. 135.

32. 'The Contagious Diseases Acts', *Gravesend and Dartford Reporter*, 9 July 1870; Editorial, *Kentish Gazette*, 15 February 1870.

33. Editorial, *Dover Express*, 11 February 1870.

34. R. D. Storch, 'The Plague of Blue Locusts: Police Reform and Popular Resistance in Northern England, 1840–57', *International Review of Social History*, 20 (1975), pp. 61–90, on p. 61.

35. C. Emsley, *The English Police: A Political and Social History* (Harlow: Longman, 1991), p. 77.

36. *Gravesend and Dartford Reporter*, 14 June 1856.

37. L. Mahood, *The Magdalenes: Prostitution in the Nineteenth Century* (London: Routledge, 1990), p. 13.

38. H. J. Self, *Prostitution, Women and Misuse of the Law: The Fallen Daughters of Eve* (London: Frank Cass, 2003), p. 12.

39. For example, the testimony given to the 1882 Select Committee by PC Thomas Cogger indicates that women were not considered to be prostitutes if they were cohabiting with one man.

40. J. Bindel, 'A Heroine for Our Age', *Guardian*, 21 September 2006, G2.

1 Prostitution, Poverty and the Makeshift Economy

1. 'Police Intelligence', *Chatham News*, 22 June 1861. Hereafter, all references to the *Chatham News, Gravesend and Dartford Reporter, Dover Express, Maidstone Telegraph, Sheerness Guardian* and *Kentish Gazette* are to the reports of petty sessions hearings, unless specified otherwise. These are variously entitled 'Police Intelligence', 'Police Court' and 'Petty Sessions'.

2. *Maidstone Telegraph, Rochester and Chatham Gazette*, 14 June 1862.

3. *Chatham News*, 28 May 1870.

4. *Gravesend and Dartford Reporter*, 20 April 1872.

5. Acton, *Prostitution*, p. 129.

6. J. Butler, *The Education and Employment of Women* (Liverpool: T. Brakell, 1868), p. 16.

7. 'The Social Evil in Gravesend', Letter to the Editor, *Gravesend and Dartford Reporter*, 9 April 1864.

8. See, for example, C. Emsley, *Crime and Society in England 1750–1900* (Harlow: Longman, 1996), pp. 21–56.
9. Returns of Judicial Statistics of England and Wales, *PP* 1859 (2508) XXVI, pp. viii–ix.
10. 'Dover Home for Young Women', *Dover Express*, 26 July 1872.
11. S. King and A. Tomkins, *The Poor in England 1700–1850: An Economy of Makeshifts* (Manchester: Manchester University Press, 2003), p. 1.
12. See, for example, Walkowitz, *Prostitution and Victorian Society*.
13. Ibid., p. 32.
14. See, for example, M. Luddy, 'Abandoned Women and Bad Characters: Prostitution in Nineteenth-Century Ireland', *Women's History Review*, 6:4 (1997), pp. 485–504, on p. 493; Henderson, *Disorderly Women*, p. 16.
15. See, for example, Finnegan, *Poverty and Prostitution*, and Walkowitz, *Prostitution and Victorian Society*.
16. S. O. Rose, 'Gender at Work: Sex, Class and Industrial Capitalism', *History Workshop Journal*, 21 (1986), pp. 113–31, on p. 115.
17. 1871 Census of England and Wales, Volume III *(Population Abstracts; Age, Civil Condition, Occupations, and Birth-Places)*, *PP* 1873 (c.872) LXXI (hereafter 1871 Census, Volume III,), pp. xxxix, xiv, 66, 69.
18. *Maidstone and Kentish Journal*, 2 September 1871.
19. J. Y. Stratton, *Hops and Hop-Pickers* (London, 1883), p. 57.
20. T. Richardson, 'Labour', in A. Armstrong (ed.), *The Economy of Kent, 1640–1914* (Woodbridge: Boydell Press and Kent County Council, 1995), pp. 233–60, on p. 251; P. Clark and L. Murfin, *The History of Maidstone: The Making of a Modern County Town* (Stroud: Alan Sutton Publishing, 1995), p. 120.
21. Select Committee 1882, p. 137.
22. Manuscript Census Returns of England and Wales 1861, RG 9 (hereafter 1861 MSS Census), 502, 143:32.
23. G. Crossick, *An Artisan Elite in Victorian Society: Kentish London 1840–1880* (London: Croom Helm, 1978), p. 39.
24. B. Joyce, *The Chatham Scandal: A History of Medway's Prostitution in the Late Nineteenth Century* (Rochester: Baggins Book Bazaar/Bruce Aubry, 1999), p. 42.
25. *Chatham News*, 9 March 1861; Letter to the Editor, *Chatham News*, 13 October 1860.
26. Cited in Joyce, *Chatham Scandal*, p. 48.
27. *Chatham News*, 23 March 1861.
28. See, for example, N. Goose, 'Working Women in Industrial England', in N. Goose (ed.), *Women's Work in Industrial England: Regional and Local Perspectives* (Hatfield: Local Population Studies, 2007), pp. 1–28, on p. 22.
29. Elizabeth Rowe, Mary Baker and Caroline Warner were each listed as 'streetwalker' in the 1851 Gravesend census, for example. Manuscript Census Returns of England and Wales 1851 (HO 107) (Hereafter 1851 MSS Census), 1608,70:26.
30. P. Murray, *Poverty and Welfare 1830–1914* (London: Hodder & Stoughton, 1999), p. 50.
31. D. Englander, *Poverty and Poor Law Reform in Britain: From Chadwick to Booth, 1834–1914* (London: Longman, 1998), p. 13.
32. Poor Rates and Pauperism, Return (B.); Paupers Relieved on 1 July 1857, *PP* 1857 XXXII, p. 16; Poor Rates and Pauperism, Return (B.); Paupers Relieved on 1 July 1886, *PP* 1986 LVI, p. 6.
33. 'Sheppey Board of Guardians', *Sheerness Times and General Advertiser*, 26 March 1870.
34. *Sheerness Times and General Advertiser*, January 1870.

35. Englander, *Poverty and Poor Law Reform*, p. 23.

36. 'Meeting of Medway Board of Guardians', *Chatham News,* 30 July 1859.

37. Taken from census materials, newspaper reports, Kent Poor Law Records and General Registration Records, 1851–1881.

38. 1851 MSS Census, 1627, 189:41; 1861 MSS Census, 470, 85:45; Kent History and Library Centre (hereafter KHLC) Gravesend Union Admission and Discharge Register (hereafter Gravesend Admission and Discharge Register), 15 March 1858; GR 21 July 1866; 1871 MSS Census, 1007, 131:44.

39. *Dover Express*, 2 December 1870.

40. Established for thirty-six named women, from census data.

41. Manuscript Census Returns of England and Wales, 1841 (HO 107) (hereafter 1841 MSS Census), 457:13; 1851 MSS Census, 1618, 39:47.

42. 1861 MSS Census, 503, 117:26.

43. *Maidstone Telegraph and West Kent Messenger* (hereafter *Maidstone Telegraph*), 8 February 1866.

44. Manuscript Census Returns of England and Wales, 1871 (RG 10) (hereafter 1871 MSS Census) 912, 58:2.

45. Ibid., 944, 94:4.

46. Maidstone Petty Sessions Records: Court Minutes (hereafter Maidstone Petty Sessions), 1871–8 (PS/Md Sm 4–6), 14 December 1871.

47. Manuscript Census Returns of England and Wales, 1881 (RG 11) (hereafter 1881 MSS Census) 931, 101:3; General Registration Office (hereafter GRO) Death Indices (Vol. 2a), September 1880.

48. GRO Birth and Death Indices (Vol. 5), March 1847; 1851 MSS Census, 1654, 470:19; 1861 MSS Census, 471:73:37.

49. *Gravesend and Dartford Reporter*, 8 November 1862.

50. Gravesend Admission and Discharge Register, 26 February 1863; 13 July 1863.

51. Gravesend Admission and Discharge Register, 27 May 1865; 12 September 1868.

52. 1871 MSS Census, 892, 46:31.

53. See Maria Luddy's similar findings for Ireland, in *Prostitution and Irish Society 1800–1940* (Cambridge: Cambridge University Press, 2007), p. 55.

54. 1871 MSS Census, 893, 12:15; GRO Death Indices (Vol. 2a), June 1871.

55. Gravesend Admission and Discharge Register, 1873–4.

56. *Gravesend and Dartford Reporter*, 28 February 1874.

57. *Gravesend and Dartford Reporter*, 25 April 1874; 21 April 1877.

58. GRO Marriage Indices, April–June 1892, Gravesend, 2a, p. 859.

59. *Dover Express*, 30 March 1861.

60. 1861 MSS Census, 550, 133:7.

61. Banks, 'Warning to Unfortunate Loiterers'; KHLC Dover Union Admission and Discharge Register, 1859–1862 (G/DO/W/I/A/10).

62. Gravesend Admission and Discharge Register, 1863.

63. 'Medway Board of Guardians', *Chatham News*, 24 May 1862.

64. Gravesend Admission and Discharge Register, 1873–4.

65. KHLC Gravesend Borough Records: Petty Sessions Records: Minutes, 1873–5 (PS/ Gr Sm 4–5) (hereafter Gravesend Petty Sessions), 3 June 1874.

66. 'Medway Board of Guardians', *Chatham News* 14 January 1860.

67. *Chatham News*, 10 May 1873.

68. 'Coroner's Court', *Gravesend and Dartford Reporter*, 15 March 1862.

69. *Gravesend and Dartford Reporter*, 6 April 1867.
70. *Gravesend and Dartford Reporter*, 23 October 1869.
71. *Gravesend and Dartford Reporter*, 23 September 1873.
72. *Gravesend and Dartford Reporter*, 11 September 1880.
73. 1881 MSS Census, 872, 34:17.
74. *Gravesend and Dartford Reporter*, 21 May 1881.
75. KHLC Gravesend Union Death Register, 1871–1914 (G/G W1d).
76. 'Medway Board of Guardians', *Chatham News*, 22 December 1866.
77. Joyce, *Chatham Scandal*, p. 122.
78. *Chatham News*, 3 May 1862.
79. Based on newspaper reports of prosecution cases in *Gravesend and Dartford Reporter*; *Dover Express and East Kent Intelligence*; and *Chatham News*.
80. *Dover Express*, 20 April 1861; *Gravesend and Dartford Reporter*, 29 November 1856; *Chatham News*, 8 June 1867.
81. Harsin, *Policing Prostitution*, p. 134.
82. Maidstone Petty Sessions, 28 January 1865; 7 February 1865; 1871 MSS Census, 912, 58:2.
83. Maidstone Museum, Maidstone Gaol Admission Register, 22 February 1883.
84. *Gravesend and Dartford Reporter*, 15 April 1871; 8 June 1874.
85. *Gravesend and Dartford Reporter*, 22 July 1871.
86. *Gravesend and Dartford Reporter*, 18 May 1872.
87. Gravesend Petty Sessions, 23 March 1874.
88. *Gravesend and Dartford Reporter*, 3 April 1874.
89. *Maidstone Telegraph*, 28 May 1870.
90. *Sheerness Guardian*, 7 January 1865; *Gravesend and Dartford Reporter*, 15 October 1870.
91. *Gravesend and Dartford Reporter*, 19 May 1860.
92. *Maidstone Telegraph*, 7 March 1874.
93. *Gravesend and Dartford Reporter*, 13 July 1867.
94. *Chatham News*, 28 December 1861.
95. *Sheerness Times and General Advertiser*, 23 July 1870.
96. *Maidstone Telegraph*, 14 April 1866.
97. D. Taylor, *Crime, Policing and Punishment in England 1750–1914* (Basingstoke: Macmillan, 1998), p. 41.
98. *Gravesend and Dartford Reporter*, 10 May 1856.
99. *Maidstone Telegraph*, 1 December 1866.
100. *Gravesend and Dartford Reporter*, 18 December 1858.
101. *Chatham News*, 23 December 1865; 6 January 1866.
102. 1871 MSS Census, 893, 9:10.
103. *Gravesend and Dartford Reporter*, 19 August 1871.
104. *Gravesend and Dartford Reporter*, 20 January 1877; 1 March 1879.
105. 'The Distress in Gravesend', *Gravesend and Dartford Reporter*, 25 January 1879.
106. See, for example, P. Keating (ed.), *Into Unknown England, 1866–1913: Selections from the Social Explorers* (Glasgow: William Collins, 1976).
107. 'Another Tragedy at Maidstone', *Gravesend and Dartford Reporter*, 18 April 1857.
108. 'Board of Health Meeting', *Dover Express*, 14 June 1862.
109. Letter to the Editor, *Gravesend and Dartford Reporter*, 16 April 1864.
110. Select Committee 1882, p. 237.
111. *Gravesend and Dartford Reporter*, 8 August 1874.

112. Walkowitz, *Prostitution and Victorian Society*, p. 3.
113. Acton, *Prostitution*, p. 128.
114. Finnegan, *Poverty and Prostitution*, p. 8.
115. Walkowitz, *Prostitution and Victorian Society*, p. 31.
116. *Gravesend and Dartford Reporter*, 3 December 1864; 7 January 1865; 3 February 1866; 23 June 1866; 25 August 1866; 3 November 1866; 10 November 1866; 23 March 1867; 24 August 1867.
117. F. B. Smith has suggested that the superior nutrition and adequate shelter provided in hospital may have been responsible for an impression of improved health. 'Ethics and Disease in the Later Nineteenth Century: The Contagious Diseases Acts', *Historical Studies*, 15 (1971), 118–35, on p. 127.
118. Report from the Select Committee on the Administration and Operation of the Contagious Diseases Acts *PP* 1881 (351) VIII (hereafter Select Committee 1881), p. 188.
119. Select Committee 1882, p. 459.
120. KHLC Sheppey Union Inmates Admission and Discharge Register, 1866 (CKS-G/Sh/WI).
121. *Sheerness Times and General Advertiser*, 20 June 1868.
122. *Sheerness Times and General Advertiser*, 7 May 1870; 23 July 1870.
123. KHLC Sheerness Police Court Register, 23 June 1871.
124. 1881 MSS Census, 954, 71:2; 1891 MSS Census, 704, 147:25.
125. GRO Death Indices (Vol. 2a), March 1900.
126. 1861 MSS Census, 1737, 122:25.
127. 1871 MSS Census, 816, 19:32.
128. KHLC Sheerness Police Court Register, 1 December 1875; 17 February, 19 June, 7 August, 26 December 1876; 1 October 1877; 6 June 1878; 3 February 1879.
129. 1881 MSS Census, 78, 43:35.
130. GRO Death Indices (Vol. 2a), June 1881.
131. Select Committee 1882, p. 348.
132. See, for example, G. S. Frost, *'Living in Sin': Cohabiting as Husband and Wife in Nineteenth-Century England* (Manchester: Manchester University Press, 2008), pp. 123–5.
133. *Gravesend and Dartford Reporter*, 29 October 1870, 28 January 1871.
134. 1871 MSS Census, 891, 57:53.
135. GRO Marriage Indices (Vol. 2a), December 1873; 1881 MSS Census, 977, 65:25.
136. GRO Death Indices (Vol. 2a), June 1888.
137. 1851 MSS Census, 1608, 223:42.
138. 1861 MSS Census, 470, 82:40.
139. *Gravesend and Dartford Reporter*, 23 February 1861; Gravesend Admission and Discharge Register, November 1861.
140. GRO Marriage Indices (Vol. 2a), December 1863; 1861 MSS Census, 471, 31:7; *Gravesend and Dartford Reporter*, 29 March 1856.
141. 1871 MSS Census, 890, 84:38.
142. *Gravesend and Dartford Reporter*, 2 August 1879.
143. 1881 MSS Census, 871, 90:35.
144. Acton, *Prostitution*, p. 129.

2 Prostitution, Lifestyle and Life Cycle

1.   *Chatham News*, 2 March 1861.
2.   *Chatham News*, 23 March 1861.

3. Ibid.
4. *Chatham News*, 8 June 1867.
5. *Chatham News*, 20 August 1864.
6. *Dover Express*, 16 September 1870.
7. *Maidstone Telegraph*, 3 February 1872.
8. *Dover Express*, 16 September 1870.
9. *Gravesend and Dartford Reporter*, 29 January 1859.
10. *Gravesend and Dartford Reporter*, 20 September 1862; 14 January 1865.
11. *Gravesend and Dartford Reporter*, 8 July 1871, 1 October 1873.
12. *Gravesend and Dartford Reporter*, 9 April 1870.
13. *Gravesend and Dartford Reporter*, 10 June 1865; 8 August 1874.
14. Gravesend Petty Sessions, 4 May 1874.
15. Royal Commission on the Administration and Operation of the Contagious Diseases Acts, *PP* 1871 (c.408, 408–1) XIX (hereafter Royal Commission 1871), p. xliv.
16. *Chatham News*, 30 January 1869.
17. 1881 MSS Census, 980, 66:16; 980, 60:4; KHLC Sheerness Police Court Register, 9 December 1878; 21 July 1879; 26 March 1877; 29 April 1878.
18. 1881 MSS Census, 980, 53:31.
19. *Gravesend and Dartford Reporter*, 27 October 1860.
20. *Gravesend and Dartford Reporter*, 29 January 1859.
21. Walkowitz, *Prostitution and Victorian Society*, p. 17.
22. 1871 MSS Census, 912, 58:1.
23. Royal Commission 1871, p. xiii.
24. Maidstone Gaol Admission Register, 1883.
25. Select Committee 1881, p. 526.
26. Select Committee 1882, p. 44.
27. Annual Report of the Assistant Commissioner of the Metropolitan Police on the Operation of the Contagious Diseases Acts, 1874 *PP* 1875 (97) LXI (hereafter Annual Report 1874), p. 5.
28. Returns of Judicial Statistics of England and Wales 1862, *PP* 1863 (3181), lxv, 347, pp. 8, 49.
29. *Folkestone Express*, 2 May 1868.
30. *Dover Express*, 3 January 1863.
31. *Chatham News*, 8 June 1867.
32. *Dover Express*, 23 May 1863.
33. *Gravesend and Dartford Reporter*, 28 January 1865; 1871 MSS Census, 971, 81:26.
34. *Dover Express*, 18 January 1863.
35. Select Committee 1882, p. 132.
36. Maidstone Petty Sessions, 22 July 1871; 28 March 1874; 15 September 1874; 13 March 1875; *Maidstone Telegraph*, 17 March 1866.
37. 'Coroner's Court', *Gravesend and Dartford Reporter*, 8 March 1879; Petty Sessions, *Gravesend and Dartford Reporter*, 2 August 1879.
38. *Gravesend and Dartford Reporter*, 18 October 1873.
39. *Dover Express*, 3 August 1861.
40. *Chatham News*, 8 June 1867.
41. *Chatham News*, 23 February 1861; 2 March 1861; 23 March 1861.
42. *Kentish Gazette*, 14 March 1871; 4 April 1871; 1851 MSS Census, 1631, 428:17; 1861 MSS Census, 542, 17:10; 1871 MSS Census, 968, 72:6; 1881 MSS Census, 996, 18:9; 1891 MSS Census, 705, 81:6.

43. 1881 MSS Census, 618, 94:34.
44. GRO Marriage Indices (Vol. 1c), December 1883.
45. 1861 MSS Census, 476, 50:46.
46. *Gravesend and Dartford Reporter*, 31 March 1860; 20 October 1860.
47. *Gravesend and Dartford Reporter*, 28 January 1865; 1 February 1862.
48. *Gravesend and Dartford Reporter*, 21 January 1866.
49. *Gravesend and Dartford Reporter*, 3 March 1866.
50. *Gravesend and Dartford Reporter*, 14 April 1866.
51. *Gravesend and Dartford Reporter*, 28 July 1866.
52. *Gravesend and Dartford Reporter*, 23 November 1867.
53. 1871 MSS Census, 971, 81:26.
54. Walkowitz, *Prostitution and Victorian Society*, p. 20.
55. *Dover Express*, 18 May 1861.
56. *Chatham News*, 10 November 1866.
57. *Maidstone Telegraph*, 28 March 1874.
58. *Gravesend and Dartford Reporter*, 22 January 1876.
59. *Shield*, 11 April 1870; 18 July 1870; 25 November 1871.
60. See, for example, *Shield*, 11 April 1870.
61. Select Committee 1869, p. 35.
62. Select Committee 1882, p. 189.
63. 'St. Bartholemew's Hospital', *Chatham News*, 20 January 1866.
64. For example, Return of Numbers of Paupers on District and Workhouse Medical Officers' Relief-Books in England and Wales, 1869–70 *PP* 1870 (468) LVIII.727, p. 70.
65. 'Medway Board of Guardians', *Chatham News*, 23 March 1861.
66. *Chatham News*, 3 May 1862.
67. *Chatham News*, 7 September 1861.
68. Select Committee 1881, p. 258.
69. Royal Commission 1871, p. 206.
70. Select Committee 1882, p. 455.
71. Luddy, *Prostitution and Irish Society*, p. 61.
72. Logan, *The Great Social Evil*, p. 56.
73. R. M. MacLeod, 'The Edge of Hope: Social Policy and Chronic Alcoholism 1870–1900', *Journal of Social Medicine and Allied Sciences*, 22 (1967), pp. 215–45, on p. 216.
74. A. E. Dingle, 'Drink and Working-Class Living Standards in Britain, 1870–1914', *Economic History Review*, 25 (1972), pp. 608–22, on pp. 609–11.
75. *Times*, 23 January 1858, quoted in MacLeod, 'Edge of Hope', p. 216; *Gravesend and Dartford Reporter*, 4 January 1873.
76. Finnegan, *Poverty and Prostitution*, p. 145.
77. MacLeod, 'Edge of Hope', p. 217.
78. *Chatham News*, 1 June 1861.
79. *Chatham News*, 11 January 1862.
80. *Dover Express*, 7 March 1863.
81. *Gravesend and Dartford Reporter*, 23 December 1865; *Sheerness Guardian*, 20 January 1866.
82. *Gravesend and Dartford Reporter*, 4 September 1858; 5 February 1859.
83. *Chatham News*, 23 November 1867.
84. *Gravesend and Dartford Reporter*, 3 July 1858; 12 March 1859.
85. *Dover Express*, 25 January 1862.

86. *Chatham News*, 27 February 1864.
87. 'Another Tragedy at Maidstone', *Gravesend and Dartford Reporter*, 18 April 1857.
88. *Gravesend and Dartford Reporter*, 29 January 1859.
89. *Gravesend and Dartford Reporter*, 23 June 1866; 28 June 1868.
90. *Chatham News*, 8 March 1862.
91. See, for example, L. Zedner, *Women, Crime and Custody in Victorian England* (Oxford: Clarendon, 1991), p. 170; Emsley, *English Police*, pp. 56–7.
92. See, for example, Walkowitz, *Prostitution and Victorian Society*, p. 204; J. Weeks, *Sex, Politics and Society: The Regulation of Sexuality since 1800*, 2nd edn (Harlow: Longman, 1989), p. 90.
93. KHLC Sheerness Police Court Register, 7 October 1878; 28 January 1879.
94. *Gravesend and Dartford Reporter*, 19 August 1871.
95. *Gravesend and Dartford Reporter*, 15 April 1865.
96. *Gravesend and Dartford Reporter*, 19 August 1871; 22 March 1873; 23 August 1873.
97. *Gravesend and Dartford Reporter*, 15 April 1865.
98. *Gravesend and Dartford Reporter*, 15 July 1865.

3 Representations of Prostitution

1. *Gravesend and Dartford Reporter*, 21 July 1860.
2. Trudgill, *Madonnas and Magdalens*, p. 283.
3. Walkowitz, *Prostitution and Victorian Society*, p. 41; Finnegan, *Poverty and Prostitution*, p. 15.
4. S. Cohen, *Folk Devils and Moral Panics: The Creation of the Mods and Rockers*, 3rd edn (Abingdon: Routledge, 2002), p. 1.
5. J. Black, *The English Press 1621–1861* (Stroud: Sutton Publishing, 2001), p. 97.
6. A. J. Lee, *The Origins of the Popular Press, 1855–1914* (London: Croom Helm, 1976), pp. 18–19.
7. S. Gunn, *The Public Culture of the Victorian Middle Class: Ritual and Authority in the English Industrial City 1840–1914* (Manchester: Manchester University Press, 2007), p. 66.
8. Ibid., p. 68.
9. *Dover Express*, 3 June 1870; *Gravesend and Dartford Reporter*, 29 June 1861; *Dover Express*, 4 April 1873; 27 December 1862; 3 January 1873.
10. *Dover Express*, 3 January 1863; 24 May 1872.
11. See, for example, B. Reay, 'The Context and Meaning of Popular Literacy: Some Evidence from Nineteenth-Century Rural England', *Past & Present*, 131 (1991), pp. 89–129; Lee, *Origins of the Popular Press*, p. 29.
12. D. Vincent, *Literacy and Popular Culture: England 1750–1914* (Cambridge: Cambridge University Press, 1989), pp. 54, 178.
13. L. Brown, *Victorian News and Newspapers* (Oxford: Oxford University Press, 1985), p. 31.
14. Ibid., pp. 28–9.
15. H. R. Pratt Boorman, *Kent Messenger Centenary* (Kent: Kent Messenger, 1959).
16. See also H. Barker, *Newspapers, Politics and English Society 1695–1855* (Harlow: Longman, 1999), who similarly concludes that newspaper readers in the eighteenth and nineteenth centuries were likely to have come from a wider section of society than the rising middle classes.

17. Advertisement duty was repealed in 1853, newspaper stamp tax in 1855, and paper duty in 1861. For a history of the nineteenth-century press, see Lee, *The Origins of the Popular Press, 1855–1914*; and Black, *The English Press 1621–1861*.

18. Lee, *Origins of the Popular Press*, p. 84.

19. 1851 MSS Census, 1632, 494:2; 'Obituary of Joseph Friend', *Dover Express*, 18 July 1902.

20. 1851 MSS Census, 1800, 320:23.

21. C. G. Smith, *The Reporter, 1856–1966* (Ilford: Gravesend and Dartford Reporter, 1966).

22. Editorial, *Gravesend and Dartford Reporter*, 22 July 1865.

23. Pratt Boorman, *Kent Messenger Centenary*.

24. Cited in Lee, *Origins of the Popular Press*, p. 27.

25. Cited in Barker, *Newspapers, Politics and English Society*, p. 225.

26. *Gravesend and Dartford Reporter*, 22 July 1865; *Dover Express*, 3 June 1870; 14 August 1858.

27. *Dover Express*, 12 April 1872.

28. *Gravesend and Dartford Reporter*, 4 October 1856; *Dover Express*, 2 February 1872; Black, *The English Press 1621–1861*, p. 198

29. L. Hartley, *Physiognomy and the Meaning of Expression in Nineteenth-Century Culture* (Cambridge: Cambridge University Press, 2001), p. 6.

30. See also M. Percival and G. Tytler (eds), *Physiognomy in Profile: Lavater's Impact on European Culture* (Cranbury, NJ: Rosemont, 2005).

31. *Gravesend and Dartford Reporter*, 4 July 1857; *Dover Express*, 13 October 1858; *Gravesend and Dartford Reporter*, 27 June 1857; 10 March 1866.

32. *Chatham News*, 29 March 1862.

33. Zedner, *Women, Crime and Custody*, p. 2.

34. Mahood, *The Magdalenes*, p. 13.

35. Self, *Prostitution, Women and Misuse of the Law*, p. 12.

36. Zedner, *Women, Crime and Custody*, p. 4.

37. *Gravesend and Dartford Reporter*, 9 November 1861; 9 August 1862.

38. *Gravesend and Dartford Reporter*, 7 February 1863; 23 May 1863; 13 July 1867.

39. *Maidstone Telegraph*, 29 August 1863.

40. See H. S. Becker, *Outsiders: Studies in the Sociology of Deviance*, rev. edn (New York: Free Press, 1997), and L. T. Wilkins, *Social Deviance: Social Policy, Action and Research* (London, Tavistock, 1964), p. 46.

41. *Gravesend and Dartford Reporter*, 2 May 1863.

42. Letter to the Editor, *Sheerness Guardian*, 13 May 1865.

43. C. Willett Cunnington, *English Women's Clothing in the Nineteenth Century* (New York: Dover, 1990), p. 238.

44. Walkowitz, *Prostitution and Victorian Society*, p. 26.

45. *Chatham News*, 12 April 1873.

46. *Gravesend and Dartford Reporter*, 5 October 1861.

47. Cohen, *Folk Devils*, p. 1.

48. D. Garland, 'On the Concept of Moral Panic', *Crime Media Culture*, 4:9 (2008), pp. 9–30, on p. 15.

49. *Gravesend and Dartford Reporter*, 3 July 1858.

50. *Gravesend and Dartford Reporter*, 6 August 1870.

51. *Dover Express*, 30 March 1861.

52. *Dover Express*, 19 September 1858; *Gravesend and Dartford Reporter*, 14 December 1861; 5 December 1857
53. *Gravesend and Dartford Reporter*, 25 March 1871.
54. For example, the demise of Esther in E. Gaskell, *Mary Barton* (1848; Harmondsworth: Penguin, 1983), p. 465.
55. *Dover Express*, 18 May 1861; 7 November 1863.
56. Greg, 'Prostitution', p. 261.
57. A. Ribeiro, *Dress and Morality* (London: B. T. Batsford, 1986), p. 127.
58. *Maidstone Telegraph*, 7 September 1867.
59. R. Fowler, *Language in the News: Discourse and Ideology in the Press* (London: Routledge, 1991), p. 20.
60. Ibid., p. 15.
61. *Dover Express*, 22 July 1870; *Maidstone and Kentish Journal*, 16 December 1871; *Gravesend and Dartford Reporter*, 14 January 1865; 19 May 1860.
62. *Maidstone Telegraph*, 28 May 1870; *Gravesend and Dartford Reporter*, 3 October 1863.
63. Ribeiro, *Dress and Morality*, p. 132; C. Breward, *The Culture of Fashion* (Manchester: Manchester University Press, 1995), p. 151.
64. Anon., *The Habits of Good Society*, cited in Ribeiro, *Dress and Morality*, p. 129.
65. Walkowitz, *Prostitution and Victorian Society*, p. 26.
66. *Dover Express*, 7 October 1870; *Kentish Mercury*, 10 September 1870.
67. *Gravesend and Dartford Reporter*, 14 September 1861.
68. *Dover Express*, 15 March 1862; Willett Cunnington, *English Women's Clothing*, p. 256.
69. *Gravesend and Dartford Reporter*, 1 August 1857.
70. *Gravesend and Dartford Reporter*, 4 June 1864.
71. Willett Cunnington, *English Women's Clothing*, p. 208.
72. C. Cooksey and A Dronsfield, 'Fuchsine or Magenta: The Second Most Famous Aniline Dye: A Short Memoir on the 150th Anniversary of the First Commercial Production of this Well-Known Dye', *Biotechnic & Histochemistry*, 84 (2009), pp. 179–83.
73. *Maidstone Telegraph and West Kent Messenger*, 20 July 1872; see Ribeiro, *Dress and Morality*, p. 137.
74. See Breward, *Culture of Fashion*, pp. 153, 155, and Willett Cunnington, *English Women's Clothing*, p. 233.
75. Breward, *Culture of Fashion*, p. 151.
76. Ribeiro, *Dress and Morality*, p. 132.
77. H. Mayhew (ed.), *London Labour and the London Poor*, 4 vols (London, 1861–2; repr. London: Penguin, 1985), cited in Breward, *Culture of Fashion*, p. 160.
78. *Gravesend and Dartford Reporter*, 12 January 1861; 28 February 1863.

4 Geographies of Prostitution

1. *Gravesend and Dartford Reporter*, 5 December 1857.
2. *Dover Express*, 8 March 1862.
3. See, for example, Howell, *Geographies of Regulation*; P. Hubbard, 'Sexuality, Immorality and the City: Red-Light Districts and the Marginalisation of Street Prostitutes', *Gender, Place and Culture*, 5:1 (1998), pp. 55–72.
4. A. Croll, *Civilizing the Urban: Popular Culture and Public Space in Merthyr, c. 1870–1914* (Cardiff: University of Wales Press, 2000), p. 3.
5. *Dover Express*, 15 August 1873.

6. Gunn, *Public Culture*, p. 67.
7. J. Batchelor, 'Industry in Distress: Reconfiguring Femininity and Labor in the Magdalen House', *Eighteenth Century Life*, 28 (2004), pp. 1–20.
8. Gunn, *Public Culture*, p. 63.
9. Gravesham Borough Council, 'The Growth of Gravesend', at www.gravesham.gov.uk/index [accessed 25 July 2008].
10. Ibid., p. 3.
11. R. H. Hiscock, *A History of Gravesend* (London: Phillimore, 1976), p. 104.
12. *Chatham News*, 12 May 1860.
13. *A Guide to Dover, Ancient and Modern* (Dover: Dover Chronicle, 1861); *The Visitor's Guide to Dover: Its History and Antiquities* (Dover: Harvey & Hemmin, 1875), p. 9.
14. *Dover Telegraph*, 12 March 1864.
15. S. Cole, *Guide to Sheerness-on-Sea and the Isle of Sheppey* (Sheerness: S. Cole, 1891), p. 3.
16. Unattributed quotation, cited in *Blue Town Remembered: The Spirit of a Community* (Sheerness: Freedom Centre Publishing, 1992), p. 87.
17. *Sheerness Guardian*, 6 September 1862.
18. *Sheerness Guardian*, 9 June 1971.
19. E. J. Brabazon, *A Month at Gravesend* (Gravesend: Godfrey John Baynes, 1863).
20. *Gravesend and Dartford Reporter*, 2 August 1879.
21. Gunn, *Public Culture*, p. 63.
22. Hiscock, *History of Gravesend*, p. 23.
23. 'Town Council', *Gravesend and Dartford Reporter*, 17 August 1878.
24. *Gravesend and Dartford Reporter*, 5 September 1857; 4 September 1858; 24 July 1858.
25. 'The Distress in Gravesend', *Gravesend and Dartford Reporter*, 25 January 1879.
26. *Gravesend and Dartford Reporter*, 10 August 1867.
27. *Gravesend and Dartford Reporter*, 22 May 1869; 13 June 1878; 5 October 1878.
28. *Gravesend and Dartford Reporter*, 22 October 1859.
29. *Gravesend and Dartford Reporter*, 25 January 1879.
30. *Gravesend and Dartford Reporter*, 26 April 1856.
31. *Gravesend and Dartford Reporter*, 10 June 1876.
32. Brabazon, *A Month at Gravesend*, p. 26.
33. Ibid.
34. *Hall's Gravesend, Milton and Northfleet Directory and Advertiser* (Gravesend: Thomas Hall, 1870–5).
35. W. T. R. Pryce (ed.), *From Family History to Community History* (Cambridge: Cambridge University Press in association with the Open University, 1994).
36. R. Rodger, 'Slums and Suburbs: The Persistence of Residential Apartheid', in P. Waller (ed.), *The English Urban Landscape* (Oxford: Oxford University Press, 2000), pp. 233–68.
37. M. Girouard, *The English Town* (New Haven, CT and London: Yale University Press, 1990), p. 72.
38. 'The Social Evil in Gravesend', Letter to the Editor, *Gravesend and Dartford Reporter*, 9 April 1864.
39. *Gravesend and Dartford Reporter*, 9 September 1865; 4 June 1864.
40. *Gravesend and Dartford Reporter*, 3 November 1860.
41. *Kentish Gazette*, 8 October 1839.
42. *Dover Express*, 22 July 1870.
43. *Dover Express*, 16 September 1870.

44. *Dover Express*, 10 June 1870.
45. *A Guide to Dover, Ancient and Modern*, p. 3.
46. *Dover Express*, 2 February 1861.
47. H. Carter and C. R. Lewis, *An Urban Geography of England and Wales in the Nineteenth Century* (London: Edward Arnold, 1990), p. 91.
48. Gunn, *Public Culture*, p. 72.
49. *Gravesend and Dartford Reporter*, 28 March 1868.
50. *Gravesend and Dartford Reporter*, 5 October 1861.
51. Croll, *Civilizing the Urban*, p. 79.
52. *Gravesend and Dartford Reporter*, 19 July 1862.
53. *Dover Express*, 29 January 1859.
54. D. Ward, 'Environs and Neighbours in the "Two Nations": Residential Differentiation in Mid-Nineteenth-Century Leeds', *Journal of Historical Geography*, 6 (1980), pp. 133–62.
55. *Gravesend and Dartford Reporter*, 28 September 1867.
56. *Gravesend and Dartford Reporter*, 7 February 1863.
57. *Gravesend and Dartford Reporter*, 12 October 1861.
58. *Gravesend and Dartford Reporter*, 17 August 1867; 17 February 1866.
59. *Gravesend and Dartford Reporter*, 18 November 1865; Gravesend Petty Sessions, 8 June 1874.
60. *Gravesend and Dartford Reporter*, 24 July 1869.
61. *Gravesend and Dartford Reporter*, 3 August 1861; 13 August 1870.
62. *Gravesend and Dartford Reporter*, 13 February 1869.
63. M. J. Daunton, 'Public Space and Private Space: The Victorian City and the Working Class Household', in D. Fraser and A. Sutcliffe (eds), *The Pursuit of Urban History* (London: Edward Arnold, 1983), pp. 212–33, on pp. 214–15.
64. Cited in *Blue Town Remembered*, p. 87; 1861 MSS Census, 531, 111:14.
65. 1871 MSS Census, 987, 51:3.
66. *Sheerness Guardian*, 4 November 1865; 20 January 1866.
67. KHLC Sheerness Police Court Register, 21 December 1869; 27 May 1870.
68. 1881 MSS Census, 980, 53:31.
69. KHLC Sheerness Police Court Register, 16 August 1870; 16 September 1870; 13 December 1870; 27 November 1870.
70. KHLC Sheerness Police Court Register, 31 December 1874; 23 May 1876; 1861 MSS Census, 531, 111:35.
71. *Chatham News*, 4 January 1873.
72. Maidstone Gaol Admission Register, 1883.
73. *Dover Express*, 7 December 1861.
74. *Dover Express*, 13 August 1859.
75. *Dover Express*, 28 June 1862.
76. *Dover Express*, 4 January 1862.
77. 1861 MSS Census, 548, 22:5.
78. *Dover Express*, 15 October 1859.
79. *Dover Express*, 7 February 1873.
80. 'Local Intelligence', *Dover Express*, 22 August 1873.
81. *Dover Express*, 28 February 1873.
82. L. Nead, *Victorian Babylon: People, Streets and Images in Nineteenth Century London* (New Haven, CT: Yale University Press, 2000), p. 67.

83. M. P. Ryan, *Women in Public: Between Banners and Ballots, 1825–1880* (Baltimore, MD: John Hopkins University Press, 1992), p. 4.
84. Croll, *Civilizing the Urban*, p. 75.
85. *Gravesend and Dartford Reporter*, 12 October 1861.
86. See Croll, *Civilizing the Urban*, p. 68.
87. David Taylor makes this observation in relation to the criminal classes, but it applies equally to women who lived by prostitution. Taylor, *Crime, Policing and Punishment*, p. 49.
88. *Sheerness Guardian*, 31 March 1866.
89. 1871 MSS Census, 987, 54:38.
90. KHLC Sheerness Police Court Register, 22 July 1870; 10 March 1871; 29 September 1871; 22 September 1871; 3 November 1871; 20 February 1871.
91. *Gravesend and Dartford Reporter*, 10 June 1876.
92. 'Auction of Property', *Gravesend and Dartford Reporter*, 18 January 1879.
93. *Gravesend and Dartford Reporter*, 2 May 1868.
94. 1861 MSS Census, 470, 195:54–6.
95. 'Coroner's Court', *Gravesend and Dartford Reporter*, 27 February 1858.
96. *Gravesend and Dartford Reporter*, 25 October 1856.
97. Gravesend Petty Sessions, 14 November 1873.
98. *Gravesend and Dartford Reporter*, 20 September 1862.
99. *Gravesend and Dartford Reporter*, 9 April 1864; 15 September 1873.
100. J. H. Johnson and C. G. Pooley (eds), *The Structure of Nineteenth Century Cities* (London: Croom Helm, 1982), p. 206.
101. 1871 MSS Census, 891, 59:57; *Gravesend and Dartford Reporter*, 18 April 1874; 2 August 1873; *Hall's Gravesend, Milton and Northfleet Directory and Advertiser* (Gravesend: Thomas Hall 1870–5); 1881 MSS Census, 877, 37:23.
102. Brabazon, *Month at Gravesend*, p. 34.
103. KHLC Sheerness Police Court Register, 5 January 1872.
104. Select Committee 1882, p. xviii.
105. See Zedner, *Women, Crime and Custody*, p. 18.

5 Policing Prostitution

1. *Gravesend and Dartford Reporter*, 21 June 1856.
2. Walkowitz, *Prostitution and Victorian Society*, pp. 14, 42.
3. Emsley, *English Police*, p. 77.
4. See, for example, D. Taylor, *The New Police in Nineteenth-Century England: Crime, Conflict and Control* (Manchester: Manchester University Press, 1997); C. Steedman, *Policing the Victorian Community: The Formation of English Provincial Police Forces, 1856–80* (London: Routledge & Kegan Paul, 1984); Emsley, *English Police*.
5. 'Dockyard Police', *Chatham News*, 1 December 1860.
6. In Dover in 1862, for example, the Head Constable had to apply to the Watch Committee to approve the expenditure to have the police station clock wound up. KHLC Centre Dover Petty Sessions Court Register (Do/JPr 01–02) (hereafter Dover Petty Sessions), 26 November 1867.
7. KHLC Folkestone Watch Committee Minutes, 1842 (Fo/AMc1), 19 September 1842; 19 December 1842.

8. KHLC Dover Watch Committee Minutes (Do/Amc 26/2) (hereafter Dover Watch Committee), 27 September 1864, 29 December 1868.

9. M. J. Phillips, *The Development of the Police Force in Gravesend 1816–1866* (unpublished thesis, 1963; Gravesend Library, L920 & 352.2), p. 32.

10. *Rules, Regulations and Directions for the Instruction and Guidance of the Police Force of the Borough of Gravesend* (Gravesend: Caddel & Son, 1851), (hereafter, *Gravesend Rules and Regulations*), clause 99.

11. 'Inspection of Police', *Maidstone Telegraph*, 22 September 1860.

12. Dover Watch Committee, 1857–1858.

13. Dover Watch Committee, 28 February 1860.

14. Letter to the Editor, *Folkestone Chronicle*, 26 November 1870.

15. Editorial, *Gravesend and Dartford Reporter*, 13 February 1869.

16. *Gravesend and Dartford Reporter*, 7 March 1857.

17. Dover Watch Committee, 28 June 1864.

18. See D. Taylor, *Policing the Victorian Town: The Development of the Police in Middlesbrough 1840–1914* (Basingstoke: Palgrave Macmillan, 2002), p. 38.

19. R. Ingleton, *Policing Kent 1800–2000: Guarding the Garden of England* (Chichester: Phillimore, 2002), p. 28.

20. *Kentish Mercury*, 15 January 1870.

21. See Steedman, *Policing the Victorian Community*, p. 17.

22. *Chatham News*, 24 March 1866.

23. Letter to the Editor, *Chatham News*, 6 April 1861.

24. 'Report of the Watch Committee', *Gravesend and Dartford Reporter*, 11 February 1865.

25. *The Times*, April 1885, quoted in Joyce, *Chatham Scandal*, p. 239.

26. C. A. Conley, *The Unwritten Law: Criminal Justice in Victorian Kent* (Oxford: Oxford University Press, 1991), p. 17. See T. Skyrme, *History of the Justices of the Peace*, 3 vols (Chichester: Barry Rose, 1991), Vol. 2: 1689–1989, p. 171.

27. *Dover Express*, 17 June 1870, p. 3.

28. *Gravesend and Dartford Reporter*, 16 January 1858.

29. Summary Jurisdiction Act 1848, an Act to Facilitate the Performance of the Duties of Justices of the Peace out of Sessions, within England and Wales, with Respect to Summary Convictions and Orders (11 & 12 Vict.) CAP. XLIII.

30. Emsley, *Crime and Society*, pp. 205–6.

31. H. Taylor, 'A Crisis of "Modernization" or Redundancy for the Police in England and Wales, 1900–39', *British Journal of Criminology*, 39 (1999), pp. 113–35, on p. 115.

32. 'Local Intelligence', *East Kent Advertiser*, 21 September 1867.

33. *Sheerness Guardian*, 26 August 1865.

34. *Sheerness Guardian*, 14 January 1865.

35. See Emsley, *Crime and Society*, p. 190.

36. Editorial, *Chatham News*, 2 July 1859.

37. *Chatham News*, 30 November 1867; 4 April 1868.

38. *Dover Express*, 27 July 1861.

39. Town Police Clauses Act 1847, an Act for Consolidating in One Act Certain Provisions Usually Contained in Acts for Regulating the Police of Towns (10 & 11 Vict.) CAP. LXXXIX (hereafter Town Police Clauses Act 1847).

40. Cited in Editorial, *Chatham News*, 24 December 1859.

41. *Chatham News*, 24 March 1866.

42. Select Committee 1882, p. 181.

43. *Chatham News*, 13 October 1866.
44. Dover Watch Committee, 27 July 1869.
45. Vagrancy Act 1824, an Act for the Punishment of Idle and Disorderly Persons and Rogues and Vagabonds, in that Part of Great Britain called England (5 Geo. 4) CAP. LXXXIII.
46. 'Vagrancy in Kent', *Maidstone and Kentish Journal*, 2 September 1871.
47. *Dover Express*, 14 August 1858; 21 August 1858.
48. KHLC Sheerness Police Court Register, 17 March 1868.
49. *Chatham News*, 8 August 1863; Dover Petty Sessions, 14 February 1881.
50. *Dover Express*, 30 October 1858; Gravesend Petty Sessions, 25 August 1873; *Gravesend and Dartford Reporter*, 19 August 1865.
51. *Maidstone Telegraph*, 17 May 1873.
52. Self, *Prostitution, Women and Misuse of the Law*, p. 38.
53. Maidstone Gaol Admission Register, 1882.
54. Municipal Corporations (England) Act 1835, an Act to Provide for the Regulation of Municipal Corporations in England and Wales (5 & 6 Will. 4) CAP. LXXVI.
55. Town Police Clauses Act 1847.
56. *Dover Express*, 18 July 1863.
57. Taylor, *The New Police*, p. 92.
58. *Bye-Laws for the Good Rule and Government of the Borough of Gravesend, Kent and for the Prevention and Suppression of Nuisances Therein* (Gravesend: T. Caddel, 1836).
59. Quoted in Phillips, *The Development of the Police Force in Gravesend*, p. 40.
60. *Borough of Maidstone Police: Instructions and Conditions* (Maidstone: J. Brown, 1836), p. 22.
61. Emsley, *English Police*, pp. 59–60.
62. Taylor, *The New Police*, p. 90. See also D. Philips and R. Storch, *Policing Provincial England 1829–1856: The Politics of Reform* (London: Leicester University Press, 1999); S. Petrow, *The Metropolitan Police and the Home Office 1870–1914* (Oxford: Clarendon Press, 1994), p. 30.
63. Taylor, *Crime, Policing and Punishment*, p. 92.
64. Conley, *The Unwritten Law*, p. 172; Emsley, *English Police*, p. 60; D. Jones, *Crime, Protest, Community and Police in Nineteenth-Century Britain* (London: Routledge & Kegan Paul, 1982), p. 131.
65. *Kentish Gazette*, 3 January 1871; KHLC Sheerness Police Court Register, 24 December 1867; *Maidstone and Kentish Journal*, 5 April 1864.
66. *Gravesend and Dartford Reporter*, 2 May 1863; *Chatham News*, 28 September 1861.
67. Maidstone Petty Sessions, 22 June 1877; *Kentish Gazette*, 24 January 1871.
68. *Gravesend and Dartford Reporter*, 3 March 1866.
69. Gravesend Petty Sessions, 25 May 1874.
70. *Maidstone Telegraph*, 29 August 1863.
71. KHLC Sheerness Police Court Register, 24 December 1867; *Chatham News*, 3 May 1862.
72. *Kentish Gazette*, 31 January 1871; *Dover Express*, 1 June 1861.
73. *Maidstone Telegraph*, 28 March 1874.
74. *Gravesend and Dartford Reporter*, 24 May 1862; 30 August 1862.
75. An 1898 amendment to the 1824 Vagrancy Act additionally made it illegal to live on the earnings of prostitution.
76. Returns of Judicial Statistics of England and Wales, 1857–1882.

77. Select Committee 1882, p. 154.
78. Direct comparisons are more difficult for Kentish London because of the way in which the statistics were compiled.
79. Croll, *Civilizing the Urban*, p. 80.
80. *Sheerness Guardian*, 20 May 1865.
81. *Maidstone Telegraph*, 26 May 1866; *Dover Express*, 6 July 1861.
82. Conley, *The Unwritten Law*, p. 175.
83. Maidstone Petty Sessions, 10 July 1872; 14 December 1871.
84. Town Police Clauses Act 1847, clause XXVIII.
85. Ibid.
86. Maidstone Petty Sessions, 4 July 1871; 29 September 1871.
87. *Gravesend Rules and Regulations*, clause 105.
88. Returns of Judicial Statistics of England and Wales, 1860–1877.
89. *Dover Express*, 5 July 1862.
90. *Gravesend and Dartford Reporter*, 8 October 1864; 25 February 1865.
91. *Sheerness Times and General Advertiser*, 26 November 1870.
92. *Gravesend and Dartford Reporter*, 29 November 1856.
93. *Gravesend and Dartford Reporter*, 12 May 1860; 9 June 1860; Gravesend Petty Sessions, 15 October 1873.
94. *Gravesend and Dartford Reporter*, 10 February 1866.
95. *Chatham News*, 15 April 1865.
96. *Gravesend and Dartford Reporter*, 6 August 1864; Gravesend Petty Sessions, 14 October 1874.
97. *Gravesend and Dartford Reporter*, 27 May 1865.
98. *Gravesend and Dartford Reporter*, 7 January 1865.
99. Gravesend Petty Sessions, 8 June 1874.
100. *Gravesend and Dartford Reporter*, 21 February 1874.
101. *Gravesend and Dartford Reporter*, 10 October 1863.
102. *Gravesend and Dartford Reporter*, 19 August 1865.
103. KHLC Sheerness Police Court Register, 23 June 1871.
104. KHLC Sheerness Police Court Register, August–December 1879.
105. KHLC Sheerness Police Court Register, 17 August 1869.
106. KHLC Sheerness Police Court Register, 27 May 1870.
107. KHLC Sheerness Police Court Register, 22 December 1870.
108. Maidstone Petty Sessions, 14 December 1871; 10 July 1871; 20 July 1872.
109. Maidstone Petty Sessions, 14 December 1871; 10 July 1872.
110. Jones, *Crime, Protest, Community*, p. 165.
111. Maidstone Petty Sessions, 26 August 1873.
112. *Maidstone Telegraph*, 22 August 1863.
113. Return of Statistics in Possession of Metropolitan Police, Showing Operation and Effects of Contagious Diseases Acts, to December 1872, *PP* 1873 (149) LIV; Annual Reports of the Assistant Commissioner of the Metropolitan Police on the Operation of the Contagious Diseases Acts, *PP* 1875 (97) LXI; *PP* 1876 (276) LXI; *PP* 1877 (255) LXIX; *PP* 1878 (96) LXIII; *PP* 1878–79 (235) LIX; *PP* 1880 (231) LIX; *PP* 1881 (140) LXXVI; *PP* 1882 (291) LIII.
114. 1871 Census, Volume III.
115. Although the Metropolitan Police statistics are likely to have under-recorded the total numbers of women who were involved in prostitution, it seems reasonable to assume

that they were under-recorded consistently from town to town, and thus these ratios accurately reflect the relative prostitute populations of the different towns.

116. *Chatham News*, 16 November 1861; 14 December 1861.
117. *Chatham News*, 15 March 1862.
118. *Chatham News*, 11 February 1865.
119. *Chatham News*, 12 June 1863.
120. *Chatham News*, 13 November 1875; 20 November 1875; 11 December 1875.
121. *Chatham News*, 2 September 1876.
122. *Dover Express*, 14 November 1863.
123. *Dover Express*, 15 August 1873; 22 August 1873; 29 August 1873.
124. *Gravesend and Dartford Reporter*, 20 June 1867.
125. *Chatham News*, 19 January 1867.
126. *Chatham News*, 7 December 1861.
127. *Gravesend and Dartford Reporter*, 20 June 1863.
128. *Gravesend and Dartford Reporter*, 16 April 1859.
129. KHLC Sheerness Police Court Register, 21 August 1876; 5 February 1877.
130. KHLC Sheerness Police Court Register, 30 April, 7 June, 3 September 1872.
131. Walkowitz, *Prostitution and Victorian Society*, pp. 154–5.
132. Town Police Clauses Act 1847, clause XXXV.
133. Licensing Act 1872, an Act for Regulating the Sale of Intoxicating Liquors (35 & 36 Vict.) CAP. XCIV, clause 15.
134. 'If any licensed person knowingly permits his premises to be the habitual resort of or place of meeting of reputed prostitutes, whether the object of their so resorting or meeting is or is not prostitution, he shall, if he allow them to remain longer than is necessary for the purpose of obtaining reasonable refreshment, be liable to a penalty for the first offence ten pounds'. Ibid., clause 14.
135. *Maidstone Telegraph*, 22 January 1876.
136. *Dover Express*, 13 August 1859.
137. Dover Petty Sessions, 9 August 1859.
138. *Gravesend and Dartford Reporter*, 28 March 1868.
139. *Gravesend and Dartford Reporter*, 2 August 1879.
140. *Gravesend and Dartford Reporter*, 10 February 1872.
141. Zedner, *Women, Crime and Custody*, p. 306.
142. Phillips, *The Development of the Police Force in Gravesend*, p. 40.
143. *Gravesend and Dartford Reporter*, 30 December 1865.
144. *Sheerness Guardian*, 31 March 1866.
145. *Chatham News*, 16 May 1863.
146. Manuscript Census Returns of England of Wales, 1861, 1871, 1881, 1891: population tables.
147. Royal Commission 1871, p. xliv.
148. Maidstone Gaol Admissions Register, 1883.
149. *Gravesend and Dartford Reporter*, 27 April 1867.
150. KHLC, *Rules Made by the Visiting Justices for the County Prison* (Maidstone: County Prison, 1866) (Q/GGw 1), p. 65.
151. Zedner, *Women, Crime and Custody*, p. 171.
152. *Gravesend and Dartford Reporter*, 2 April 1859.
153. *Dover Express*, 27 December 1862.
154. *Gravesend and Dartford Reporter*, 20 September 1856.

155. *Gravesend and Dartford Reporter*, 21 July 1866.
156. *Gravesend and Dartford Reporter*, 9 April 1870.
157. Taylor, *Crime, Policing and Punishment*, p. 160.

6 The Contagious Diseases Acts in Kent

1.   Select Committee 1882, pp. 52–4.
2.   Select Committee 1882, p. 158, Appendix 5.
3.   Coppin, it may be remembered from Chapter 1, had begun her career with petty theft at the age of sixteen, had spent four years in a reformatory and at least one period at the Chatham Lock Hospital undergoing treatment for venereal disease, and is recorded being admitted once again to Maidstone Gaol in the early 1880s.
4.   See Joyce, *Chatham Scandal*, p. 113.
5.   Metropolitan Police Orders, 1865 (MEPO/7), 'Dockyards'.
6.   KHLC Sheerness Police Court Register, 1871–9.
7.   Maidstone Petty Sessions, 1871.
8.   Maidstone Petty Sessions, 24 June 1871; 10 July 1872.
9.   Josephine Butler, speech made at Gravesend, 5 July 1870, reported in *Shield*, 18 July 1870, p. 163.
10. *Shield*, 1 August 1900, p. 59.
11. *Shield*, 18 January 1873, p. 22.
12. 1861 MSS Census, 320, 131:44; 1871 MSS Census, 1006, 46:33.
13. *Dover Express*, 23 December 1870.
14. McHugh, *Prostitution and Victorian Social Reform*, pp. 148–9.
15. *Shield*, 14 December 1878, pp. 291–2.
16. Ibid.
17. Ibid., p. 293.
18. Select Committee 1882, p. 195.
19. 'Watch Committee', *Dover Express*, 2 February 1872.
20. *Shield*, 4 April 1870, p. 36; 3 December 1870, p. 315.
21. *Chatham Observer*, 19 June 1875, quoted in Conley, *The Unwritten Law*, p. 38.
22. Joyce, *Chatham Scandal*, p. 67.
23. 1871 MSS Census, 912, 58:2; 1881 MSS Census, 894, 45:5.
24. 1871 MSS Census, 890, 46:23; 1881 MSS Census, 871, 56:47.
25. *Shield*, 19 November 1870.
26. *Maidstone Telegraph*, 19 November 1870.
27. *Maidstone Telegraph*, 17 February 1872.
28. 1871 MSS Census, 945, 68:31.
29. Royal Commission 1871, p. 462.
30. Joyce, *Chatham Scandal*, pp. 177, 185.
31. Ibid., p. 67.
32. Annual Report of the Assistant Commissioner of the Metropolitan Police on the Operation of the Contagious Diseases Acts, *PP* 1882 (291) LII (hereafter Annual Report 1882), pp. 8–9.
33. Royal Commission 1871, p. 637; Annual Report of the Assistant Commissioner of the Metropolitan Police on the Operation of the Contagious Diseases Acts, *PP* 1881 (140) LXXVI (hereafter Annual Report 1881), pp. 8–12.
34. Annual Report 1881, pp. 8–12.

35. Walkowitz, *Prostitution and Victorian Society*, p. 108; *Shield*, 27 November 1871, p. 740.
36. Select Committee 1882, p. 153.
37. Whilst operation of the legislation was not suspended until 1883, the final report by the Assistant Commissioner of the Metropolitan Police on the operation of the Acts was produced in 1882, reporting statistics for the year 1881.
38. *Shield*, 18 July 1870, p. 163.
39. *Shield*, 3 September 1870, p. 209.
40. Select Committee 1882, p. 248.
41. Ibid., p. 152.
42. Select Committee 1881, p. 596; Royal Commission 1871, p. lix.
43. *Shield*, 27 May 1871, p. 507
44. Royal Commission 1871, p. lix.
45. *Shield*, March 1871, quoted in Joyce, *Chatham Scandal*, p. 82.
46. Joyce, *Chatham Scandal*, p. 79.
47. *Chatham News*, 12 May 1866.
48. *Shield*, 9 May 1870, p. 75; *Chatham News*, 26 March 1870.
49. *Chatham News*, 2 February 1867.
50. *Chatham News*, 13 April 1867.
51. *Chatham News*, 30 March 1867; 13 April 1867.
52. *Chatham News*, 21 April 1866.
53. *Chatham News*, 2 March 1867.
54. *Chatham News*, 28 April 1866.
55. *Chatham News*, 15 December 1866.
56. Select Committee 1882, p. 153.
57. Annual Reports of the Assistant Commissioner of the Metropolitan Police on the Operation of the Contagious Diseases Acts, *PP* 1875 (97) LXI; *PP* 1876 (276) LXI; *PP* 1877 (255) LXIX; *PP* 1878 (96) LXIII; *PP* 1878–79 (235) LIX; *PP* 1880 (231) LIX; *PP* 1881 (140) LXXVI; *PP* 1882 (291) LIII. As a point of comparison, there were 2,634 prosecutions of prostitutes in the county of Kent (excluding Kentish London) in the twelve years of 1866–1877 under local policing, according to Parliamentary Annual Returns of Judicial Statistics.
58. Select Committee 1882, p. 453.
59. Dover Petty Sessions, January–December 1882.
60. *Kentish Gazette*, 19 July 1870.
61. KHLC Sheerness Police Court Register, 2 May 1878; 5 May 1879.
62. Maidstone Petty Sessions, 1 April–22 July 1871.
63. Royal Commission 1871, p. xlv.
64. Walkowitz, *Prostitution and Victorian Society*, p. 237; Weeks, *Sex, Politics and Society*, p. 89.
65. Gravesend Petty Sessions; Annual Report 1881, p. 13.
66. The wording used in these convictions is taken from the surviving KHLC Sheerness Police Court Register, 1867–1879.
67. KHLC Sheerness Police Court Register, 30 August 1870; 9 September 1871.
68. *Shield*, 10 December 1870, p. 322: 'The Garrison Towns of Kent', *Shield*, April–May 1870, cited in J. Jordan, *Josephine Butler* (London: John Murray, 2001), p. 116.
69. Maidstone Gaol Admission Register, 1883.
70. *Folkestone Chronicle*, 10 July 1869.
71. *Gravesend and Dartford Reporter*, 15 July 1873.

72. *Chatham News*, 18 December 1869; 9 July1870; *Gravesend and Dartford Reporter*, 1 July 1871; 30 September 1871; 24 May 1873; KHLC Sheerness Police Court Register, December 1871, 6 February 1872.
73. Select Committee 1882, p. 175.
74. Walkowitz, *Prostitution and Victorian Society*, p. 89; Weeks, *Sex, Politics and Society*, p. 237.
75. KHLC Sheerness Police Court Register, 29 January 1870; *Sheerness Times and General Advertiser*, 1 February 1870.
76. *Maidstone Telegraph*, 15 January 1870.
77. Letter to the Editor, *Maidstone Telegraph*, 28 May 1870; 11 June 1870.
78. The *Lancet*, cited in *Chatham News*, 5 January 1867.
79. *Shield*, 2 December 1871.
80. Cited in M. Pearson, *The Age of Consent: Victorian Prostitution and its Enemies* (Newton Abbott: David & Charles, 1972), p. 65.
81. Royal Commission 1871, p. liii.
82. *Shield*, 2 December 1871.
83. Select Committee 1882, Appendix 4, pp. 598, 438.
84. B. O. Taithe, *From Danger to Scandal, Debating Sexuality in Victorian England: The Contagious Diseases Act (1864–1869) and the Morbid Imagery of Victorian Society* (Manchester: University of Manchester Press, 1992), p. 83.
85. *Shield*, 20 July 1972, p. 1012.
86. Select Committee 1866, p. 36.
87. Select Committee 1882, p. 375.
88. *Shield*, 2 May 1870, p. 72.
89. Royal Commission 1871, p. lix.
90. *Shield*, 2 May 1870, p. 71.
91. Select Committee 1881, p. 597.
92. Select Committee 1882, p. 162.
93. *Shield*, 14 January 1871, p. 71.
94. McHugh, *Prostitution and Victorian Social Reform*, p. 144.
95. Select Committee 1881, pp. 477–8.
96. Letter to the Editor, *Kentish Gazette*, 12 April 1870.
97. Return of Statistics in Possession of Metropolitan Police, Showing Operation and Effects of Contagious Diseases Acts, to December 1871, *PP* 1872 (114) XLVII, pp. 3–4.
98. Royal Commission 1871, p. 554.
99. 'Letter to the Editor from the Governor of a County Prison', *Kentish Gazette*, 17 May 1870.
100. Royal Commission 1871, p. 554.
101. Ibid., p. lix.
102. Ibid., p. 816.
103. 'Letter to the Editor from the Governor of a County Prison', *Kentish Gazette*, 17 May 1870.
104. Ibid.
105. Ibid.
106. Royal Commission 1871, p. 818.
107. *Kentish Gazette*, 26 April 1870.
108. Annual Report 1881, p. 11.
109. *Gravesend and Dartford Reporter*, 25 January 1873.

110. *Gravesend and Dartford Reporter*, 11 April 1868.
111. *Gravesend and Dartford Reporter*, 20 May 1871; 4 April 1874; 25 January 1879; 8 February 1879.
112. *Gravesend and Dartford Reporter*, 18 June 1870.
113. *Gravesend and Dartford Reporter*, 25 January 1873.
114. Ibid.
115. *Gravesend and Dartford Reporter*, 1 February 1873.
116. *Gravesend and Dartford Reporter*, 26 June 1880.
117. Select Committee 1881, p. 331.
118. Select Committee 1866, p. 35.
119. Statistics taken from Annual Report 1881, pp. 9–13.
120. Select Committee 1882, p. 599.
121. Hansard Parliamentary Debates (Commons), Third Series, vol. 278 (1883), cols 828–9.

Afterword

1. For a summary of legislative measures, see J. Laite, 'Paying the Price Again: Prostitution Policy in Historical Perspective', in *History and Policy*, at www.historyandpolicy.org/papers/policy-paper-46.html [accessed 2 September 2012].
2. *A Coordinated Prostitution Strategy*, Home Office Communication Directorate: January 2006.
3. 'Prostitutes are Victims Not Criminals', *Independent*, 13 April 2007.
4. 'The Coordinated Prostitution Strategy', *Focus on Women*, 4 (2006), p. 4, at www.row.org.uk [accessed 15 August 2008].
5. '33 Reasons Why the Clients of Sex Workers Should Not Be Criminalized', SCOT-PEP, at http://www.scot-pep.org.uk [accessed 31 July 2008].
6. Joyce, *Chatham Scandal*, p. 112.
7. *Gravesend and Dartford Reporter*, 6 August 1864.

WORKS CITED

Primary Sources

Manuscript Sources

General Register Office (Office for National Statistics)
Civil Registration Birth, Marriage and Death Indices for England and Wales, 1840–1900.

Kent History and Library Centre, Maidstone
Dover Watch Committee Minutes, 1857–82 (Do/Amc 26/2).
Dover Petty Sessions Court Register, 1880–4 (Do/JPr 01–02).
Dover Union Admission and Discharge Register, 1859–62 (G/DO/W/I/A/10).
Folkestone Watch Committee Minutes, 1842 (Fo/AMc1).
Gravesend Borough Records: Petty Sessions Special Sessions (Gr/JP 3).
Gravesend Borough Records: Watch Committee Records (Gr/Aw).
Gravesend Borough Records: Gaol/2 (Gr/Ag 2).
Gravesend Petty Sessions Records: Minutes, 1873–5 (PS/ Gr Sm 4–5).
Gravesend Union Outdoor Relief Order Books, 1873–5 (G/G AR 3–4).
Gravesend Union Inmates Admission and Discharge Register, March 1873–October 1874 (G/G W1a 13).
Gravesend Union Death Register, 1871–1914 (G/G W1d).
Maidstone Petty Sessions Records: Court Minutes, 1859–65; 1871–8 (PS/Md Sm 4–6).
Sheerness Police Court Register, 1867–79 (PS/Shr 1–1a).
Sheppey Union Inmates Admission and Discharge Register, 1866 (CKS-G/Sh/WI).

Maidstone Museum
Maidstone Gaol Admission Register, 1882–3.

National Archives
Manuscript Census Returns of England and Wales: 1841 (HO 107), 1851 (HO 107), 1861 (RG 9), 1871 (RG 10), 1881 (RG 11), 1891 (RG 12), 1901 (RG 13).
Metropolitan Police Orders, 1865 (MEPO/7), 'Dockyards'.

Printed and Published Sources

Official Publications

A Coordinated Prostitution Strategy, Home Office Communication Directorate, January 2006.

Parliamentary Records

1871 Census of England and Wales, Volume III (*Population Abstracts; Age, Civil Condition, Occupations, and Birth-Places*), *PP* 1873 (c.872) LXXI.

Annual Reports of the Assistant Commissioner of the Metropolitan Police on the Operation of the Contagious Diseases Acts, *PP* 1875 (97) LXI; *PP* 1876 (276) LXI; *PP* 1877 (255) LXIX; *PP* 1878 (96) LXIII; *PP* 1878–9 (235) LIX; *PP* 1880 (231) LIX; *PP* 1881 (140) LXXVI; *PP* 1882 (291) LIII.

Contagious Diseases Prevention Act 1864, an Act for the Prevention of Contagious Diseases at Certain Naval and Military Stations (27 & 28 Vict.) CAP. LXXXV.

Contagious Diseases Act 1866, an Act for the Better Prevention of Contagious Diseases at Certain Naval and Military Stations (29 & 30 Vict.) CAP. XXXV.

Contagious Diseases Act 1869, an Act to Amend the Contagious Diseases Act 1866 (32 & 33 Vict.) CAP. XCVI.

Hansard Parliamentary Debates (Commons), Third Series, vol. 278 (1883).

Licensing Act 1872, an Act for Regulating the Sale of Intoxicating Liquors (35 & 36 Vict.) CAP. XCIV.

Municipal Corporations (England) Act 1835, an Act to Provide for the Regulation of Municipal Corporations in England and Wales (5 & 6 Will. 4) CAP. LXXVI.

Poor Rates and Pauperism, Return (B.); Paupers Relieved on 1 July 1857, *PP* 1857 (461) XXXII.

Poor Rates and Pauperism, Return (B.); Paupers Relieved on 1 July 1886, *PP* 1986 (645) LVI.

Reports from the Select Committee on the Administration and Operation of the Contagious Diseases Acts: *PP* 1868–69 (306–306.1) VII; *PP* 1878–79 (323) VIII; *PP* 1880 (114) VIII; *PP* 1881 (351) VIII; *PP* 1882 (340) IX.

Return of Numbers of Paupers on District and Workhouse Medical Officers' Relief-Books in England and Wales, 1869–70 *PP* 1870 (468) LVIII.727.

Returns of Judicial Statistics of England and Wales, *PP* 1857–58 (2407) LVII; *PP* 1859 (2508) XXVI; *PP* 1860 (2692) LXIV; *PP* 1861 (2860) LX; *PP* 1862 (3025) LVI; *PP* 1863 (3181) LXV; *PP* 1864 (3370) LVII; *PP* 1865 (3534) LII; *PP* 1866 (3726) LXVIII; *PP* 1867 (3919) LXVI; *PP* 1867–68 (4062) LXVII; *PP* 1868–69 (4196) LVIII; *PP* 1870 (c.195) LXIII; *PP* 1871 (c.442) LXIV; *PP* 1872 (c.600) LXV; *PP* 1873 (c.871) LXX; *PP* 1874 (c.1055) LXXI; *PP* 1875 (c.1315) LXXXI; *PP* 1876 (c.1595) LXXIX; *PP* 1877 (c.1871) LXXXVI; *PP* 1878 (c.2154) LXXIX; *PP* 1878–79 (c.2418) LXXVI; *PP* 1880 (c.2726) LXXVII; *PP* 1881 (c.3088) XCV; *PP* 1882 (c.3333) LXXV.

Returns of Statistics in Possession of the Metropolitan Police, Showing Operation and Effects of Contagious Diseases Acts, to December 1871, *PP* 1872 (114) XLVII; to December 1872, *PP* 1873 (149) LIV.

Royal Commission on the Administration and Operation of the Contagious Diseases Acts, *PP* 1871 (c.408, 408–1) XIX.

Summary Jurisdiction Act 1848, an Act to Facilitate the Performance of the Duties of Justices of the Peace out of Sessions, within England and Wales, with Respect to Summary Convictions and Orders (11 & 12 Vict.) CAP. XLIII.

Town Police Clauses Act 1847, an Act for Consolidating in One Act Certain Provisions Usually Contained in Acts for Regulating the Police of Towns (10 & 11 Vict.) CAP. LXXXIX.

Vagrancy Act 1824, an Act for the Punishment of Idle and Disorderly Persons and Rogues and Vagabonds, in that Part of Great Britain called England (5 Geo. 4) CAP. LXXXIII.

Newspapers and Journals

Chatham News, 1859–70; 1873–6.

Dover Express and East Kent Intelligence, 1858–63.

Dover Telegraph, 1864.

East Kent Advertiser, 1867.

Folkstone Chronicle, 1869–70.

Folkestone Express, 1868.

Gravesend and Dartford Reporter, 1856–81.

Independent, April 2007.

Kentish Gazette, 1870.

Kentish Mercury, 1870.

Maidstone and Kentish Journal, 1864; 1871.

Maidstone Telegraph and West Kent Messenger, 1866–7; 1870–4.

Maidstone Telegraph, Rochester and Chatham Gazette, 1862.

Sheerness Guardian, 1864–5.

Sheerness Times and General Advertiser, 1870.

Shield, 1870–7.

Contemporary Printed and Published Sources

A Guide to Dover, Ancient and Modern (Dover: Dover Chronicle, 1861).

Acton, W., *Prostitution*, ed. P. Fryer (1857; London: Macgibbon & Kee, 1968).

Brabazon, E. J., *A Month at Gravesend* (Gravesend: Godfrey John Baynes, 1863).

Butler, J., *The Education and Employment of Women* (Liverpool: T. Brakell, 1868).

Clark, P., and L. Murfin, *The History of Maidstone: The Making of a Modern County Town* (Stroud: Alan Sutton Publishing, 1995).

Gaskell, E., *Mary Barton* (1848; Harmondsworth: Penguin, 1983).

Greg, W. R., 'Prostitution', *Westminster Review*, 53 (July 1850), pp. 238–68.

Logan, W., *The Great Social Evil: Its Causes, Extent, Results and Remedies* (London: Hodder and Stoughton, 1871).

Mayhew, H. (ed.), *London Labour and the London Poor*, 4 vols (London, 1861–2; repr. London: Penguin, 1985).

Miller, T., *The Poetical Language of Flowers; or the Pilgrimage of Love*, 2nd edn (London: David Bogue, 1885).

Stratton, J. Y., *Hops and Hop-Pickers* (London, 1883).

The Visitor's Guide to Dover: Its History and Antiquities (Dover: Harvey & Hemmin, 1875).

Kent History and Library Centre, Maidstone

Borough of Maidstone Police: Instructions and Conditions (Maidstone: J. Brown, 1836).

Rules Made by the Visiting Justices for the County Prison (Maidstone: County Prison, 1866) (Q/GGw 1).

Rules, Regulations and Directions for the Instruction and Guidance of the Police Force of the Borough of Gravesend (Gravesend: Caddel & Son, 1851).

Dover Public Library

Pike's Blue Book and Dover Directory (Brighton: Robinson, Son and Pike, 1888–9).

Gravesend Public Library

Bye-Laws for the Good Rule and Government of the Borough of Gravesend, Kent and for the Prevention and Suppression of Nuisances Therein (Gravesend: T. Caddel, 1836).

Hall's Gravesend, Milton and Northfleet Directory and Advertiser (Gravesend: Thomas Hall, 1870–5).

Secondary Sources

'33 Reasons Why the Clients of Sex Workers Should Not Be Criminalized', SCOT-PEP, at http://www.scot-pep.org.uk [accessed 31 July 2008].

Banks, J. K. A., 'Warning to Unfortunate Loiterers', *History of Dover*, at http://www.doverhistory.co.uk/warning-to-unfortunate-loiterers.html [accessed 30 May 2012].

Barker, H., *Newspapers, Politics and English Society 1695–1855* (Harlow: Longman, 1999).

Batchelor, J., 'Industry in Distress: Reconfiguring Femininity and Labor in the Magdalen House', *Eighteenth Century Life*, 28 (2004), pp. 1–20.

Becker, H. S., *Outsiders: Studies in the Sociology of Deviance*, rev. edn (New York: Free Press, 1997).

Black, J., *The English Press 1621–1861* (Stroud: Sutton Publishing, 2001).

Breward, C., *The Culture of Fashion* (Manchester: Manchester University Press, 1995).

Bindel, J., 'A Heroine for Our Age', *Guardian*, 21 September 2006, G2.

Blue Town Remembered: The Spirit of a Community (Sheerness: Freedom Centre Publishing, 1992).

Brown, L., *Victorian News and Newspapers* (Oxford: Oxford University Press, 1985).

Carter, H., and C. R. Lewis, *An Urban Geography of England and Wales in the Nineteenth Century* (London: Edward Arnold, 1990).

Cohen, S., *Folk Devils and Moral Panics: The Creation of the Mods and Rockers*, 3rd edn (Abingdon: Routledge, 2002).

Cole, S., *Guide to Sheerness-on-Sea and the Isle of Sheppey* (Sheerness: S. Cole, 1891).

Conley, C. A., *The Unwritten Law: Criminal Justice in Victorian Kent* (Oxford: Oxford University Press, 1991).

Cooksey, C., and A. Dronsfield, 'Fuchsine or Magenta: The Second Most Famous Aniline Dye. A Short Memoir on the 150th Anniversary of the First Commercial Production of this Well-Known Dye', *Biotechnic & Histochemistry*, 84 (2009), pp. 179–83.

Croll, A., *Civilizing the Urban: Popular Culture and Public Space in Merthyr, c. 1870–1914* (Cardiff: University of Wales Press, 2000).

Crossick, G., *An Artisan Elite in Victorian Society: Kentish London 1840–1880* (London: Croom Helm, 1978).

Daunton, M. J., 'Public Space and Private Space: The Victorian City and the Working Class Household', in D. Fraser and A. Sutcliffe (eds), *The Pursuit of Urban History* (London: Edward Arnold, 1983), pp. 212–33.

Dingle, A. E., 'Drink and Working-Class Living Standards in Britain, 1870–1914', *Economic History Review*, 25 (1972), pp. 608–22.

Emsley, C., *Crime and Society in England 1750–1900* (Harlow: Longman, 1996).

—, *The English Police: A Political and Social History* (Harlow: Longman, 1991).

Englander, D., *Poverty and Poor Law Reform in Britain: From Chadwick to Booth, 1834–1914* (London: Longman, 1998).

Finnegan, F., *Poverty and Prostitution: A Study of Victorian Prostitutes in York* (Cambridge: Cambridge University Press, 1979).

Fowler, R., *Language in the News: Discourse and Ideology in the Press* (London: Routledge, 1991).

Frost, G. S., *'Living in Sin': Cohabiting as Husband and Wife in Nineteenth-Century England* (Manchester: Manchester University Press, 2008).

Garland, D., 'On the Concept of Moral Panic', *Crime Media Culture*, 4:9 (2008), pp. 9–30.

Girouard, M., *The English Town* (New Haven, CT and London: Yale University Press, 1990).

Goose, N., 'Working Women in Industrial England', in N. Goose (ed.), *Women's Work in Industrial England: Regional and Local Perspectives* (Hatfield: Local Population Studies, 2007), pp. 1–28, on p. 22.

Gravesham Borough Council, 'The Growth of Gravesend', at http://www.gravesham.gov.uk/index [accessed 25 July 2008].

Gunn, S., *The Public Culture of the Victorian Middle Class: Ritual and Authority and the English Industrial City 1840–1914* (Manchester: Manchester University Press, 2007).

Harsin, J., *Policing Prostitution in Nineteenth-Century Paris* (Princeton, NJ: Princeton University Press, 1985).

Hartley, L., *Physiognomy and the Meaning of Expression in Nineteenth-Century Culture* (Cambridge: Cambridge University Press, 2001).

Henderson, T., *Disorderly Women in Eighteenth-Century London: Prostitution and Control in the Metropolis 1730–1830* (London: Pearson Education, 1999).

Hiscock, R. H., *A History of Gravesend* (London: Phillimore, 1976).

Howell, P., *Geographies of Regulation: Policing Prostitution in Nineteenth-Century Britain and the Empire* (Cambridge: Cambridge University Press, 2009).

Hubbard, P., 'Sexuality, Immorality and the City: Red-Light Districts and the Marginalisation of Female Street Prostitutes', *Gender, Place and Culture*, 5:1 (1998), pp. 55–72.

Ingleton, R., *Policing Kent 1800–2000: Guarding the Garden of England* (Chichester: Phillimore, 2002).

Johnson, J. H., and C. G. Pooley (eds), *The Structure of Nineteenth Century Cities* (London: Croom Helm, 1982).

Jones, D., *Crime, Protest, Community and Police in Nineteenth Century Britain* (London: Routledge & Kegan Paul, 1982).

Jordan, J., *Josephine Butler* (London: John Murra, 2001).

Joyce, B., *The Chatham Scandal: A History of Medway's Prostitution in the Late Nineteenth Century* (Rochester: Baggins Book Bazaar/Bruce Aubry, 1999).

Keating, P. (ed.), *Into Unknown England, 1866–1913: Selections from the Social Explorers* (Glasgow: William Collins, 1976).

King, S., and A. Tomkins, *The Poor in England 1700–1850: An Economy of Makeshifts* (Manchester: Manchester University Press, 2003).

Laite, J., 'Paying the Price Again: Prostitution Policy in Historical Perspective', in *History and Policy*, at www.historyandpolicy.org/papers/policy-paper-46.html [accessed 2 September 2012].

Lee, A. J., *The Origins of the Popular Press in England, 1855–1914* (London: Croom Helm, 1976).

Luddy, M., 'Abandoned Women and Bad Characters: Prostitution in Nineteenth-Century Ireland', *Women's History Review*, 6:4 (1997), pp. 485–504.

—, *Prostitution and Irish Society 1800–1940* (Cambridge: Cambridge University Press, 2007).

MacLeod, R. M., 'The Edge of Hope: Social Policy and Chronic Alcoholism 1870–1900', *Journal of Social Medicine and Allied Sciences*, 22 (1967), pp. 215–45.

Mahood, L., *The Magdalenes: Prostitution in the Nineteenth Century* (London: Routledge, 1990).

McHugh, P., *Prostitution and Victorian Social Reform* (London: Croom Helm, 1980).

Murray, P., *Poverty and Welfare 1830–1914* (London: Hodder & Stoughton, 1999).

Nead, L., *Victorian Babylon: People, Streets and Images in Nineteenth-Century London* (New Haven, CT: Yale University Press, 2000).

Pearson, M., *The Age of Consent: Victorian Prostitution and its Enemies* (Newton Abbott: David & Charles, 1972).

Percival, M., and G. Tytler (eds), *Physiognomy in Profile: Lavater's Impact on European Culture* (Cranbury, NJ: Rosemont, 2005).

Petrow, S., *The Metropolitan Police and the Home Office 1870–1914* (Oxford: Clarendon Press, 1994).

Philips, D., and R. Storch, *Policing Provincial England 1829–1856: The Politics of Reform* (London: Leicester University Press, 1999).

Phillips, M. J., *The Development of the Police Force in Gravesend 1816–1866* (unpublished thesis, 1963; Gravesend Library, L920 & 352.2).

Pratt Boorman, H. R., *Kent Messenger Centenary* (Kent: Kent Messenger, 1959).

Pryce, W. T. R. (ed.), *From Family History to Community History* (Cambridge: Cambridge University Press in association with the Open University, 1994).

Reay, B., 'The Context and Meaning of Popular Literacy: Some Evidence from Nineteenth-Century Rural England', *Past & Present*, 131 (1991), pp. 89–129.

Ribeiro, A., *Dress and Morality* (London: B. T. Batsford, 1986).

Richardson, T., 'Labour', in A. Armstrong (ed.), *The Economy of Kent, 1640–1914* (Woodbridge: Boydell Press and Kent County Council, 1995), pp. 233–60.

Rodger, R., 'Slums and Suburbs: The Persistence of Residential Apartheid', in P. Waller (ed.), *The English Urban Landscape* (Oxford: Oxford University Press, 2000), pp. 233–68.

Rose, S. O., 'Gender at Work: Sex, Class and Industrial Capitalism', *History Workshop Journal*, 21 (1986), pp. 113–31.

Ryan, M. P., *Women in Public: Between Banners and Ballots, 1825–1880* (Baltimore, MD: John Hopkins University Press, 1992).

Self, H. J., *Prostitution, Women and Misuse of the Law: The Fallen Daughters of Eve* (London: Frank Cass, 2003).

Skyrme, T., *History of the Justices of the Peace*, 3 vols (Chichester: Barry Rose, 1991), Vol. 2: 1689–1989.

Smith, C. G., *The Reporter, 1856–1966* (Ilford: Gravesend and Dartford Reporter, 1966).

Smith, F. B., 'Ethics and Disease in the Later Nineteenth Century: The Contagious Diseases Acts', *Historical Studies*, 15 (1971), pp. 118–35.

Steedman, C., *Policing the Victorian Community: The Formation of English Provincial Police Forces, 1856–80* (London: Routledge & Kegan Paul, 1984).

Storch, R. D., 'The Plague of Blue Locusts: Police Reform and Popular Resistance in Northern England, 1840–57', *International Review of Social History*, 20 (1975), pp. 61–90.

Taithe, B. O., *From Danger to Scandal, Debating Sexuality in Victorian England: The Contagious Diseases Act (1864–1869) and the Morbid Imagery of Victorian Society* (Manchester: University of Manchester Press, 1992).

Taylor, D., *Policing the Victorian Town: The Development of the Police in Middlesbrough 1840–1914* (Basingstoke: Palgrave Macmillan, 2002).

—, *The New Police in Nineteenth-Century England: Crime, Conflict and Control* (Manchester: Manchester University Press, 1997).

—, *Crime, Policing and Punishment in England 1750–1914* (Basingstoke: Macmillan, 1998).

Taylor, H., 'A Crisis of "Modernization" or Redundancy for the Police in England and Wales, 1900–39', *British Journal of Criminology*, 39 (1999), pp. 113–35.

'The Coordinated Prostitution Strategy', *Focus on Women*, 4 (2006), p. 4, at www.row.org.uk [accessed 15 August 2008].

Trudgill, E., *Madonnas and Magdalens: The Origins and Development of Victorian Sexual Attitudes* (London: Heinemann, 1976).

Vincent, D., *Literacy and Popular Culture: England 1750–1914* (Cambridge: Cambridge University Press, 1989).

Walkowitz, J. R., *Prostitution and Victorian Society: Women, Class and the State* (Cambridge: Cambridge University Press, 1980).

Ward, D., 'Environs and Neighbours in the "Two Nations": Residential Differentiation in Mid-Nineteenth-Century Leeds', *Journal of Historical Geography*, 6 (1980), pp. 133–62.

Weeks, J., *Sex, Politics and Society: The Regulation of Sexuality since 1800*, 2nd edn (Harlow: Longman, 1989).

Wilkins, L. T., *Social Deviance: Social Policy, Action and Research* (London: Tavistock, 1964).

Willett Cunnington, C., *English Women's Clothing in the Nineteenth Century* (New York: Dover, 1990).

Zedner, L., *Women, Crime and Custody in Victorian England* (Oxford: Clarendon, 1991).

INDEX

Lightning Source UK Ltd.
Milton Keynes UK
UKHW020227261119
354241UK00007B/34/P